Teaching U.S. History Thematically

Document-Based Lessons for the Secondary Classroom

Rosalie Metro

Teachers College Press
TEACHERS COLLEGE | COLUMBIA UNIVERSITY
NEW YORK AND LONDON

Published by Teachers College Press, 1234 Amsterdam Avenue, New York, NY 10027

Copyright © 2017 by Teachers College, Columbia University

Cover design by Laura Duffy. All cover images in the public domain. Photos, top to bottom, left to right: Ronald Reagan, John Calhoun, George Washington, Sojourner Truth, Cesar Chavez, Frederick Douglass, Abraham Lincoln, Thomas Jefferson, Martin Luther King Jr., Sandra Day O'Connor, Barack Obama, Japanese internment camp. Documents, left to right: Executive Order 9066, Resulting in the Relocation of Japanese (1942); *Plessy v Ferguson*.

Permissions lines for the documents featured in Lessons 2.12, 4.12, and 5.10 appear in the text within the relevant lessons.

All rights reserved. No part of this publication may be reproduced or transmitted in any form or by any means, electronic or mechanical, including photocopy, or any information storage and retrieval system, without permission from the publisher. For reprint permission and other subsidiary rights requests, please contact Teachers College Press, Rights Dept.: tcpressrights@tc.columbia.edu

Library of Congress Cataloging-in-Publication Data

Names: Metro, Rosalie, author.
Title: Teaching U.S. history thematically : document-based lessons for secondary classrooms / Rosalie Metro.
Description: New York, NY : Teachers College Press, [2017] | Includes bibliographical references and index.
Identifiers: LCCN 2017029992 (print) | LCCN 2017033134 (ebook) | ISBN 9780807776636 (ebook) | ISBN 9780807758687 (pbk. : alk. paper)
Subjects: LCSH: United States—History—Study and teaching (Secondary) | United States—History—Sources.
Classification: LCC E175.8 (ebook) | LCC E175.8 .T416 2017 (print) | DDC 973/.0712—dc23
LC record available at https://lccn.loc.gov/2017029992

ISBN 978-0-8077-5868-7 (paper)
ISBN 978-0-8077-7663-6 (ebook)

Printed on acid-free paper
Manufactured in the United States of America

24 23 22 21 20 19 18   8 7 6 5 4 3

Contents

Acknowledgments	vii
Introduction: Why Use a Thematic, Document-Based Approach for Teaching U.S. History?	1
Why Thematic?	1
Why Document-Based?	3
Meeting Common Core and High-Quality State Standards	4
What Do We Mean When We Say "We"?	6
Structure of a Unit	8
Structure of a Lesson	10
Assessment	14
Accounting for Grade Level and Differentiating Instruction	15
Classroom Climate	16
Designing Your Own Thematic Units	19
1. American Democracy: What Is American Democracy, and What Should It Be?	21
Lesson 1.1: How Do Ordinary Americans Define Democracy in the 21st Century?	22
Lesson 1.2: How Did Native American Traditions Influence American Democracy?	23
Lesson 1.3: How Did Thomas Paine Argue for Independence from Britain?	26
Lesson 1.4: What Was James Madison's Argument for Representative Democracy?	28
Lesson 1.5: What Did Thomas Jefferson Believe Were the Main Responsibilities of Government?	30
Lesson 1.6: How Did Andrew Jackson Represent the "Common Man"?	32
Lesson 1.7: How Did Frederick Douglass Criticize American Democracy?	36
Lesson 1.8: How Did Abraham Lincoln Define Democracy?	37
Lesson 1.9: How Did Susan B. Anthony Interpret the Constitution?	39
Lesson 1.10: What Did John F. Kennedy Believe the United States Should Do for the World?	41
Lesson 1.11: Why Did Ronald Reagan Believe America Was Great?	44
Lesson 1.12: Why Did Barack Obama Think the United States Was Not Yet a Perfect Union?	46

2. Diversity and Discrimination: What Does Equality Mean?   50

Lesson 2.1: What Was the Supreme Court's Argument for Allowing Same-Sex Marriage?   51
Lesson 2.2: What Did the Constitution Say About Slavery?   53
Lesson 2.3: How Did Native Americans Argue for Equal Rights?   55
Lesson 2.4: How Did Sojourner Truth Define Equality?   57
Lesson 2.5: What Was the Supreme Court's Rationale for Denying Black People Citizenship?   58
Lesson 2.6: Why Did John Brown Think Violence Was Justified to End Slavery?   61
Lesson 2.7: What Was the Supreme Court's Reasoning for "Separate but Equal" Facilities?   63
Lesson 2.8: Why Did Elizabeth Cady Stanton Believe Women Deserved the Same Rights as Men?   65
Lesson 2.9: What Was the Supreme Court's Argument for Excluding Chinese People from U.S. Citizenship?   67
Lesson 2.10: What Was the Ku Klux Klan's Argument for White Supremacy?   69
Lesson 2.11: How Did the Supreme Court Explain Its Decision to Overturn the "Separate but Equal" Doctrine?   72
Lesson 2.12: How Did Malcolm X Think Racial Equality Could Be Achieved?   74

3. States' Rights and Federal Power: How Should Power Be Distributed Among Local, State, and Federal Governments?   77

Lesson 3.1: On What Basis Did the NAACP Argue That North Carolina Law Violated the Voting Rights Act?   77
Lesson 3.2: What Was the Balance of Power Between the States and Congress in the Articles of Confederation?   80
Lesson 3.3: How Did the Constitution Compare with the Articles of Confederation?   82
Lesson 3.4: How Did George Washington Explain His Decision to Suppress the Whiskey Rebellion?   85
Lesson 3.5: How Did States' Rights and Federalist Interpretations of the Constitution Differ?   87
Lesson 3.6: Who Is Responsible for Protecting Native American Nations: State or Federal Governments?   89
Lesson 3.7: How Did Daniel Webster Argue That States Couldn't Nullify Federal Laws?   92
Lesson 3.8: How Did the Southern States Explain Their Decision to Secede from the Union?   94
Lesson 3.9: Why Did Dwight Eisenhower Enforce Desegregation?   97
Lesson 3.10: How Did Orval Faubus Argue for Segregation as a "State's Right"?   99
Lesson 3.11: Does the State or Federal Government Protect Individuals from Environmental Harm?   100

4. Government, Business, and Workers: What Role Should Government and Business Play in Promoting Citizens' Well-Being?   104

Lesson 4.1: How Did Donald Trump Think the Government Should Promote a
    Strong Economy? 105
Lesson 4.2: What Were Christopher Columbus's Economic and Social Goals? 107
Lesson 4.3: Why Did John Calhoun Define Slavery as a "Positive Good"? 109
Lesson 4.4: Why Did the Lowell Mill Women Go on Strike? 111
Lesson 4.5: How Did W. E. B. Du Bois Think That the Government Succeeded and
    Failed in Helping Former Slaves? 113
Lesson 4.6: What Was Andrew Carnegie's Argument for Social Darwinism? 115
Lesson 4.7: How Did the "Other Half" Live in Jacob Riis's Photos? 117
Lesson 4.8: How Did Upton Sinclair Want to Change the Meatpacking Industry? 120
Lesson 4.9: What Was Henry Ford's Plan for Ending Poverty? 122
Lesson 4.10: What Were the Aims of the New Deal? 124
Lesson 4.11: Why Did Lyndon Johnson Launch a War on Poverty? 127
Lesson 4.12: Why Did Cesar Chavez Believe Farmworkers Should Unionize? 129
Lesson 4.13: What Was Reaganomics? 131

**5. Foreign Policy: Under What Circumstances Should
    the United States Intervene in World Events? 135**
Lesson 5.1: How Did Donald Trump Explain His Decision to Bomb Syria? 135
Lesson 5.2: Why Did George Washington Believe
    the United States Should Stay Neutral? 138
Lesson 5.3: How Did the Monroe Doctrine Change U.S. Foreign Policy? 139
Lesson 5.4: How Was the Idea of Manifest Destiny Used to Justify Taking Over
    Foreign Lands? 141
Lesson 5.5: Why Did Mark Twain Oppose U.S. Colonization of the Philippines? 143
Lesson 5.6: How Did Woodrow Wilson Try to Convince Americans to Stay Neutral
    in World War I? 145
Lesson 5.7: How Did Franklin D. Roosevelt Explain His Decision to Involve the
    United States in World War II? 147
Lesson 5.8: How Did Eleanor Roosevelt Explain the Purpose of the United Nations? 149
Lesson 5.9: How Did the Truman Doctrine Change U.S. Foreign Policy? 151
Lesson 5.10: Why Did Martin Luther King Jr. Oppose the Vietnam War? 153
Lesson 5.11: On What Basis Did Henry Kissinger Advise Richard Nixon to Oppose
    Chilean President Salvador Allende? 156
Lesson 5.12: How Did Bill Clinton Explain His Decision to Intervene in the
    Genocide of Bosnian Muslims? 158
Lesson 5.13: What Was George W. Bush's Strategy in the War on Terror? 161

**6. Civil Liberties and Public Safety: Under What Conditions,
    If Any, Should Citizens' Freedoms Be Restricted? 164**
Lesson 6.1: What Was Barack Obama's Plan to Reduce Gun Violence? 164
Lesson 6.2: How Did the United States Explain Its Decision to Declare
    Independence from Britain? 167
Lesson 6.3: What Does the Bill of Rights Guarantee? 168

Lesson 6.4: How Did John Adams Restrict Freedom of the Press? 171
Lesson 6.5: What Was Abraham Lincoln's Argument for Suspending
   Habeas Corpus Rights During the Civil War? 172
Lesson 6.6: Was Carrie Nation's Temperance Activism Protected by the Constitution? 174
Lesson 6.7: How Did Herbert Hoover Explain His Decision to Disperse
   the Bonus Army? 176
Lesson 6.8: How Did Franklin D. Roosevelt Justify the Internment of Japanese
   Americans? 178
Lesson 6.9: How Did Paul Robeson Defend Himself Against Joseph McCarthy's
   Accusation That He Was a Communist? 180
Lesson 6.10: How Did COINTELPRO Justify Its Surveillance of U.S. Citizens? 182
Lesson 6.11: What Rights Did the Black Panther Party Demand, and Why? 185
Lesson 6.12: How Did the U.S. Government Defend the USA PATRIOT Act? 187

7. Identity: What Do We Mean When We Say "We"? **191**
Lesson 7.1: Declaration of Independence, Thomas Jefferson, 1776 191
Lesson 7.2: Our Hearts Are Sickened, John Ross, 1838 192
Lesson 7.3: Declaration of Immediate Causes, South Carolina Legislature, 1860 192
Lesson 7.4: On Women's Right to Vote, Susan B. Anthony, 1872 192
Lesson 7.5: Appeal for Neutrality, Woodrow Wilson, 1914 193
Lesson 7.6: *The Klan's Fight for Americanism*, Hiram W. Evans, 1926 193
Lesson 7.7: Day of Infamy, Franklin D. Roosevelt, 1941 193
Lesson 7.8: By Any Means Necessary, Malcolm X, 1964 194
Lesson 7.9: Why I Am Opposed to the War in Vietnam, Martin Luther King, Jr., 1967 194
Lesson 7.10: A Shining City on a Hill, Ronald Reagan, 1974 194
Lesson 7.11: The War on Terror, George W. Bush, 2001 194
Lesson 7.12: A More Perfect Union, Barack Obama, 2008 195

Appendixes **196**
Appendix A: Quick Reference Guide 196
Appendix B: Course Entry Survey 204
Appendix C: Course Exit Survey 204
Appendix D: Unit Entry Survey 205
Appendix E: Biographical Research Paper Instructions 205
Appendix F: Summit Research Worksheet 205
Appendix G: Unit Exit Survey 206
Appendix H: Current Issue Letter Instructions 207
Appendix I: Designing Your Own Thematic Units 207
Appendix J: Discussion Guidelines 207
Appendix K: Online Content 208

References **209**

Index **210**

About the Author **216**

Acknowledgments

This book has been many years in the making, and I have accumulated many debts of gratitude.

Douglas Fix, my adviser at Reed College, provided a role model for dedicated and innovative history teaching. Jason Bricker, Diane Bruckerhoff, and other colleagues at Columbia Independent School supported me in developing and implementing this curriculum. Teacher friends like Jason Wagner have engaged me in ongoing dialogue about the goals of education. Sam Wineburg gave me helpful feedback on this project early on. Diana Laufenberg encouraged me to make this material available to teachers. Colleagues at the University of Missouri–Columbia, including Tony Castro and LaGarrett King, have broadened my views on social studies education.

Jean Ward, my editor at Teachers College Press, believed in this book from the beginning. TCP staff including Christina Brianik, Karl Nyberg, Romaine Perin, Nancy Power, and Jamie Rasmussen shepherded it along.

Thanks are also due to my husband, Sean Franzel; my mother, Judy Metro; my father, Alexander Metro; my dear friend Rebecca Tuhus-Dubrow; and Jane Levey, who first inspired me to study history. For my kids, Mae and Louis: I hope your generation can work for justice through understanding.

Finally, my students taught me more than I can express, and they challenged me to make history matter.

INTRODUCTION

Why Use a Thematic, Document-Based Approach for Teaching U.S. History?

"Open your textbooks to page 254. Read the sections on *McCulloch v. Maryland*, the Missouri Compromise, and the Monroe Doctrine. Answer the questions at the end of each section."

Read these words out loud to yourself, and you can almost hear the students' bored sighs, the rustling of pages, the clock ticking toward the end of the period.

If you listen harder, you can hear the questions going through the students' minds as they bend over their textbooks: Who cares? Why do we have to read about this endless string of names and dates that have nothing to do with each other? What does any of it have to do with my life?

Listen even harder, and you might be able to hear the teacher's silent questions, too, as she looks out at her class. Didn't I start teaching history because I wanted to make a difference? Why don't the students realize how important this is? And how am I going to meet those Common Core State Standards?

This book contains the tools teachers need to get started with an innovative approach to teaching history, one that develops literacy and higher-order thinking skills, connects the past to students' lives, and meets Common Core State Standards. I developed this approach during my time as a secondary-level social studies teacher, and I refined it while writing my doctoral dissertation. This approach is the product of both research and practice, and I'm eager to share it with teachers who are tired of hearing students say that history is boring.

WHY THEMATIC?

The standard way to teach history is to start with the earliest event to be covered and proceed forward in time toward the present. This approach does have some advantages: Moving chronologically helps students sequence events; it allows them to understand what was happening in the country or around the world during a given period of time. But I think the main reason history is taught chronologically is out of habit. We do it because that's the way we learned; that's the way textbooks are organized; that's what students and parents expect.

However, teaching history chronologically has several drawbacks. First, it's difficult to forge the past-present connections that make history relevant to students' daily lives. Often, the school year ends before teachers make it to the present (or even the past 30 years) (Loewen, 2008). Second, teaching chronologically makes history feel like a barrage of events, connected to one another only insofar as they happened around the same time. So much happens in a day, a year, a century. How do teachers decide what's important and what's not? Without some organizing principles, criteria for what's included in the curriculum and what's left out can feel random.

Organizing a history curriculum by theme, on the other hand, allows students to develop an understanding of how an issue develops over time. Take foreign policy, the theme of Chapter 5. Under what circumstances should the United States intervene in world events? This question has recurred throughout our history. Leaders have answered it differently in every era, but those answers build on one another. How can students understand Woodrow Wilson's hesitance to get involved in World War I without referring back to George Washington's Proclamation of Neutrality? How can they evaluate Henry Kissinger's advice that Richard Nixon should depose Chilean president Salvador Allende without considering the Monroe and Truman doctrines? If we want students to make these connections, let's structure our curriculum in a way that facilitates comparison, rather than burying these relationships under a landslide of other facts.

Teaching history thematically doesn't mean that we let go of chronology. Having students keep personal timelines of the events they study, and keeping a timeline on the classroom wall, keeps the sequence of events clear in students' minds. Apps such as Timeline Eons, which students can use to construct and annotate illustrated timelines, can also be helpful. Revisiting each era multiple times over the course of the school year allows students to gradually build an understanding of historical periodization. Each theme provides a new journey through the past, another opportunity to see continuity and change.

There is a dearth of research comparing outcomes of thematic versus chronological approaches to teaching history. Moving chronologically is likely preferable if the goal is for students to memorize dates. Yet most of us have greater purposes: inspiring intellectual curiosity, promoting deep engagement with the past, empowering students to find their own answers to the questions that have haunted this nation. In that sense, teaching thematically provides exciting opportunities.

As someone who taught chronologically early in my career and thematically later, I can say that it would be hard for me to go back. Teachers who use this approach may find the same is true for them.

WHY DOCUMENT-BASED?

Ask any student who dislikes history why, and you'll hear, "The textbook. It's boring." Textbooks can be useful for reference, but they don't make history come alive. History curricula that use textbooks as the main or only source of information not only bore students but also deaden their curiosity and mislead them about the nature of historical inquiry.

Why do we use textbooks? Because they simplify decisions about what to teach. We may believe that in most cases they contain a reasonably accurate representation of events. The idea that there is one correct interpretation of U.S. history may be comforting.

But traditional textbooks speak with a monolithic voice of authority, concealing the debates historians have with one another about the meaning of sources and about theories of cause and effect. Many textbooks have made strides toward including primary documents interspersed through the text or in an appendix. Yet these documents are treated as supplements to the main narrative, rather than as constitutive of its meaning.

For that reason, textbooks do not build the habit of engaging critically with every source, a habit that is essential to historical inquiry (Wineburg, 2001). Scholars who study historical thinking with the Stanford History Education Group (SHEG, n.d.), have come up with a set of questions students should bring to every source they read, including: "Who wrote this?" "What is the author's perspective?" and "What do other documents say?"

It is certainly possible to ask these questions of a textbook. Some teachers do engage their students in critical analysis of their textbook as a document that illustrates the biases of its authors. Yet most of the time, the textbook is taken to be a neutral collection of facts, to be the objective truth. Students are expected to accept their textbooks wholesale, rather than treat them as products of specific historical circumstances (Loewen, 2008). In this sense, textbooks are not the best resource for helping students develop the literacy and higher-order thinking skills that they will need to be critical consumers of information.

Finally, most U.S. history textbooks available today present what Ronald Takaki (Takaki & Steffof, 2012, p. 6) calls the "master narrative" of our nation: "that our country was settled by European immigrants, and that Americans are white." Takaki's work shows that this narrative is inaccurate; Native Americans, African Americans, Asian Americans, and Latino Americans have been central to, not on the sidelines of, U.S. history. Textbooks convey this master narrative, not only in overt ways, but also subtly. Most textbooks "whitewash" the racist views of many of our nation's leaders by including only the details that make them seem heroic to people today (Loewen, 2008). Many textbooks leave out the stories of poor people and other marginalized groups (Zinn, 2003). One scholar found that the grammar and wording of textbooks recently used in Texas downplayed the brutality of slavery, humanizing the slave owners while portraying slaves as cogs in an economic system (Rockmore, 2015). Whether the master narrative is implicit or explicit, it is damaging to our increasingly diverse country when students' cultures and histories are left out or misrepresented. A document-based* approach makes it easier to incorporate the contradictory viewpoints of diverse Americans, as well as to consider the founders and presidents in a new light.

That said, this book, like most U.S. history textbooks, over-represents the views of White, wealthy men. Because of racism, sexism, and class hierarchy, that demographic has dominated our government, and thus their words have been preserved (and are available without copyright protection).† However, I do hope that the juxtaposition of their words with strategically chosen documents by women, people of color, and those with less socioeconomic power will bring to the surface the very dynamics that have led to this discrepancy in historical representation.

Basing the curriculum on documents also addresses a related issue of bias. Any U.S. history curriculum is open to accusations of partiality. In document-based approaches, curriculum designers' biases influence the selection of documents and the questions asked about them (as do mine in this book). However, a document-based approach allows students significant freedom to interpret the material according to their own values and emerging political orientations. Some students may be inspired by Ronald Reagan's call to reduce corporate taxes and deregulate private enterprises; other students may prefer Franklin D. Roosevelt's plans to tax the wealthy and increase government spending. The important thing is that students have direct access to Reagan's and Roosevelt's words, rather than being limited to the interpretations of a textbook author, whose own opinions invariably creep in. Moreover, as students examine historical documents—Supreme Court cases, speeches by politicians and activists, political cartoons—they come to understand multiple perspectives on history and develop a healthy sense of skepticism about the claims they encounter.

MEETING COMMON CORE AND HIGH-QUALITY STATE STANDARDS

More than 40 states have adopted the Common Core State Standards (CCSS), which aim to "provide teachers, parents, and students with a set of clear

---

*I use the term *documents* instead of *primary sources* because even a secondary source such as a textbook can be analyzed in the same manner that "primary" sources can.

† The expense and time of securing permissions prevented me from including many of the modern historical figures I would have liked to, especially women, advocates for the poor, and racial and ethnic minorities. For instance, I would have loved to include works by James Baldwin, Jeanne Wakatsuki Houston, Angela Davis, and leaders of the Young Lords and AIM movements. I explain this not to excuse the under-representation of marginalized people in this curriculum but to point out that teachers are free to supplement this curriculum with documents from these and other historical figures under educational use provisions.

expectations to ensure that all students have the skills and knowledge necessary to succeed in college, career, and life upon graduation from high school, regardless of where they live" (Common Core State Standards Initiative, 2016). Specific standards for history/social studies outline the disciplinary skills that students are supposed to gain. While many states have since decided to write their own standards, most have written them with an eye toward the same objectives seen in the CCSS, including interrogating documents and thinking critically.

It would be difficult to meet these new standards while teaching in the traditional manner, chronologically and solely from a textbook. Moreover, the standards' focus on skills rather than content gives teachers more freedom about which topics to teach and in what order. Therefore, I hope this book can be a useful as a main text, or as a resource for teachers who are trying to incorporate document analysis into their curriculum in a focused, organized manner. This book could also work well for homeschoolers. It is also possible to use the documents in this book selectively as one of many supplemental texts. Several standards listed below are particularly well-suited to thematic, document-based teaching. I've highlighted the ways in which this book encourages students to develop the skills below.

CCSS.ELA-LITERACY.RH.9-10.1

Cite specific textual evidence to support analysis of primary and secondary sources, attending to such features as the date and origin of the information.

Students answer questions such as "Who created this document?" and "Choose a quotation that shows how different the author's perspective is from most people's today," which draw their attention to sourcing and historical context.

CCSS.ELA-LITERACY.RH.9-10.6

Compare the point of view of two or more authors for how they treat the same or similar topics, including which details they include and emphasize in their respective accounts.

Organizing the curriculum thematically is well-suited to this standard. For instance, students compare the details that Henry Ford, Franklin D. Roosevelt, and Andrew Carnegie include in their discussion of businesses' and government's role in promoting citizens' well-being.

CCSS.ELA-LITERACY.RH.9-10.9

Compare and contrast treatments of the same topic in several primary and secondary sources.

For example, students can compare the treatment of democracy in the writings of Susan B. Anthony, Frederick Douglass, and Thomas Jefferson.

CCSS.ELA-LITERACY.RH.11-12.4

Determine the meaning of words and phrases as they are used in a text, *including analyzing how an author uses and refines the meaning of a key term over the course of a text (e.g., how Madison defines* faction *in Federalist Paper No. 10).*

James Madison's Federalist Paper No. 10 is included in this book, and students are prompted to answer this exact question. This is not an isolated activity, separate from the rest of the curriculum; students hone their skills at understanding the vocabulary that is used in all the texts they read.

CCSS.ELA-LITERACY.RH.11-12.7

Integrate and evaluate multiple sources of information presented in diverse formats and media *(e.g., visually, quantitatively, as well as in words) in order to address a question or solve a problem.*

Students examine visual sources such as political cartoons about Andrew Jackson and photographs by Jacob Riis in order to build an understanding of the questions at hand.

CCSS.ELA-LITERACY.RH.11-12.8

Evaluate an author's premises, claims, and evidence by corroborating or challenging them with other information.

Students are prompted to cross-reference documents in order to evaluate the claims authors make. They are asked to consider what kind of proof authors would need to provide in order to support their assertions.

CCSS.ELA-LITERACY.RH.11-12.9

Integrate information from diverse sources, both primary and secondary, into a coherent understanding of an idea or event, noting discrepancies among sources.

Over the course of a unit, students build toward exactly such a "coherent understanding" of ideas such as democracy and equality. As they compare what is written in traditional textbooks with the documents herein, they bring the same critical attitude to primary and secondary sources.

WHAT DO WE MEAN WHEN WE SAY "WE"?

This book is constructed around seven "essential questions" that are especially meaningful when teaching U.S. history. Essential questions are not intended to yield final or correct answers, but rather to promote critical thinking (McTighe & Wiggins, 2013). They are questions that have preoccupied the greatest minds in our country for centuries. These questions engage students because they remain relevant today, and because the stakes in answering them are high.

One of these essential questions serves as a touchstone for students' entire inquiry into U.S. history: What do we mean when we say "we"? This question allows students to consider how American identity has evolved over the course of the past three centuries. I arrived at this question because I found that students—and I—often used the word *we* without considering who is included and who is excluded (Levstik, 2000). For instance, a White student might say, "We treated slaves badly," or "We moved the Native Americans from their land," or "We won the Mexican-American War," without considering whether Black, indigenous, or Mexican American students would feel part of that "we." A middle-class student might say, "We had to collect more taxes from the rich to help the poor," without considering the range of socioeconomic statuses in the classroom. A male student might say, "We gave women the right to vote," without realizing that the other half of the class might say, "Men denied us the right to vote." As the teacher, I might say, "We have passed on a large national debt to the next generation," without realizing that the next generation is sitting right in front of me.

When we expand this question beyond our classrooms, it takes on even more meaning. Whom did Thomas Jefferson intend to include when he wrote, "We hold these truths to be self-evident"? Which "us" was George W. Bush talking about when he said, "Either you are with us, or you are with the terrorists?" The meaning of the American "we" has shifted depending on who is speaking and when. Therefore, it is a great question to get students thinking about continuity and change.

Teachers can introduce this essential question at the beginning of the school year, alongside activities designed to elicit students' backgrounds and prior knowledge. A Course Entry Survey (Appendix B) prompts students to reflect on their own experiences of belonging (or not) in the United States, and the extent to which they feel part of the historical or current "we." Students can discuss their responses to this survey, and even create collages or multimedia projects describing their identities as insiders/outsiders in U.S. history.* Those projects could serve as visual reminders of the "classroom we" that informs how students interpret the many versions of the "American we" they will encounter in the documents.

The seventh and final unit, in which students return to documents that highlight concepts of "we" and "us," circles back to this essential question. As students reflect on the material they have read in previous units, they have a chance to synthesize what they've learned about the multi-dimensional and ever-changing nature of American identity. A Course Exit Survey (Appendix C) allows students to reflect on how their own views of what it means to be American have changed over the course of the year.

---

*Teachers should be aware when choosing whether or not to have students complete this project that students might reveal family citizenship status or other information that might compromise their safety. Teachers should take measures to protect students from the consequences of these disclosures.

STRUCTURE OF A UNIT

Each of the seven units is structured around an essential question that highlights one theme in U.S. history. For example, Chapter 6, on the theme of civil liberties and public safety, asks, "Under what conditions, if any, should citizens' freedoms be restricted?" Each unit begins with a Current Issue Question that highlights the topic's importance to the present; for the Civil Liberties unit, it is, "Can reforming gun laws make Americans safer?" Teachers introduce these questions, and students complete a Unit Entry Survey (Appendix D) in which they report their personal views. (I have selected a current issue for each unit, but times change quickly, and teachers may find that other topics are more salient in their contexts.) Beginning with a current issue enables students to see what is at stake in the unit. Students' first concern when studying history is often "Why does this matter?" or "How does this affect me today?," and starting with a current issue addresses those questions.

Students then rewind history to the earliest point covered in the unit and proceed to analyze 10 to 13 documents, chronologically arranged, that address the essential question in some way. Each document is linked with a historical event and with a historical figure (often, but not always, the document's author). These linkages provide context for the documents and focus any background reading that students might do.

At the beginning of the unit, each student (or pairs or trios, depending on class size) should choose a historical figure represented in the documents to research. They become experts on these historical figures and represent them in a "summit" at the end of the unit. Students' task is to understand how their historical figure would have answered the Unit Question, and how they would answer the Current Issue Question if they were alive today. The documents students read in class provide the basis for their answers, but students may also conduct independent research and/or supplementary assignments such as a Biographical Paper (see Appendix E for Biographical Research Paper Instructions and Appendix F for the Summit Research Worksheet).

Once students have discussed the current issue and chosen their historical figures, they start with the earliest document in the unit and continue toward the present day, analyzing each source. The structure of individual lessons is explained in detail below, but briefly, teachers introduce the topic, place the document in context, highlight key vocabulary, and then guide students in analyzing the document, applying the knowledge they've gained, and reflecting on what they've learned.

Every unit culminates in a "summit," in which each student (or team of students) represents the historical figure they've chosen (see instructions below). Students imagine that all the historical figures they've discussed could travel through time to be in the same place—their classroom. Each historical figure makes an opening statement, providing brief biographical details and presenting his or her answers to the Unit Question and Current Issue

Question. Students must stay in character, while also citing evidence from the documents they've read to support their positions. Then there is time for questions and answers, during which the historical figures interact spontaneously. Students must consider what these historical figures would have to say to each other. Would James Madison agree with Barack Obama's proposal for reforming gun laws? Would John Adams respect Abraham Lincoln's rationale for suspending habeas corpus rights during the Civil War?

Summit Instructions

You will participate in a summit representing a historical figure. During this summit, you have three tasks:

1. Make an "opening statement" in which you:
   - introduce yourself and provide relevant biographical information in order to explain your importance in U.S. history.
   - present your answer to the Unit Question and give an example of something you did or said that proves you would answer that way.
   - present your view on the Current Issue Question for this unit and explain why you have this view.

2. Listen attentively to other students' presentations.

3. Participate in a question–and-answer session in which you address your classmates as the historical figures they represent, challenging or agreeing with their ideas.
   - Prepare at least two questions for other historical figures.
   - Anticipate two questions you are likely to be asked and provide answers.

Cite the document we read in class linked to your historical figure and at least one other source.

In order to provide plenty of material for discussion, the historical figures in each unit represent a range of views. For instance, Chapter 2, which centers on diversity and discrimination, includes both activists for equality, such as Sojourner Truth and Thurgood Marshall, and those who sought to maintain social and racial hierarchies, such as the Supreme Court justices who supported "separate but equal" policies and the exclusion of Chinese people from U.S. citizenship. Discussions are more thought-provoking when there are stark contrasts between historical figures' positions.

A summit can be as low-key or as elaborate as students and teachers want it to be. Students may bring in a theatrical element by dressing in costume or respectfully reproducing the way their historical figure would have spoken and acted, or they may do a more bare-bones presentation. Either way, the students' critical thinking skills are engaged as they separate their own viewpoint from that of their historical figure, provide evidence to support their views, and predict how their historical figure would respond extemporaneously to questions.

In my experience, the first summit of the year is quite challenging for students. They tend to ask questions not relevant to the theme, or questions that reflect their own experience rather than that of their historical figure. For instance, James Madison might ask Barack Obama what it was like to live in the White House. Yet over the course of the year, students become increasingly adept at setting aside their own views in order to represent historical figures from a very different time and place from their own.

The summit ends with students dropping their characters and discussing the Unit Question and Current Issue Question as themselves. This was always the most rewarding part of the unit for me as a teacher—I got to see how much students had learned from history. It was wonderful to hear them considering a range of perspectives and articulating their own emerging views, informed by the documents we had read.

Students can consolidate these reflections in a Unit Exit Survey (Appendix G), in which they consider how their answers to the Unit Question and Current Issue Question have either changed or been confirmed by their studies. They identify the event, historical figure, or document that most affected their own view, and they can also bring their learning into the present by writing a letter to a leader regarding the current issue (see Appendix H, Current Issue Letter Instructions). Thus, students end each unit by finding their own answers to the big questions that have occupied the greatest minds in our nation. They also gain practice in the essential learning skill of metacognition, or thinking about their own thinking.

Each unit might take 3 to 4 weeks to complete, allowing class time for background reading, drafting Biographical Research Papers, and preparing for the summit. Therefore, there would be adequate time in a school year for students to complete each of the seven units included in this book, in addition to other projects. Teachers who wish for a slower pace might pick and choose which units or documents to include. Homeschool families would have even more freedom to adapt the curriculum to their interests.

STRUCTURE OF A LESSON

Within the previously described architecture of a unit, individual lessons also have a dependable structure, making it easier for teachers and students to settle in. Each document is incorporated into a lesson that sets it in context and connects it to the other documents in the unit. These lessons are planned to take from 45 to 90 minutes, depending on whether teachers assign some or all of the questions and activities. Teachers may wish to spread one lesson out over 2 days, depending on the length of their class periods and their students' needs.

Setting Up the Lesson

Before the lesson, teachers may wish to assign background reading on events, concepts, or historical figures related to the document. For instance, before having students read South Carolina's Declaration of Immediate Causes, teachers will want students to have some information about the Civil War. Such readings are widely available in traditional textbooks, and teachers will have their own preferred or required secondary sources. This background information could be conveyed in a prior lesson or assigned as homework the day before. It is also possible to pre-teach the vocabulary related to each document in a prior class period or through homework exercises.

Lesson Question

Each lesson is titled with a question that students should be able to answer by the lesson's conclusion, for example, "How did Thomas Paine argue for independence from Britain?"* These questions are different from the essential questions that title each unit in that they have specific (although not always straightforward) answers. By the end of the lesson, students should be able to answer the question by citing specific passages in the document. Students may well come to different conclusions, but they should be able to support their interpretations.

It is important to differentiate the kind of questions asked here from those in comparable approaches to teaching history. For example, the Stanford History Education Group has designed a fantastic collection of document-based lessons for their Reading like a Historian program (SHEG, n.d.). Their approach is to provide students with multiple documents pertaining to the same event, and to ask students to compare these documents in order to arrive at a conclusion about history. For example, their "central historical question" for one lesson is "Why were Japanese Americans interned during World War II?" They provide students with several documents related to this question. In contrast, my lesson on Japanese internment asks, "How did Franklin D. Roosevelt justify the internment of Japanese Americans?" I provide only one document, Roosevelt's explanation of Japanese internment. In other words, I focus on what students can learn from what one historical figure said or wrote instead of asking students to arrive at a broader conclusion about cause and effect in history based on multiple sources.

The kind of questions that SHEG asks are certainly valuable, and teachers could use SHEG's lessons to complement mine (or vice versa). Although I don't provide multiple documents about each event, in the Resources section of each lesson, I do suggest other accounts teachers could use to

---

*Lesson Questions can be transformed into objectives: "Students will analyze how Thomas Paine argued for independence from Britain."

deepen students' perspective. Indeed, outside research will be essential for students to begin questioning the claims that historical figures make in these documents.

Historical Figure and Event

Following the Lesson Question, teachers will find a historical figure and an event connected to the document. The event is described in or related to the document. Students should keep a personal and/or class timeline on which these events are added before, during, or after each lesson. Teachers may wish to choose background readings that provide more information on these historical figures and events.

Introduction

Each lesson begins with an introductory question or activity designed to capture students' attention, connect with their prior knowledge, and/or relate the topic to their lives. These questions do not have right or wrong answers, but are intended to spark thought and discussion and to connect each student's current understandings with the knowledge they will gain.

Mini-Lecture

Following the introduction, the teacher delivers a mini-lecture that puts the document in context. These mini-lectures are intended to review information students have gained from background readings and provide specific information about the document itself. In other words, they are not intended to convey a breadth and depth of historical understanding but rather to refresh students' memories and prepare them to analyze the document. These mini-lectures can be delivered orally and/or in digital format (e.g., PowerPoint). Teachers may wish to have students take notes on these lectures, or teachers might create fill-in notes for students to complete as they listen. These lectures take 5 to 10 minutes, unless students have many questions or teachers want to take time to delve into certain topics in more detail.

Vocabulary

A list of vocabulary words pulled from each document accompanies the lesson. I provide simple definitions addressing how the words are used in context. Some teachers may find that their students don't need these lists to comprehend the documents; others may find that some students require more assistance with reading comprehension. Teachers might pre-teach vocabulary through homework or class activities, present it during the course of the lesson, and/or review it afterward.

Document

The next step is for students to read the document. Each document is prefaced with its title, its author, and the year in which it was created or published. Teachers may want to read it aloud as students follow along; have students read it aloud, as a class or in pairs; or have students read it silently. Active reading strategies, such as predicting, visualizing, and asking questions, may be helpful. Several documents are in the form of images. In those cases, teachers can use Visual Thinking Strategies (VTS), including speculating, questioning, and analyzing (Visual Thinking Strategies, 2016), to have students examine the photo or political cartoon. Most documents are excerpts of approximately 500 words that were originally part of a longer text. I have abridged them to omit details unrelated to the unit's theme and to make them manageable for students and teachers to analyze within a class period or two. A source follows each document so that teachers can locate the complete version. Printable versions of all documents (arranged chronologically by historical event), along with the instructions and handouts included in Appendixes B–J, are available for download at www.tcpress.com/Metro (see Appendix K for a list of materials available there).

Comprehension Questions

Comprehension questions follow each document. These questions are aimed at the lower levels of Revised Bloom's Taxonomy (Iowa State University of Science and Technology, 2016), and they allow teachers to assess whether students have understood the document thoroughly enough to proceed to analysis, synthesis, and evaluation. Students might answer these in writing and/or orally, individually or in groups. The answers to some of these questions might be debatable, but in general, teachers should be able to easily determine correct or incorrect responses and use students' responses to pinpoint misunderstandings.

Activities

Once teachers are confident that students have comprehended the document's main points, students complete activities that allow them to apply, analyze, and evaluate what they have learned from the document. Students can consider these questions individually or through group and partner activities. Often there are not clear correct or incorrect answers to these questions; students could arrive at various conclusions, depending on their interpretation of the documents and their own views. The activities I suggest include: writing letters from one historical figure to another, role-playing or creating cartoons illustrating conversations between historical figures, creating Venn diagrams to compare historical figures' views, finding evidence to support arguments, conducting research and making presentations, and participating in small-group discussions or class debates. These activities scaffold students' learning to build toward the summit at the end of the unit. Teachers may want to adapt these activities (for instance, turning a group assignment into an individual one, or asking for a written dialogue instead of having students act it out), or they may want to generate additional activities, depending on their own preferences; on student needs; on district or school guidelines; or on constraints of time, space, or resources. For more activity ideas, books on group work (Cohen & Lotan, 2014) and active learning strategies (Casale-Giannola & Green, 2013) are helpful.

The questions I ask require students to use "historical thinking skills" identified by SHEG and others: sourcing, contextualization, corroboration, and close reading of documents. For students who need support in developing these skills prior to engaging with documents in this book, I suggest SHEG's introductory materials for the Reading Like a Historian program (SHEG, n.d.), which break down each skill into easy-to-follow steps.

Reflection

Each lesson ends with a question or set of questions for students to reflect on as they synthesize what they've learned and make connections to the rest of the unit. Teachers might have students complete these questions on an exit ticket or have them discuss answers in pairs, in small groups, or with the whole class.

Resources

Rounding out each lesson are one or two resources that teachers can use to build their own knowledge or create extension activities for students. These resources may contain different or broader perspectives than the documents do, so they can be helpful for corroboration or contextualization and for assisting students in connecting history to current events.

ASSESSMENT

This approach to teaching history provides rich opportunities for both formative and summative assessment. Comprehension questions allow for confirmation that students have understood the documents at a basic level. Observations of and artifacts from activities show whether students are engaging with the material at a higher level by applying, analyzing, and evaluating what they've learned. Reflections show teachers whether students are connecting new information to what they've already learned in the unit. Teachers may also wish to conduct weekly or bimonthly quizzes covering historical figures and events.

The summit that ends each unit is a great opportunity for summative assessment, as it enables students to use the analysis and evaluation they've done to create something new: an interpretation of a historical figure's perspective. Students might also write Biographical Research Papers on the historical figures they've chosen (Appendix E). The Unit Exit Survey (Appendix G) shows how much students have gained from the unit. Students can also write letters about the Current Issue Question to local, state, federal, or school leaders. For instance, at the conclusion of the unit on foreign policy, students might write to President Donald Trump to express their views on his decision to bomb Syria or on a more current foreign policy decision. After the unit on civil liberties, students might write to their superintendent about what policy they believe is appropriate regarding guns in schools (see Appendix H, Current Issue Letter Instructions). These letters not only allow teachers to assess students' synthesis of the material covered but also encourage students to become active citizens. Teachers may wish to create tests covering the historical figures and events in the unit, and/or to test students' comprehension of the documents.

ACCOUNTING FOR GRADE LEVEL AND DIFFERENTIATING INSTRUCTION

I recommend this approach to teaching history in Grades 7 to 12. I know it can be done in 8th grade from my own experience; as Levstik and Barton (2005) show, the capacity of young students for historical inquiry is often underestimated. It would be possible to adapt this method to younger grades, or even college-level courses, but this book is intended for use in 7th–12th grade and is most appropriate toward the middle of that range. Teachers of younger students would need to provide simpler background reading and more support in comprehending the documents, while 11th- or 12th-grade teachers might want to offer students more independence and additional and/or more complex primary and secondary sources, as well as opportunities for extension.

The design of this book makes it easy for teachers to adapt this material to various grade levels or to differentiate instruction within a class. Most documents are abridged, both to focus on the parts that refer to the Unit Question and to remove details that may require additional explanations that aren't directly related to the topic at hand. For instance, in Barack Obama's speech "The President's Remarks on Common-Sense Gun Safety Reform" in Chapter 6, I took out the line "Contrary to claims of some presidential candidates, apparently, before this meeting, this is not a plot to take away everybody's guns." This line would require an explanation of the intricacies of the 2016 presidential campaign. This type of allusion to events or people outside the main topic at hand is one reason, I find, that teachers hesitate to use primary source documents—it takes too much time to explain every detail, and students' curiosity often takes the conversation in directions tangential to the lesson's objectives.

However, for higher grade levels or more advanced students, teachers might assign original documents in their entirety alongside the excerpts in this book. Links to the full documents can be found following the excerpts and at www.tcpress.com/Metro (arranged chronologically by historical event). On the other hand, some teachers may wish to abridge the documents further or scaffold understanding for English language learners or students who struggle with comprehension (see Gibbons, 2015, for ideas on working with ELLs). There's no scientific process to abridging documents, so teachers should feel free either to restore parts of the document that I have cut or to simplify them further. The important thing is that students have direct access to the ideas.

CLASSROOM CLIMATE

In order for this approach to teaching history to work well, teachers need to create a classroom climate in which students respect one another's differing opinions and discuss facts and values in a civil manner. This climate can be difficult to establish in a country as politically divided as the United States is in 2017. However, political polarization makes it all the more important that kids learn to listen to one another, consider evidence, and disagree without name-calling. Some teachers try to sidestep potential problems by avoiding current events altogether. But although conversations about racial, economic, social, and gender inequality can be difficult, avoiding them makes us more likely to reproduce these structures (Milner, 2010). I agree with Hess and McAvoy (2015) that U.S. history is most meaningful to students when it is connected to the debates that animate our country today. I would go further and say that to analyze history without relating it to the present is to rob the past of its meaning.

Nonetheless, some teachers may not find it prudent to reference current events as much as this book does. Their administrations or school communities may not be supportive. Teachers may not feel confident about managing the difficult conversations that could arise. Or the dynamics of their classrooms and communities might make discussing sensitive issues too risky.

I would advise teachers who do use the approach I describe in this book to reflect on how their own political and social positions may affect how they teach this material. For example, I grew up in a left-leaning White family in an urban Democratic stronghold. My first teaching experiences, in New York City, required me to consider how my Black, Latino, and West Indian students would interpret the colonization of the Americas and the racial hierarchies that continue today. When I moved to a "red state," on the other hand, I had to design a curriculum that helped students from conservative, rural backgrounds feel welcome. In keeping with those experiences, I have tried to include documents in this book that reflect perspectives across the political and social spectrum.

Of course, teachers have their own opinions about politics and history. They will have to decide for themselves how much is appropriate to share with their students. However, in using this approach, it is important that teachers do not predetermine which historical figures students should agree with and which they should condemn, especially along the conservative-liberal divide.

Seeking to understand a historical figure is distinct from accepting his or her arguments. That said, many students, parents, and administrators are likely to feel uncomfortable with extreme views such as Hiram W. Evans's praise of the Ku Klux Klan or John C. Calhoun's defense of slavery. I feel strongly that leaving these elements out of U.S. history impedes students' ability to understand the past and the present. Nevertheless, teachers should carefully evaluate the racial and socioeconomic dynamics of their classes when covering these topics. LaGarrett King (2016), a specialist in social studies education and Black history, has pointed out that simulations (such as the summits) run the risk of retraumatizing Black students by exposing them to documents that disparage members of their race or force them into the role of victims. Students of any race might feel uncomfortable representing the views of White supremacists; and unfortunately, some students may consciously or unconsciously embrace these views. From another angle, some White students might feel awkward representing the views of Black nationalists like Malcolm X or Huey Newton. Some students might be upset by Andrew Carnegie's social Darwinism or by the socialist views of Upton Sinclair, while others would admire them.

I encourage teachers to have conversations with students and their families, and with colleagues and administrators, about how best to navigate these challenges. Creating an atmosphere of trust and respect is key when discussing issues that are currently controversial, such as racism, LGBTQ (lesbian, gay, bisexual, transgender, and queer or questioning) rights, and civil liberties. Teachers can give students the right to "pass" when answering questions during class discussions, and follow up with them later about their discomfort. Teachers can also provide explicit examples of how to disagree respectfully. In that vein, the Discussion Guidelines shown in the box on page 18 may be useful (also see Appendix J).

Discussion Guidelines

1. Assume positive intentions and give classmates the benefit of the doubt—disagree with ideas, don't attack people.

    NO: If you don't believe in background checks on gun sales, you don't care about public safety!

    NO: If you believe in background checks on gun sales, you don't care about civil liberties!

    YES: I know we both care about public safety and civil liberties; I think we disagree on the effect of background checks on gun sales.

2. Speak to your classmates as you would to a role model you respect.

    NO: You idiot!

    YES: I strongly disagree with you.

3. Don't blame your classmates for what members of a group they belong to have done, and don't ask classmates to speak for all members of a group they belong to.

    NO: Why do you Black people think violence is necessary?

    NO: Why do you White people always take Native Americans' land?

    YES: I have questions about Malcolm X's idea of armed self-defense.

    YES: As a Native American, I feel upset when I learn that White people took my ancestors' land.

4. Reflect on how your own experiences and biases affect your views—avoid blame and shame.

    NO: I don't see why we need to study women in history; men did most of the important stuff.

    NO: Men should feel guilty about how they have treated women.

    YES: As a male, I realize that I've been seeing history through the eyes of men.

5. If you feel upset, angry, or confused during a discussion, take a break. Take care of yourself and take care of each other.

It is also helpful for teachers to consider their goals in teaching history. Some teach to promote social justice, others to promote patriotism; some teach to prepare students to be active citizens, others to help students succeed in the society that exists. The purposes served by the approach of this text are as follows: to expose students to a wide range of viewpoints in our country's history, which provides context for contemporary life; to teach them to consider evidence carefully; and to encourage them to decide for themselves what resonates with their values, experiences, and logic.

DESIGNING YOUR OWN THEMATIC UNITS

The units in this book are only examples of what teachers could do with a thematic, document-based approach. In my own classes, I have taught other thematic units—for instance,

- Checks and Balances: How Should Power Be Distributed Among the Three Branches of Government?
- Separation of Church and State: What Role Should Religion Play in Public Life?
- American Expansionism: How Should the Country Grow?

For more ideas, see the blog "Big Questions Many Answers," on my website at rosaliemetro.com/bigquestionsmanyanswers. Here you will find lists of documents that could be included in thematic units like these, as well as blog posts about developing your own units.

Adding additional topics or units can be helpful, because the content included here is by no means exhaustive. The units in this book touch on key themes in U.S. history, and I've tried to cover major events and important historical figures while also drawing attention to lesser-known people and ideas. Teachers may wish to replace or supplement units with additional material that reflects their students' communities.

I hope that this book will inspire teachers to create their own thematic units for U.S. history—or for other courses, such as world history, women's history, or Black history. Doing so is fairly straightforward and quite rewarding, although planning takes time (see Appendix I, Designing Your Own Thematic Units). Regardless of how teachers choose to use this book, I hope that they and their students find the reading and critical interrogation of these documents and themes a rich and stimulating way to study history together.

CHAPTER 1

American Democracy

UNIT QUESTION: What Is American Democracy, and What Should It Be?

Current Issue Question: What does democracy mean to you today?

Unit Introduction: In this unit, students will explore the roots of democracy in North America, from Native American innovations to the ideas of our 44th president. They will read not only the perspectives of leaders such as Thomas Jefferson and John F. Kennedy but also the views of critics of the U.S. government, including Frederick Douglass and Susan B. Anthony. Thomas Paine and James Madison will tell students how democracy is supposed to work, and political cartoons about Andrew Jackson may give them a sense of how it has not worked for marginalized people or Native Americans. They will end by considering the criteria upon which the United States could be considered a great democracy.

Students will also gain exposure to the contemporary political spectrum, from the liberal views of Barack Obama to the conservative outlook of Ronald Reagan. It is important to emphasize that the meanings of the terms *liberal* and *conservative* have changed over time and are used in different ways today around the world; likewise, political parties in the United States have shifted significantly over the past 200 years. Nevertheless, the "Basic U.S. Political Spectrum circa 2017" diagram (see Figure 1.5 in Lesson 1.11) provides a sketch of current political orientations in the United States, which students may find helpful as they try to relate the views of historical figures to the vocabulary of the present. Teachers may wish to elaborate on this diagram, introducing terms such as *libertarian* or *progressive* if students' inquiries direct discussion there, or adding terms such as *socialist* or *communist* as students encounter these terms in the documents.

As these discussions can be controversial, it is a good idea to prepare parents and administrators that students will be making connections between the material they study and their own opinions. In order to make all students and families comfortable, it is important to emphasize that there are no "correct" or "incorrect" answers when it comes to these questions. Exposing students to a variety of views will make them better-informed as citizens.

Students begin this unit by considering how ordinary Americans on Twitter today define democracy. This connection to contemporary social media is intended to help them see the ongoing relevance of the questions they will be considering. Over the course of this unit, they will have a chance to build up their own understandings of our form of government and how it influences their lives.

LESSON 1.1
How Do Ordinary Americans Define Democracy in the 21st Century?

Historical Figures: Ordinary Americans

Event: 240th anniversary of the start of the Revolutionary War, 2015

Introduction: What does democracy mean to you? Try to express your view in 140 characters or less.

Mini-Lecture:

- In 2015, a nonprofit organization called Everyday Democracy asked people to publicly share their definitions of democracy via Twitter.
- Everyday Democracy invited people to share their views in honor of the 240th anniversary of the start of the Revolutionary War, through which the United States became independent from Britain.
- Our document consists of tweets from ordinary Americans.

Vocabulary:

mob rule: control by a group of people who do not have legal powers and may use violence

vaccination: treatment intended to prevent disease

state schooling: education provided through public schools

GE: General Electric, a corporation involved in many different industries that has received tax breaks from the government

The Fed: Federal Reserve, a central banking system run by the federal government that sets interest rates and regulates banks

Document: What Does Democracy Mean to You? various authors, 2015

1. Democracy means equality. @evdem
2. Democracy means stopping the violence. @evdem
3. Democracy means power and possibility. @evdem
4. Democracy means freedom to be me. @evdem
5. Democracy means everyone has the power to create change. @evdem
6. Democracy means to me . . . majority rules. @WhenInDoughtSigh
7. Democracy without a Constitution is mob rule. @MrTugwit
8. Democracy means being able to disagree. @JRwaratah

UNIT QUESTION: What Is American Democracy, and What Should It Be?

9. Democracy means no forced vaccinations, no state schooling, no taxes propping up banks & GE and no central banking aka "The Fed." @GlendaMcRose
10. To me democracy means we're in this together & we share responsibility for the outcomes of govt. @socialcap

Source: Everyday Democracy. (2015). What does democracy mean to you? Retrieved from everyday-democracy.org/news/what-does-democracy-mean-you

Comprehension Questions:

1. In tweet 9, what are @GlendaMcRose's criticisms of the federal government?
2. Who is the intended audience for these statements?

Activities:

1. Find two tweets that seem to contradict each other, and two tweets whose authors would probably agree.
2. How would Americans' answers to these questions have differed in 1775, at the start of the Revolutionary War? Based on what you know of history, work with a small group to write two tweets about democracy that could have been written by ordinary Americans from 1775.

Reflection: Have your views on democracy changed after reading other Americans' views and considering the country's history? Why or why not?

Resources:

Everyday Democracy. (n.d.). History of everyday democracy. Retrieved from everyday-democracy.org/about/history

Pew Research Center. (2017). Large majorities see checks and balances, right to protest as essential to Democracy. Retrieved from people-press.org/2017/03/02/large-majorities-see-checks-and-balances-right-to-protest-as-essential-for-democracy/

LESSON 1.2

HOW DID NATIVE AMERICAN TRADITIONS INFLUENCE AMERICAN DEMOCRACY?

Historical Figure: Dekanawidah

Event: Haudenosaunee Confederacy established, circa 1500

Introduction: What kind of government or political organization do you think Native Americans had before European settlers came to the United States? On what sources are you basing your idea?

Mini-Lecture:

- The Haudenosaunee (or Iroquois) Confederacy is a group of five Native American nations (Mohawk, Oneida, Onondaga, Cayuga, Seneca) that agreed long ago to live by common laws.

- Historians believe these nations formed the confederacy around 1500 in what is now the northeastern United States.
- Our document is the Great Law of Peace, an oral constitution of the confederacy, which was written down by historians.
- Some historians believe that the confederacy and its constitution influenced the writers of the U.S. Constitution.
- Similar principles can be found in both documents, including popular sovereignty, separation of powers, limited government, checks and balances, and federalism.

Vocabulary:

popular sovereignty: people have the power to choose their government

separation of powers: having a legislative branch of government to make laws, a judicial branch to interpret laws, and an executive branch to enforce laws

limited government: leaders cannot do whatever they want; people can replace them if necessary

checks and balances: each part of government has different powers so that none becomes too powerful

federalism: power is shared by a central government and local governments

confederacy: a group of nations, states, or people that join to achieve common goals

irregular: different from what it usually is

upbraid: to criticize

erring: mistaken

unanimous: with every person agreeing after discussion

contumacious: stubborn

divest: to take away

Document: Great Law of Peace, Dekanawidah, circa 1500

> I am Dekanawidah and with the Five Nations' Confederate Lords I plant the Tree of Great Peace....
>
> Roots have spread out from the Tree of the Great Peace, one to the north, one to the east, one to the south and one to the west. The name of these roots is The Great White Roots and their nature is Peace and Strength. We place at the top of the Tree of the Long Leaves an Eagle who is able to see afar. If he sees in the distance any evil approaching or any danger threatening he will at once warn the people of the Confederacy....
>
> The Council of the Mohawk shall be divided into three parties as follows:... The third party is to listen only to the discussion of the first and second parties and if an error is made or the proceeding is irregular they are to call attention to it, and when the case is right and properly decided by the two parties they shall confirm the decision of the two parties and refer the case to the Seneca Lords for their decision....
>
> In all cases the procedure must be as follows: when the Mohawk and Seneca Lords have unanimously agreed upon a question, they shall report their decision to the Cayuga and Oneida Lords who shall deliberate upon the question and

report a unanimous decision to the Mohawk Lords. The Mohawk Lords will then report the standing of the case to the Firekeepers, who shall render a decision as they see fit in case of a disagreement by the two bodies, or confirm the decisions of the two bodies if they are identical. The Firekeepers shall then report their decision to the Mohawk Lords who shall announce it to the open council. . . .

If at any time it shall be manifest that a Confederate Lord has not in mind the welfare of the people or disobeys the rules of this Great Law, the men or women of the Confederacy, or both jointly, shall come to the Council and upbraid the erring Lord through his War Chief. If the complaint of the people through the War Chief is not heeded the first time it shall be uttered again and then if no attention is given a third complaint and warning shall be given. If the Lord is contumacious the matter shall go to the council of War Chiefs. The War Chiefs shall then divest the erring Lord of his title by order of the women in whom the titleship is vested. . . . The women will then select another of their sons as a candidate and the Lords shall elect him. Then shall the chosen one be installed by the Installation Ceremony. . . .

Five arrows shall be bound together very strong and each arrow shall represent one nation. As the five arrows are strongly bound this shall symbolize the complete union of the nations. Thus are the Five Nations united completely and enfolded together, united into one head, one body and one mind. Therefore they shall labor, legislate and council together for the interest of future generations. . . .

Source: Halsall, P. (1997). Modern history sourcebook: The Constitution of the Iroquois Confederacy. Retrieved from sourcebooks.fordham.edu/mod/iroquois.asp

Comprehension Questions:

1. Identify one quotation that illustrates each of the five principles listed in the mini-lecture.

Activities:

1. Some historians believe that the founders of the United States knew about the Iroquois Constitution and used some of the concepts in writing their own constitution. Others think it is just a coincidence that the constitutions are similar. What do you think? Write down your reasons. Then find someone who thinks differently and have a conversation, sharing your views and making a list together of what else you would need to know to make a more informed decision.
2. Based on your knowledge or research about the U.S. Constitution, how does it differ from the Iroquois Constitution?

Reflection: How did the document change or confirm your idea about the government of Native Americans before European settlement?

Resources:

Haudenosaunee Confederacy. (2016). Haudenosaunee Confederacy. Retrieved from haudeno-
sauneeconfederacy.com/

National Museum of the American Indian. (2009). Haudenosaunee guide for educators. Retrieved from nmai.si.edu/sites/1/files/pdf/education/HaudenosauneeGuide.pdf

LESSON 1.3
How Did Thomas Paine Argue for Independence from Britain?

Historical Figure: Thomas Paine

Event: Declaration of Independence, 1776

Introduction: Name one situation in which you believe people in the United States today would be justified in trying to overthrow their government, and one situation in which they would not be justified.

Mini-Lecture:

- Thomas Paine was a political philosopher who was born in England and moved to the colonies just before the Revolutionary War.
- In the Revolutionary War, American colonists rebelled against King George III of Britain and won independence.
- Paine's ideas were part of the Enlightenment, an 18th-century philosophical and political movement that promoted reason and science.
- Paine believed that popular government (by the people) was better than absolute governments like monarchies (in which kings and queens had all the power).
- Our document is from *Common Sense*, which was widely read in 1776 and played a key role in creating support for independence.

Vocabulary:

distinction: difference
subject: someone who is under the power of a ruler
exalted: respected
assert: to claim
fallacious: false

precedent: example for the future
roundly: enthusiastically
at variance with: in conflict with
doth: does
havoc: chaos
defective: broken or incomplete

Document: Common Sense, Thomas Paine, 1776

> . . . But there is another and great distinction for which no truly natural or religious reason can be assigned, and that is the distinction of men into KINGS and SUBJECTS. Male and female are the distinctions of nature, good and bad the distinctions of Heaven; but how a race of men came into the world so exalted above the rest, and distinguished like some new species, is worth

inquiring into, and whether they are the means of happiness or of misery to mankind. . . .

I have heard it asserted by some, that as America has flourished under her former connection with Great Britain, the same connection is necessary towards her future happiness, and will always have the same effect. Nothing can be more fallacious than this kind of argument. We may as well assert that because a child has thrived upon milk, that it is never to have meat, or that the first twenty years of our lives is to become a precedent for the next twenty. But even this is admitting more than is true; for I answer roundly that America would have flourished as much, and probably much more, had no European power taken any notice of her. . . .

I challenge the warmest advocate for reconciliation to show a single advantage that this continent can reap by being connected with Great Britain. I repeat the challenge; not a single advantage is derived. Our corn will fetch its price in any market in Europe, and our imported goods must be paid for buy them where we will.

But the injuries and disadvantages which we sustain by that connection, are without number; and our duty to mankind at large, as well as to ourselves, instruct us to renounce the alliance: because, any submission to, or dependence on, Great Britain, tends directly to involve this Continent in European wars and quarrels, and set us at variance with nations who would otherwise seek our friendship, and against whom we have neither anger nor complaint. . . .

But where says some is the King of America? I'll tell you Friend, he reigns above, and doth not make havoc of mankind like the Royal Brute of Britain. Yet that we may not appear to be defective even in earthly honors, let a day be solemnly set apart for proclaiming the charter; let it be brought forth placed on the divine law, the word of God; let a crown be placed thereon, by which the world may know, that so far as we approve as monarchy, that in America THE LAW IS KING. For as in absolute governments the King is law, so in free countries the law ought to be King; and there ought to be no other.

Source: ushistory.org. (2016). Common Sense by Thomas Paine.
Retrieved from ushistory.org/paine/commonsense/

Comprehension Questions:

1. According to Paine, how is the difference between kings and subjects different from the difference between men and women?
2. In Paine's analogy about the child in paragraph 2, what does milk symbolize and what does meat symbolize?

Activities:

1. Work with a partner to write and act out a dialogue between Thomas Paine and King George III about whether America should remain a British colony.

2. According to Paine, who should be king of America, God or the law? Support your answer with a quotation.

Reflection: Think back to the two situations you described in the introduction. What advice do you think Thomas Paine would give us in those situations, and why?

Resources:

Library of Congress. (n.d.). King George III's address to Parliament, October 27, 1775. Retrieved from loc.gov/teachers/classroommaterials/presentationsandactivities/presentations/timeline/amrev/shots/address.html

LESSON 1.4
What Was James Madison's Argument for Representative Democracy?

Historical Figure: James Madison

Event: Constitution created, 1787

Introduction: You and five friends are deciding which movie to see together. If three people want to see one movie and the other three want to see a different one, how do you decide?

Mini-Lecture:

- James Madison helped to write the Constitution and was president from 1809 to 1817.
- The Constitution was written in 1787, and it came into effect in 1789 after the states ratified, or approved, it.
- James Madison and two other founders, Alexander Hamilton and John Jay, wrote 85 essays—the Federalist Papers—under the pseudonym "Publius," to convince states to ratify the Constitution.
- Our document is Federalist Paper No. 10, which discusses direct democracy and representative democracy.
- In direct (or pure) democracy, citizens vote on which laws to pass.
- In representative democracy, citizens elect representatives who then make laws. This form of government is called a republic.
- The US is a representative democracy, or republic, but some laws are passed by direct democracy (ballot initiatives) at state and local levels.

Vocabulary:

faction: a group with strong views opposed to views of another group
actuated: motivated
adversed: opposed
aggregate: taken all together

popular government: rule by the people, for instance, democracy
desideratum: desirable goal
opprobrium: bad reputation
inducement: temptation

UNIT QUESTION: What Is American Democracy, and What Should It Be?

turbulence: instability
contention: fighting
pure democracy: direct rule by the people
republic: society with representative democracy
partial: biased

Document: Federalist Paper No. 10, James Madison, 1787

Among the numerous advantages promised by a well constructed Union, none deserves to be more accurately developed than its tendency to break and control the violence of faction. . . .

By a faction, I understand a number of citizens, whether amounting to a majority or a minority of the whole, who are united and actuated by some common impulse of passion, or of interest, adversed to the rights of other citizens, or to the permanent and aggregate interests of the community. . . .

To secure the public good and private rights against the danger of such a faction, and at the same time to preserve the spirit and the form of popular government, is then the great object to which our inquiries are directed. Let me add that it is the great desideratum by which this form of [popular] government can be rescued from the opprobrium under which it has so long labored, and be recommended to the esteem and adoption of mankind. . . .

From this view of the subject it may be concluded that a pure democracy, by which I mean a society consisting of a small number of citizens, who assemble and administer the government in person, can admit of no cure for the mischiefs of faction. A common passion or interest will, in almost every case, be felt by a majority of the whole; a communication and concert result from the form of government itself; and there is nothing to check the inducements to sacrifice the weaker party or an obnoxious individual. Hence it is that such democracies have ever been spectacles of turbulence and contention; have ever been found incompatible with personal security or the rights of property; and have in general been as short in their lives as they have been violent in their deaths. . . .

A republic, by which I mean a government in which the scheme of representation takes place, opens a different prospect, and promises the cure for which we are seeking. Let us examine the points in which it varies from pure democracy, and we shall comprehend both the nature of the cure and the efficacy which it must derive from the Union.

The two great points of difference between a [direct] democracy and a republic are: first, the delegation of the government, in the latter, to a small number of citizens elected by the rest; secondly, the greater number of citizens, and greater sphere of country, over which the latter may be extended.

The effect of the first difference is, on the one hand, to refine and enlarge the public views, by passing them through the medium of a chosen body of citizens, whose wisdom may best discern the true interest of their country, and whose patriotism and love of justice will be least likely to sacrifice it to temporary or partial considerations. Under such a regulation, it may well happen that the public voice, pronounced by the representatives of the people, will be more consonant to the public good than if pronounced by the people themselves, convened for the purpose. On the other hand, the effect may be inverted.

Source: Lillian Goldman Law Library. (2008). The Federalist Papers: No. 10. Retrieved from avalon.law.yale.edu/18th_century/fed10.asp

Comprehension Questions:

1. Put Madison's definition of *faction* into your own words.
2. According to Madison, what are two advantages of a republic over a direct democracy?

Activities:

1. Identify a decision about curriculum or class rules that students could make together. Divide the class in half. Half the class will elect one person to make the decision for them. Half will vote using direct democracy. Students should have time to try to convince one another of their points of view or decide whom to elect.
2. Which process, direct or representative democracy, worked better? More quickly? Did factions emerge? How would this process be different if the decision had to be made by the whole school, or the whole district?

Reflection: Do you think representative democracy is working today as Madison intended? Why or why not?

Resources:

University of Groningen. (2012). The Federalist Papers. Retrieved from let.rug.nl/usa/documents/1786-1800/the-federalist-papers/

LESSON 1.5
What Did Thomas Jefferson Believe Were the Main Responsibilities of Government?

Historical Figure: Thomas Jefferson

Event: Thomas Jefferson elected, 1800

Introduction: Make a list of what you think are the five most important things government should do, and five things the government should never do.

Mini-Lecture:

- Thomas Jefferson helped to write the Declaration of Independence and the Constitution and was president from 1801 to 1809.
- He supported the idea of "limited government," which means that the government should not have too much power over people's lives.
- The document is from Jefferson's inaugural address.

- Although Jefferson talked about "equal justice and exact justice for all men," he owned slaves and expressed racist views. At times he also advocated for an end to the slave trade.

Vocabulary:

frugal: not wasteful
regulate: to manage and have rules for
felicities: joys
comprehend: to include
deem: to believe
persuasion: belief
commerce: business
bulwark: defense
antirepublican: against the will of the people
sheet anchor: something one can rely on in an emergency; the term comes from sailing, the sheet being a sail, the anchor something to tie it to

jealous: careful
acquiescence: giving in to
despotism: political system in which a ruler has all the power
militia: an unofficial army
burthened: burdened
arraignment: holding someone accountable for a crime
handmaid: helper
diffusion: spread
habeas corpus: the right of people accused of a crime not to be imprisoned indefinitely without being charged or tried

Document: First Inaugural Address, Thomas Jefferson, 1801

Still one thing more, fellow citizens—a wise and frugal Government, which shall restrain men from injuring one another, shall leave them otherwise free to regulate their own pursuits of industry and improvement, and shall not take from the mouth of labor the bread it has earned. This is the sum of good government, and this is necessary to close the circle of our felicities.

About to enter, fellow-citizens, on the exercise of duties which comprehend everything dear and valuable to you, it is proper you should understand what I deem the essential principles of our Government. . . . Equal and exact justice to all men, of whatever state or persuasion, religious or political, peace, commerce, and honest friendship with all nations, entangling alliances with none; the support of the State governments in all their rights, as the most competent administrations for our domestic concerns and the surest bulwarks against antirepublican tendencies; the preservation of the General Government in its whole constitutional vigor, as the sheet anchor of our peace at home and safety abroad; a jealous care of the right of election by the people—a mild and safe corrective of abuses which are lopped by the sword of revolution where peaceable remedies are unprovided; absolute acquiescence in the decisions of the majority, the vital principle of republics, from which is no appeal but to force, the vital principle and immediate parent of despotism; a well-disciplined militia, our best reliance in peace and for the first moments of war till regulars may relieve them; the supremacy of the civil over the military authority; economy in the public expense, that labor may be lightly burthened; the honest payment of our debts and sacred preservation of the public faith; encouragement of agriculture, and of commerce as its handmaid; the diffusion of information and arraignment of all abuses at the bar of the public reason; freedom of religion; freedom of the press, and freedom of person under the protection of the habeas corpus, and trial by juries impartially selected.

Source: Lillian Goldman Law Library. (2008). Thomas Jefferson first inaugural. Retrieved from avalon.law.yale.edu/19th_century/jefinau1.asp

Comprehension Questions:

1. In the first paragraph, what does bread symbolize?
2. List five things Jefferson says the government should do, and five things the government should not do.

Activities:

1. Would Jefferson approve of the following policies? With a small group, find a quotation to support one of these claims, then present it to the class.
   a. Make an alliance of mutual defense with three other countries so that "an attack on one is an attack on all."
   b. Tax wealthy citizens' income and redistribute it to the poor.
   c. Enforce laws that keep every citizen safe.
   d. Presidents can overrule the decisions of state governments.
   e. Protect the rights of people whose opinions are different from the majority's.

Reflection: Look back at the things you thought government should and shouldn't do and compare them with the list you generated from Jefferson's speech. Would you say that you, like Jefferson, are in favor of limited government? Why or why not?

Resources:

Whitehouse.gov. (2016). Thomas Jefferson. Retrieved from whitehouse.gov/1600/presidents/thomasjefferson

---

LESSON 1.6

HOW DID ANDREW JACKSON REPRESENT THE "COMMON MAN"?

Historical Figure: Andrew Jackson

Event: Election of Andrew Jackson, 1828

Introduction: Are wealth, education, and sophistication necessary for becoming president of the United States? What evidence do you have to support your opinion?

Mini-Lecture:

- Andrew Jackson was president from 1829 to 1837.

UNIT QUESTION: What Is American Democracy, and What Should It Be?   33

- Unlike previous presidents, who were all wealthy, well educated, and from the Northeast, Jackson grew up in a poor family in the Waxhaws area of North Carolina and did not attend a prestigious university.
- Jackson fought in the War of 1812 and was said to have stood up to British soldiers as a child during the Revolutionary War.
- Jackson, nicknamed "Old Hickory," was a populist: He promised to fight for the "common man" instead of the wealthy elite.
- Jackson forced Native Americans to move from their ancestral lands to reservations in Oklahoma. Their journey was called the Trail of Tears, because so many people died along the way.
- Once Jackson was in office, some people accused him of taking too much power for himself.
- Jackson thought the Constitution did not give Congress permission to charter a national bank, and he vetoed Congress's decision to recharter the bank; Nicholas Biddle, president of the Second Bank of the United States, opposed him.

Vocabulary:

set to: fight   *bully:* brave or aggressive

Document: Political cartoons about Andrew Jackson, various artists, 1830s

Figure 1.1. *Brave Boy of the Waxhaws*, Currier and Ives, 1876

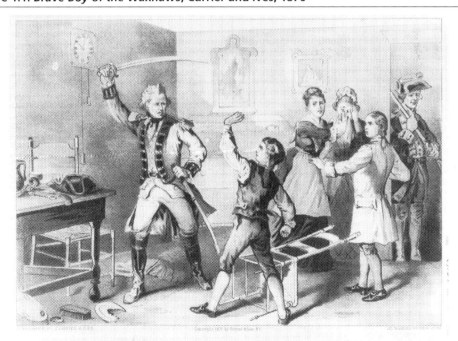

Figure 1.2. *Set To Between Old Hickory and Bully Nick*, Anthony Imbert, 1834

Figure 1.3. *King Andrew*, anonymous, 1832

UNIT QUESTION: What Is American Democracy, and What Should It Be? 35

Figure 1.4. *Great Father Andrew Jackson*, artist unknown, circa 1835

Comprehension Questions:

1. Match each political cartoon with the way it portrays Jackson:
   a. Jackson was a tyrant who did not respect the Constitution.
   b. Jackson bravely stood up to a British soldier.
   c. Jackson fought against the national bank.
   d. Jackson took care of Native Americans.

Activities:

1. For each cartoon, find three adjectives to describe how the cartoonist portrays Jackson. Do you agree with the cartoonists' views? Why or why not?
2. For each cartoon, find two objects that have symbolic meaning. What do they symbolize?
3. With a small group, create a new cartoon about Jackson that illustrates your views of him.

Reflection: How do you think Jackson defined the "common man"? Do you agree with his definition?

Resources:

Roy Rosenzweig Center. (2016). Interpreting political cartoons in the history classroom. Retrieved from teachinghistory.org/teaching-materials/teaching-guides/21733

LESSON 1.7

HOW DID FREDERICK DOUGLASS CRITICIZE AMERICAN DEMOCRACY?

Historical Figure: Frederick Douglass

Event: Frederick Douglass escapes from slavery, 1838

Introduction: What does Independence Day (Fourth of July) mean to you? How do you celebrate, if at all?

Mini-Lecture:

- Frederick Douglass was born into slavery in Maryland; his mother was a slave and his father was an unknown White man.
- Unlike most slaves, he learned to read and write as a child.
- In 1838, he escaped to Massachusetts and become involved with the abolitionist (antislavery) movement there.
- He wrote an autobiography explaining what he had suffered as a slave.
- Our document is from a speech Douglass gave in New York to an abolitionist audience.

Vocabulary:

devout: showing deep religious feeling
would to God: I wish
affirmative: yes
disparity: difference
within the pale: included in
bequeathed: given
fetters: chains used on slaves
gross: severe

sham: something falsely claimed to be the truth
license: freedom
denunciation: condemnation or insult
impudence: disrespect
bombast: fancy language without much meaning
impiety: not showing respect to religion

Document: What to the Slave is the Fourth of July? Frederick Douglass, 1852

> Fellow-citizens, pardon me, allow me to ask, why am I called upon to speak here to-day? What have I, or those I represent, to do with your national independence? Are the great principles of political freedom and of natural justice, embodied in that Declaration of Independence, extended to us? and am I, therefore, called upon to bring our humble offering to the national altar, and to confess the benefits and express devout gratitude for the blessings resulting from your independence to us?
>
> Would to God, both for your sakes and ours, that an affirmative answer could be truthfully returned to these questions! Then would my task be light, and my burden easy and delightful. . . .
>
> But, such is not the state of the case. I say it with a sad sense of the disparity between us. I am not included within the pale of this glorious anniversary! Your

high independence only reveals the immeasurable distance between us. The blessings in which you, this day, rejoice, are not enjoyed in common.—The rich inheritance of justice, liberty, prosperity and independence, bequeathed by your fathers, is shared by you, not by me. The sunlight that brought life and healing to you, has brought stripes and death to me. This Fourth [of] July is yours, not mine. You may rejoice, I must mourn. To drag a man in fetters into the grand illuminated temple of liberty, and call upon him to join you in joyous anthems, were inhuman mockery and sacrilegious irony. . . .

What, to the American slave, is your 4th of July? I answer: a day that reveals to him, more than all other days in the year, the gross injustice and cruelty to which he is the constant victim. To him, your celebration is a sham; your boasted liberty, an unholy license; your national greatness, swelling vanity; your sounds of rejoicing are empty and heartless; your denunciations of tyrants, brass fronted impudence; your shouts of liberty and equality, hollow mockery; your prayers and hymns, your sermons and thanksgivings, with all your religious parade, and solemnity, are, to him, mere bombast, fraud, deception, impiety, and hypocrisy—a thin veil to cover up crimes which would disgrace a nation of savages. There is not a nation on the earth guilty of practices, more shocking and bloody, than are the people of these United States, at this very hour.

Source: Foner, P. S. (Ed.). (1999). *Frederick Douglass: Selected speeches and writings.* Chicago, IL: Lawrence Hill.

Comprehension Questions:

1. Who is the "you" that Douglass addresses in his speech?
2. Why does Douglass mourn on the Fourth of July?

Activities:

1. With a partner, write and act out a dialogue between Thomas Jefferson and Frederick Douglass in which they each try to describe American democracy.

Reflection: Have your own views on Fourth of July changed or been reinforced after reading Douglass's speech? Why?

Resources:

Douglass, F. (2014). *Narrative of the life of Frederick Douglass, an American slave.* New York, NY: Library of America.

LESSON 1.8

How Did Abraham Lincoln Define Democracy?

Historical Figure: Abraham Lincoln

Event: Battle of Gettysburg, 1863

Introduction: What do you know already about the Civil War? What questions do you have?

Mini-Lecture:

- Abraham Lincoln was president from 1861 to 1865, during the Civil War.
- In 1861, Southern states seceded from the Union in order to protect the institution of slavery, and joined together to form the Confederacy.
- Lincoln took a variety of positions on slavery throughout his political career: In 1862, he said his goal was to preserve the Union, not free the slaves; at other times, he said slavery was morally wrong.
- The Battle of Gettysburg, Pennsylvania, was the largest battle of the Civil War, and Union forces won.
- Our document is taken from a speech Lincoln gave in Gettysburg several months after the battle.

Vocabulary:

fourscore and seven: 87
conceive: to begin
proposition: idea
endure: to last a long time

consecrate: to make special or holy
hallow: to make special or holy
detract: to reduce the importance of
in vain: for no reason

Document: Gettysburg Address, Abraham Lincoln, 1863

> Fourscore and seven years ago our fathers brought forth on this continent a new nation, conceived in liberty and dedicated to the proposition that all men are created equal. Now we are engaged in a great civil war, testing whether that nation or any nation so conceived and so dedicated can long endure. We are met on a great battlefield of that war. We have come to dedicate a portion of that field as a final resting-place for those who here gave their lives that that nation might live. It is altogether fitting and proper that we should do this. But in a larger sense, we cannot dedicate, we cannot consecrate, we cannot hallow this ground. The brave men, living and dead who struggled here have consecrated it far above our poor power to add or detract. The world will little note nor long remember what we say here, but it can never forget what they did here. It is for us the living rather to be dedicated here to the unfinished work which they who fought here have thus far so nobly advanced. It is rather for us to be here dedicated to the great task remaining before us—that from these honored dead we take increased devotion to that cause for which they gave the last full measure of devotion—that we here highly resolve that these dead shall not have died in vain, that this nation under God shall have a new birth of freedom, and that government of the people, by the people, for the people shall not perish from the earth.
>
> *Source:* Lillian Goldman Law Library. (2008). Gettysburg Address. Retrieved from avalon.law.yale.edu/19th_century/gettyb.asp

UNIT QUESTION: What Is American Democracy, and What Should It Be?   39

Comprehension Questions:

1. What event does Lincoln reference that occurred 87 years before he gave the speech?
2. Whom does Lincoln seem to be addressing in this speech?

Activities:

1. Lincoln's definition of American democracy ("of the people, by the people, for the people") is often quoted. How do you think Lincoln defined *the people* differently from how presidents did before him? How might he define *the people* differently from how current leaders do?
2. Lincoln does not mention slavery explicitly in this speech. Find two quotations where readers can infer his views on slavery.

Reflection: Lincoln says the work of creating a nation "dedicated to the proposition that all men are created equal" is "unfinished." Do you think that work is still unfinished today? Why or why not?

Resources:

National Park Service. (n.d.). Lincoln on slavery. Retrieved from nps.gov/liho/learn/history-culture/slavery.htm

Ibis Communications, Inc. (n.d.). The Battle of Gettysburg, 1863. Retrieved from eyewitnesstohistory.com/gtburg.htm

LESSON 1.9

HOW DID SUSAN B. ANTHONY INTERPRET THE CONSTITUTION?

Historical Figure: Susan B. Anthony

Event: Susan B. Anthony arrested for voting, 1872

Introduction: If you were a middle-class White woman living in the United States in 1872, which groups would have more political power than you did? Which groups would have less political power than you did?

Mini-Lecture:

- Before 1920, when the 19th Amendment was passed, women did not have the right to vote.
- Susan B. Anthony was an activist for women's rights and a leader of the suffragists, women who believed they should have *suffrage*, or the right to vote.
- This document is from a speech Anthony gave after she was arrested for casting an illegal vote in the presidential election of 1872.
- She was tried and then fined $100, but she refused to pay.

Vocabulary:

indictment: accusation in court
alleged: supposed
preamble: introduction
posterity: children
disfranchisement: denial of the right to vote
bill of attainder: law that allows punishment without trial
ex post facto law: legal order making something illegal only after the thing has been done

odious: terrible
aristocracy: high social class
oligarchy: rule by a small group of people over a larger group
Saxon: White person, of European heritage
ordain: to declare
dissension: disagreement
hardihood: strength
immunities: protections
null and void: having no legal power

Document: On Women's Right to Vote, Susan B. Anthony, 1872

Friends and fellow citizens: I stand before you tonight under indictment for the alleged crime of having voted at the last presidential election, without having a lawful right to vote. It shall be my work this evening to prove to you that in thus voting, I not only committed no crime, but, instead, simply exercised my citizen's rights, guaranteed to me and all United States citizens by the National Constitution, beyond the power of any state to deny.

The preamble of the Federal Constitution says: "We, the people of the United States, in order to form a more perfect union, establish justice, insure domestic tranquility, provide for the common defense, promote the general welfare, and secure the blessings of liberty to ourselves and our posterity, do ordain and establish this Constitution for the United States of America."

It was we, the people; not we, the white male citizens; nor yet we, the male citizens; but we, the whole people, who formed the Union. And we formed it, not to give the blessings of liberty, but to secure them; not to the half of ourselves and the half of our posterity, but to the whole people—women as well as men. And it is a downright mockery to talk to women of their enjoyment of the blessings of liberty while they are denied the use of the only means of securing them provided by this democratic-republican government—the ballot.

For any state to make sex a qualification that must ever result in the disfranchisement of one entire half of the people, is to pass a bill of attainder, or, an ex post facto law, and is therefore a violation of the supreme law of the land. By it the blessings of liberty are forever withheld from women and their female posterity.

To them this government has no just powers derived from the consent of the governed. To them this government is not a democracy. It is not a republic. It is an odious aristocracy; a hateful oligarchy of sex; the most hateful aristocracy ever established on the face of the globe; an oligarchy of wealth, where the rich govern the poor. An oligarchy of learning, where the educated govern the ignorant, or even an oligarchy of race, where the Saxon rules the African, might be endured; but this oligarchy of sex, which makes father, brothers, husband, sons, the oligarchs over the mother and sisters, the wife and daughters, of every household—which ordains all men sovereigns, all women subjects, carries dissension, discord, and rebellion into every home of the nation. . . .

The only question left to be settled now is: Are women persons? And I hardly believe any of our opponents will have the hardihood to say they are not. Being persons, then, women are citizens; and no state has a right to make any law, or to enforce any old law, that shall abridge their privileges or immunities. Hence, every discrimination against women in the constitutions and laws of the several states is today null and void, precisely as is every one against Negroes.

Source: The History Place. (2012). Susan B. Anthony: On women's right to vote. Retrieved from historyplace.com/speeches/anthony.htm

Comprehension Questions:

1. List three points Anthony makes to support her argument that women have the right to vote.
2. Find two quotations that show how Anthony compares the situations of women and Black people, and put them in your own words.

Activities:

1. Thomas Paine argues in *Common Sense* (Lesson 1.3) that the difference between men and women is a "distinction of nature," whereas the difference between kings and their subjects is not. How would Anthony respond to Paine's claim? Create a cartoon with speech bubbles and thought bubbles for both figures.

Reflection: Look back at your answer from the Introduction. What has changed since 1872? What has remained the same?

Resources:

Federal Judicial Center. (n.d.). The trial of Susan B. Anthony. Retrieved from fjc.gov/history/home.nsf/page/tu_anthony_narrative.html

---

LESSON 1.10

What Did John F. Kennedy Believe the United States Should Do for the World?

Historical Figure: John F. Kennedy

Event: Cold War, 1946–1991

Introduction: What role do you believe the United States should play in the world?

Mini-Lecture:

- John F. Kennedy was president from 1961 until his assassination in 1963.
- He was president during the Cold War, a rivalry between capitalist countries, led by the United States, and communist countries, led by the Soviet Union.
- During the Cold War, the United States and the Soviet Union participated in an "arms race" to accumulate nuclear weapons, competed for influence around the world, and intervened in wars in countries such as Vietnam.
- Capitalism is an economic theory that people should sell their labor and their products, competing to accumulate wealth in the marketplace.
- Communism is an economic theory that there should be a classless society instead of economic inequality, and that workers should control their workplaces and own natural resources in common.
- In 1991, the Cold War ended when the Soviet Union broke apart into individual republics, including Russia.

Vocabulary:

forebears: ancestors
foe: enemy
tempered: tested

adversary: enemy
tribulation: difficulties

Document: Inaugural address, John F. Kennedy, 1961

> The world is very different now [from how it was when the United States was founded]. For man holds in his mortal hands the power to abolish all forms of human poverty and all forms of human life. And yet the same revolutionary beliefs for which our forebears fought are still at issue around the globe—the belief that the rights of man come not from the generosity of the state, but from the hand of God.
>
> We dare not forget today that we are the heirs of that first revolution. Let the word go forth from this time and place, to friend and foe alike, that the torch has been passed to a new generation of Americans—born in this century, tempered by war, disciplined by a hard and bitter peace, proud of our ancient heritage, and unwilling to witness or permit the slow undoing of those human rights to which this nation has always been committed, and to which we are committed today at home and around the world. . . .
>
> To those people in the huts and villages of half the globe struggling to break the bonds of mass misery, we pledge our best efforts to help them help themselves, for whatever period is required—not because the Communists may be doing it, not because we seek their votes, but because it is right. If a free society cannot help the many who are poor, it cannot save the few who are rich. . . .
>
> Finally, to those nations who would make themselves our adversary, we offer not a pledge but a request: that both sides begin anew the quest for peace,

before the dark powers of destruction unleashed by science engulf all humanity in planned or accidental self-destruction. . . .

Now the trumpet summons us again—not as a call to bear arms, though arms we need—not as a call to battle, though embattled we are—but a call to bear the burden of a long twilight struggle, year in and year out, "rejoicing in hope; patient in tribulation," a struggle against the common enemies of man: tyranny, poverty, disease, and war itself.

Can we forge against these enemies a grand and global alliance, North and South, East and West, that can assure a more fruitful life for all mankind? Will you join in that historic effort?

In the long history of the world, only a few generations have been granted the role of defending freedom in its hour of maximum danger. I do not shrink from this responsibility—I welcome it. I do not believe that any of us would exchange places with any other people or any other generation. The energy, the faith, the devotion which we bring to this endeavor will light our country and all who serve it. And the glow from that fire can truly light the world. And so, my fellow Americans, ask not what your country can do for you; ask what you can do for your country. My fellow citizens of the world, ask not what America will do for you, but what together we can do for the freedom of man.

Source: Voices of Democracy. (n.d.). John Fitzgerald Kennedy, inaugural address. Retrieved from voicesofdemocracy.umd.edu/kennedy-inaugural-address-speech-text/

Comprehension Questions:

1. Name three groups Kennedy is addressing in this speech.
2. What is his main message to each of them?

Activities:

1. Work with a partner to create and illustrate a list of technologies that existed in 1961 for "abolishing human poverty" and "abolishing all forms of human life" that did not exist during the Revolutionary War; then list technologies for those purposes that exist today but didn't exist in 1961.
2. Find three quotations in which Kennedy alludes to the Cold War without mentioning it directly.

Reflection: What do you think you can do for the United States? For the world?

Resources:

John F. Kennedy Presidential Library and Museum. (n.d.). Curricular resources. Retrieved from jfklibrary.org/Education/Teachers/Curricular-Resources.aspx

LESSON 1.11

WHY DID RONALD REAGAN BELIEVE AMERICA WAS GREAT?

Historical Figure: Ronald Reagan

Event: Ronald Reagan elected, 1980

Introduction: What factors do you think are most important in evaluating a country's "greatness"? Choose your top three from this list, and compare with a partner: 1. Wealth 2. Health Outcomes 3. Military Power 4. Spiritual Strength 5. Equality of Opportunity 6. Advanced Technology 7. Generosity to Other Countries 8. Education 9. Civil Liberties 10. Some Other Factor: _____

Mini-Lecture:

- Ronald Reagan was president from 1981 to 1989.
- Before he was president, he was governor of California from 1967 to 1975.
- Our document is from a speech he gave at the Conservative Political Action Conference while he was governor.
- Reagan defined himself as a conservative. The meaning of that term has changed over time, but currently in the United States, conservatives favor an economic

Figure 1.5. Basic U.S. Political Spectrum circa 2017

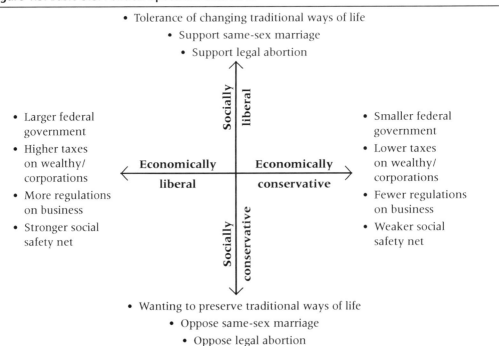

system in which a small federal government places lower tax rates on wealthy people and corporations and reduces regulations on businesses in order to promote economic growth (see Figure 1.5). People who are socially conservative favor ways of life they define as traditional. For instance, they may oppose same-sex marriage and legal abortion for religious reasons. Conservatives can be described as toward "the right" on the political spectrum, and may be represented by the Republican Party.
- At the other end of the spectrum, liberals favor an economic system in which the federal government places higher tax rates on wealthy people and corporations in order to create a social safety net (see Lessons 4.10 and 4.11) for poorer people, and regulates businesses in order to protect public well-being. People who are socially liberal favor what they define as tolerance of changing traditional ways of life. Currently in the United States, liberals can be described as toward "the left" on the political spectrum, and may be represented by the Democratic Party.
- People toward the middle of the spectrum economically or socially can be called moderate. People can be socially liberal, but economically conservative; or vice versa.

Vocabulary:

abiding: long-lasting
materialism: quality of valuing money more than people

charged with: accused of

Document: A City on a Hill, Ronald Reagan, 1974

> I have always believed that there was some divine plan that placed this great continent between two oceans to be sought out by those who were possessed of an abiding love of freedom and a special kind of courage. This was true of those who pioneered the great wilderness in the beginning of this country, as it is also true of those later immigrants who were willing to leave the land of their birth and come to a land where even the language was unknown to them.
>
> . . . One-half of all the economic activity in the entire history of man has taken place in this republic. We have distributed our wealth more widely among our people than any society known to man. Americans work less hours for a higher standard of living than any other people. Ninety-five percent of all our families have an adequate daily intake of nutrients—and a part of the five percent that don't are trying to lose weight! Ninety-nine percent have gas or electric refrigeration, 92 percent have televisions, and an equal number have telephones. There are 120 million cars on our streets and highways—and all of them are on the street at once when you are trying to get home at night.
>
> But isn't this just proof of our materialism—the very thing that we are charged with? Well, we also have more churches, more libraries, we support

voluntarily more symphony orchestras, and opera companies, non-profit theaters, and publish more books than all the other nations of the world put together.

. . . We cannot escape our destiny, nor should we try to do so. The leadership of the free world was thrust upon us two centuries ago in that little hall of Philadelphia. . . . We are indeed, and we are today, the last best hope of man on earth.

Source: TributetoRonaldReagan.com. (2004). A city on a hill, 1974. Retrieved from jeffhead.com/reagantribute/speech02.htm
Courtesy Ronald Reagan Library.

Comprehension Questions:

1. According to Reagan, whose plan led to the creation of the United States?
2. List five pieces of evidence Reagan provides to support his claim that the United States is the greatest country on earth.

Activities:

1. For three of the five pieces of evidence you listed above, find current statistics. Work with a partner to create a bar graph showing the change in these figures.
2. Compare Reagan's evidence that the United States was great in 1974 to what you think the United States needs to be great today. Create a Venn diagram showing the common factors that you and Reagan use to evaluate greatness and the factors that are different.

Reflection: Do you believe the United States was greater in the past that it is now, or will be greater in the future than it is now? Why?

Resources:

Central Intelligence Agency. CIA world factbook. Retrieved from cia.gov/library/publications/the-world-factbook/

Pew Research Center. (2017). Political Typology Quiz. Retrieved from people-press.org/quiz/political-typology/

LESSON 1.12

WHY DID BARACK OBAMA THINK THE UNITED STATES WAS NOT YET A PERFECT UNION?

Historical Figure: Barack Obama

Event: Barack Obama elected, 2008

Introduction: What do you think are the United States' major flaws in the present or mistakes in the past?

UNIT QUESTION: What Is American Democracy, and What Should It Be?

Mini-Lecture:

- Barack Obama was president from 2009 to 2017.
- He represented Illinois in the U.S. Senate from 2005 to 2008.
- Obama was the son of a White American woman and a Black man from Kenya; he was the first Black or biracial U.S. president.
- This document is from a speech he gave during his campaign for president in 2008.
- Obama made this speech after facing controversy because the pastor at his church, Jeremiah Wright, made comments critical of the United States.

Vocabulary:

improbable: unlikely to happen, rare
bondage: lack of freedom
successive: one after another
Jim Crow: legal and informal discrimination against African Americans between the late 1800s and the civil rights movement of the 1960s.

Brown v. Board of Education: a 1954 court case that made racial segregation in schools illegal
pervasive: widespread
achievement gap: difference between academic attainment of two groups of students

Document: A More Perfect Union, Barack Obama, 2008

> "We the people, in order to form a more perfect union." Two hundred and twenty one years ago, in a hall that still stands across the street, a group of men gathered and, with these simple words, launched America's improbable experiment in democracy. . . .
>
> The document [the Constitution] they produced was eventually signed but ultimately unfinished. It was stained by this nation's original sin of slavery, a question that divided the colonies and brought the convention to a stalemate until the founders chose to allow the slave trade to continue for at least twenty more years, and to leave any final resolution to future generations.
>
> Of course, the answer to the slavery question was already embedded within our Constitution—a Constitution that had at i[t]s very core the ideal of equal citizenship under the law; a Constitution that promised its people liberty, and justice, and a union that could be and should be perfected over time.
>
> And yet words on a parchment would not be enough to deliver slaves from bondage, or provide men and women of every color and creed their full rights and obligations as citizens of the United States. What would be needed were Americans in successive generations who were willing to do their part—through protests and struggle, on the streets and in the courts, through a civil war and civil disobedience and always at great risk—to narrow that gap between the promise of our ideals and the reality of their time. . . .
>
> As William Faulkner once wrote, "The past isn't dead and buried. In fact, it isn't even past." We do not need to recite here the history of racial injustice in

this country. But we do need to remind ourselves that so many of the disparities that exist in the African-American community today can be directly traced to inequalities passed on from an earlier generation that suffered under the brutal legacy of slavery and Jim Crow.

Segregated schools were, and are, inferior schools; we still haven't fixed them, fifty years after Brown v. Board of Education, and the inferior education they provided, then and now, helps explain the pervasive achievement gap between today's black and white students. . . .

In the white community, the path to a more perfect union means acknowledging that what ails the African-American community does not just exist in the minds of black people; that the legacy of discrimination—and current incidents of discrimination, while less overt than in the past—are real and must be addressed. . . .

For we have a choice in this country. We can accept a politics that breeds division, and conflict, and cynicism. . . . Or, at this moment, in this election, we can come together and say, "Not this time." This time we want to talk about the crumbling schools that are stealing the future of black children and white children and Asian children and Hispanic children and Native American children. . . . This union may never be perfect, but generation after generation has shown that it can always be perfected.

Source: Huffington Post. (2008, March 18). Obama race speech. Retrieved from huffingtonpost.com/2008/03/18/obama-race-speech-read-th_n_92077.html

Comprehension Questions:

1. Why does Obama think the Constitution was unfinished when it was ratified?
2. According to Obama, why is there an achievement gap between Black and White students?

Activities:

1. Obama identified as liberal or progressive, whereas Reagan (Lesson 1.10) identified as conservative. Imagine a debate between them about what makes American great and what could be improved today. One half of the class can represent Reagan's views, and the other half can represent Obama's views.

Reflection: Do you agree with Obama that our union (the United States) isn't currently perfect? Do you agree that it can be perfected? Why or why not?

Resources:

Ross, R., & El Buri, R. (2008, March 13.) Obama's pastor: God damn America, US to blame for 9/11. ABC News. Retrieved from abcnews.go.com/Blotter/DemocraticDebate/story?id=4443788&page=1

UNIT CONCLUSION

Over the course of this unit, students have gained a sense of the foundations of American democracy and how those foundations have been shaken and rebuilt by those originally excluded from its protections. Students may be left with a sense of pride in what the country has accomplished, disappointment in the ways it has fallen short, or enthusiasm to improve our democracy in the future. They may be considering where they fit into the political spectrum they have learned about.

The classroom summit will help students process and integrate these ideas. Because this will be the first summit, they may need extra support in preparing for it. They already have some practice imagining dialogues between historical figures, and their Summit Research Worksheet (Appendix F) will give them a chance to consider what their character would say. Teachers may wish to introduce this summit as a "practice round" for skills they will be perfecting all year. It is normal for students to struggle at first to represent their historical figure's views instead of their own—teachers can "pause" the summit to ask the class questions like "Would Frederick Douglass say that?" if their answers veer too far from the historical record. After gathering some constructive criticism, teachers can "rewind" and allow "Frederick Douglass" to give his answer again. Teachers may even want to record the summit to allow students to reflect back on it later.

Be sure to take time at the end of the summit for students to drop their characters and discuss the Unit Question and Current Issue Question from their own perspectives; this is a good opportunity to re-emphasize the Discussion Guidelines (see p. 18 and Appendix J). In most units, there will be a historical figure associated with the Current Issue Question. However, since the "historical figures" whose tweets are quoted in Lesson 1.1 are a group of ordinary Americans, no one will need to represent them. Nevertheless, when the students come out of character to discuss their own views at the end of the summit, they may wish to refer to the tweets from Lesson 1.1.

CHAPTER 2

Diversity and Discrimination
UNIT QUESTION: What Does Equality Mean?

Current Issue Question: What are your views on same-sex marriage?

Unit Introduction: In this unit, students will investigate how ideas about equality have changed over the past two hundred years. They will see how the Constitution created a basis both for equality and inequality, leading to a string of Supreme Court cases that restricted people's rights based on race or ethnicity: *Dred Scott v. Sandford*, *Plessy v. Ferguson*, and *Fong Yue Ting v. US*. They will consider John Brown's and Malcolm X's arguments that violence may be necessary to defend groups that have been denied their rights. Elizabeth Cady Stanton will argue that women should not only have the right to vote but also have social equality with men. *Brown v. Board of Education* will prompt students to consider the progress the United States has made and how much work is still to be done to create equal opportunities for all.

The Current Issue Question on same-sex marriage makes it clear that debates about the meaning of equality are far from over. This topic can be polarizing, so teachers may consult with parents and administrators in advance and reiterate Discussion Guidelines for students (see Appendix J). If there are LGBTQ students or families, teachers will want to take special care that their needs and wishes are respected. If some students or families hold strong religious views against same-sex marriage, it may be helpful to remind them that the purpose of the discussion is not to reach consensus on the issue, but to understand the constitutional arguments for and against same-sex marriage and how it fits into a history of Supreme Court decisions.

This unit may also prompt some difficult conversations about race and gender, of which parents and administrators may wish to be informed in advance. Extreme views, such as Hiram W. Evans's argument for the superiority of White Europeans, are likely to shock and dismay many students. Students of marginalized ethnicities, races, or genders may feel anger about how their ancestors were treated and how that marginalization carries over into contemporary life. Teachers might give these students the choice to opt out of some discussions or activities and provide alternate assignments that convey the same content. White or male students may feel guilty, on the one hand, or

Unit Question: What Does Equality Mean?

defensive, on the other, when confronted with the way their ancestors treated other groups or when considering the privileges they have today. It will be important for teachers to remind students that it is only by discussing these difficult topics that we can hope to move toward a more just society.

LESSON 2.1
What Was the Supreme Court's Argument for Allowing Same-Sex Marriage?

Historical Figure: Anthony Kennedy

Event: Supreme Court allows same-sex marriage, 2015

Introduction: How do you think attitudes toward LGBTQ (lesbian, gay, bisexual, transgender, and queer or questioning) people have changed over the past 50 years?

Mini-Lecture:

- Same-sex marriage is marriage between two men or two women.
- The Federal Defense of Marriage Act (DOMA), passed in 1996, defined marriage as between one man and one woman.
- In 2013, the Supreme Court decided that DOMA was unconstitutional, and the federal government began recognizing same-sex marriages.
- Same-sex marriages were legal in some states but not others.
- In 2013, two men, James Obergefell and John Arthur, got married in Maryland, because same-sex marriage was not legal in their home state of Ohio.
- Obergefell sued so the state of Ohio would recognize their marriage.
- The case went to the Supreme Court, and in 2015 the court decided in favor of Obergefell, and same-sex couples from other states, that all states had to recognize same-sex marriage.
- Justice Anthony Kennedy, who joined the Supreme Court in 1989, wrote the majority opinion in the case.

Vocabulary:

petitioner: person suing in court
respondent: person being sued in court
held: decided by the court
Fourteenth Amendment: an amendment to the Constitution that protects people from losing "life, liberty, or property" without "due process of law" (for instance, a trial) and that grants all people "equal protection of the laws."
demean: to disrespect

coverture: laws that, until the 20th century in the United States, gave wives fewer legal rights than their husbands
intimacy: what couples do in private
autonomy: ability to make decisions about one's own life
discord: inconsistency
stricture: restriction

Document: *Obergefell v. Hodges*, Supreme Court, 2015

Michigan, Kentucky, Ohio, and Tennessee define marriage as a union between one man and one woman. The petitioners, 14 same-sex couples and two men whose same-sex partners are deceased, filed suits in Federal District Courts in their home States, claiming that respondent state officials violate the Fourteenth Amendment by denying them the right to marry or to have marriages lawfully performed in another State given full recognition. . . .

Held: The Fourteenth Amendment requires a State to license a marriage between two people of the same sex and to recognize a marriage between two people of the same sex when their marriage was lawfully licensed and performed out-of-State. . . .

(1) The history of marriage as a union between two persons of the opposite sex marks the beginning of these cases. To the respondents, it would demean a timeless institution if marriage were extended to same-sex couples. But the petitioners, far from seeking to devalue marriage, seek it for themselves because of their respect—and need—for its privileges and responsibilities, as illustrated by the petitioners' own experiences. . . .

(2) The history of marriage is one of both continuity and change. Changes, such as the decline of arranged marriages and the abandonment of the law of coverture, have worked deep transformations in the structure of marriage, affecting aspects of marriage once viewed as essential. These new insights have strengthened, not weakened, the institution. Changed understandings of marriage are characteristic of a Nation where new dimensions of freedom become apparent to new generations.

This dynamic can be seen in the Nation's experience with gay and lesbian rights. Well into the 20th century, many States condemned same-sex intimacy as immoral, and homosexuality was treated as an illness. Later in the century, cultural and political developments allowed same-sex couples to lead more open and public lives. Extensive public and private dialogue followed, along with shifts in public attitudes. Questions about the legal treatment of gays and lesbians soon reached the courts, where they could be discussed in the formal discourse of the law. In 2003, this Court overruled its 1986 decision in *Bowers v. Hardwick*, . . . which upheld a Georgia law that criminalized certain homosexual acts, concluding laws making same-sex intimacy a crime "demea[n] the lives of homosexual persons." . . .

(1) The fundamental liberties protected by the Fourteenth Amendment Due Process Clause extend to certain personal choices central to individual dignity and autonomy, including intimate choices defining personal identity and beliefs. . . . Courts must exercise reasoned judgment in identifying interests of the person so fundamental that the State must accord them its respect. History and tradition guide and discipline the inquiry but do not set its outer boundaries. When new insight reveals discord between the Constitution's central protections and a received legal stricture, a claim to liberty must be addressed.

Source: Legal Information Institute. (n.d.). *Obergefell v. Hodges.* Retrieved from law.cornell.edu/supct/pdf/14-556.pdf

UNIT QUESTION: What Does Equality Mean?

Comprehension Questions:

1. According to the Supreme Court, how has marriage changed over the years?
2. According to the Supreme Court, how have views about gays and lesbians changed over the years?

Activities:

1. With a small group, generate a list of laws that would deprive people of (a) life, (b) liberty, and (c) property WITH due process of law. Then generate a list of laws that would deprive people of (a) life, (b) liberty, and (c) property WITHOUT due process of law. Place Ohio's law banning same-sex marriage, which the Supreme Court overturned with its decision in *Obergefell v. Hodges*, in an appropriate place on the list.
2. Four out of nine of the justices on the Supreme Court disagreed with the majority in *Obergefell v. Hodges*. What argument do you think they made about why bans on same-sex marriage did not violate the Due Process and Equal Protection Clauses?

Reflection: Do you believe that LGBTQ people need the right to get married in order to have equality? Why or why not?

Resources:

Legal Information Institute. (n.d.). Dissent in Obergefell v. Hodges. Retrieved from law.cornell.edu/supremecourt/text/14-556#writing-14-556_DISSENT_4

National LGBTQ Task Force. (2016). National LGBTQ Task Force. Retrieved from thetaskforce.org/

LESSON 2.2

WHAT DID THE CONSTITUTION SAY ABOUT SLAVERY?

Historical Figure: Roger Sherman

Event: Constitutional Convention, 1787

Introduction: Think of a time in your life when you and a friend or family member made a compromise. Did it work out well? Why or why not?

Mini-Lecture:

- When the delegates to the Constitutional Convention were drafting the Constitution, they had disagreements about slavery, and especially about whether slaves should be counted for the purposes of taxation and representation.
- In the late 1700s, all Southern states allowed slavery, while some Northern states did not.
- Delegates from states that allowed slavery wanted slaves to be counted when it was being considered how many representatives the delegates should get in Congress, so those states could have more power.

- Delegates from states that allowed slavery did not want slaves to be counted for purposes of taxation, because then slave owners would have to pay higher taxes.
- Delegates from states where slavery was illegal wanted the opposite: for slaves to be counted for taxation but not representation.
- As a compromise, the delegates agreed that slaves would count as three-fifths of a person for the purposes of taxation and representation; this compromise was based on the racist idea that Black people were not equal to Whites.
- Roger Sherman, a delegate from Connecticut, helped to gain agreement on the compromise.
- Sherman was personally opposed to slavery on moral grounds, but he did not want the issue to prevent Southern states from ratifying the Constitution.

Vocabulary:

apportioned: assigned or given out
importation: bringing goods for sale into the country
discharged: freed
party: person

Document: U.S. Constitution, 1787

> Article I, Section 2, Clause 3: Representatives and direct Taxes shall be apportioned among the several States which may be included within this Union, according to their respective Numbers, which shall be determined by adding to the whole Number of free Persons, including those bound to Service for a Term of Years, and excluding Indians not taxed, three fifths of all other Persons. . . .
>
> Article I, Section 9, Clause 1: The Migration or Importation of such Persons as any of the States now existing shall think proper to admit, shall not be prohibited by the Congress prior to the Year one thousand eight hundred and eight, but a Tax or duty may be imposed on such Importation, not exceeding ten dollars for each Person. . . .
>
> Article IV, Section 2, Clause 3: No Person held to Service or Labour in one State, under the Laws thereof, escaping into another, shall, in Consequence of any Law or Regulation therein, be discharged from such Service or Labour, but shall be delivered up on Claim of the Party to whom such Service or Labour may be due.

Comprehension Questions:

1. Why aren't Indians given representation in Congress?
2. Who are the "other Persons" referred to in Article I, Section 2, Clause 3?
3. After what date could Congress end the slave trade?
4. What would happen to a slave who escaped to a state where slavery was illegal?

Activities:

1. Why do you think indentured servants (people "bound to Service for a Term of Years") were counted as whole people for the purposes of taxation and representation?

Unit Question: What Does Equality Mean?

2. Come up with a list of words to describe how the writers of the Constitution saw slaves. Write your answers on posters around the room and do a gallery walk to see other students' responses.

Reflection: Do you see Roger Sherman as a hero, for arranging a compromise that allowed the Constitution to be ratified by all states? Or do you see him in a negative light because he allowed slaves to be counted as less than whole people?

Resources:

Takaki, R., & Steffof, R. (2012). The hidden origins of slavery. In *A different mirror for young people* (chap. 3). New York, NY: Seven Stories Press.

LESSON 2.3

How Did Native Americans Argue for Equal Rights?

Historical Figure: John Ross

Event: Trail of Tears, 1838

Introduction: What would you guess were the similarities and differences between the lives of Native Americans and White people in the United States in the early 1800s?

Mini-Lecture:

- John Ross was a leader of the Cherokee nation in Georgia.
- Many Native American nations had practiced agriculture for hundreds of years before the arrival of Europeans.
- However, many Europeans considered agriculture and permanent settlements to be elements of civilization that they had invented, so they called some Native Americans who had this lifestyle (the Cherokee, Creek, Seminole, Chickasaw, and Choctaw Nations) the "Five Civilized Tribes."
- Andrew Jackson, who became U.S. president in 1828, wanted the Cherokee to leave Georgia so the Whites could use their land.
- Jackson forced some Cherokee leaders to sign the Treaty of New Etocha, which stated that the Cherokee people had to move to "Indian Territory" that the government had created in Oklahoma.
- Cherokee people call their journey to Oklahoma the Trail of Tears, because 4,000 out of 15,000 people died along the way.
- This document is from a letter than John Ross wrote to Congress in 1836, protesting the treaty.

Vocabulary:

stipulation: a point written down in a document
despoil: to steal
indefeasible: not to be defeated or lost

plundered: stolen
utterance: ability to speak
audacious: daring and bold
stratagem: a clever, tricky plan

dexterity: skillfulness
reiterated: repeated
gloried: felt pride
veneration: great respect

precept: belief or rule
manifest: clearly seen
industrious: hard-working
rude: uncivilized

Document: To the Senate and House of Representatives, John Ross, 1838

By the stipulations of this instrument [the treaty], we are despoiled of our private possessions, the indefeasible property of individuals. We are stripped of every attribute of freedom and eligibility for legal self-defence. Our property may be plundered before our eyes; violence may be committed on our persons; even our lives may be taken away, and there is none to regard our complaints. We are denationalized; we are disfranchised. We are deprived of membership in the human family! We have neither land nor home, nor resting place that can be called our own. . . .

We are overwhelmed! Our hearts are sickened, our utterance is paralyzed, when we reflect on the condition in which we are placed, by the audacious practices of unprincipled men, who have managed their stratagems with so much dexterity as to impose on the Government of the United States, in the face of our earnest, solemn, and reiterated protestations.

In truth, our cause is your own; it is the cause of liberty and of justice; it is based upon your own principles, which we have learned from yourselves; for we have gloried to count your [George] Washington and your [Thomas] Jefferson our great teachers; we have read their communications to us with veneration; we have practised their precepts with success. And the result is manifest. The wildness of the forest has given place to comfortable dwellings and cultivated fields, stocked with the various domestic animals. Mental culture, industrious habits, and domestic enjoyments, have succeeded the rudeness of the savage state.

Source: PBS. (n.d.). Cherokee letter protesting the Treaty of New Etocha. Retrieved from pbs.org/wgbh/aia/part4/4h3083t.html

Comprehension Questions:

1. Who is Ross addressing in this document?
2. What are Ross's problems with the Treaty of New Etocha?
3. According to Ross, how have the Cherokee people applied the teachings of Jefferson and Washington?

Activities:

1. How do you think Andrew Jackson (Lesson 1.6) would respond to this letter? Work with a partner to write Jackson's possible response.
2. Look back at the Three-Fifths Compromise (Lesson 2.2). Could John Ross use it to support his points, or could Andrew Jackson use it to contradict Ross's points?

UNIT QUESTION: What Does Equality Mean?

Reflection: Were the similarities and differences you thought might exist between the lives of Native Americans and White Americans in the early 1800s corroborated or contradicted by this document? How so?

Resources:

PBS. (n.d.). Indian removal. Retrieved from pbs.org/wgbh/aia/part4/4p2959.html
PBS. (n.d.). Andrew Jackson's second annual message. Retrieved from pbs.org/wgbh/aia/part4/4h3437t.html

LESSON 2.4
HOW DID SOJOURNER TRUTH DEFINE EQUALITY?

Historical Figure: Sojourner Truth

Event: Ohio Women's Rights Convention, 1851

Introduction: Are men and women different, apart from biological differences in their bodies?

Mini-Lecture:

- Sojourner Truth (c. 1797–1883) was an activist for women's rights and the abolition of slavery.
- She was born into slavery and escaped just before New York, where she was living, emancipated slaves.
- She became a Christian and traveled the country speaking out against slavery and the oppression of women.
- This document comes from a speech she gave at the Ohio Women's Rights Convention.

Vocabulary:

ain't: aren't
out of kilter: wrong, out of balance
'twixt: between
in a fix: having a problem

head: to outperform
lash: whip
mean: stingy
obliged: grateful

Document: Ain't I a Woman? Soujourner Truth, 1851

> Well, children, where there is so much racket there must be something out of kilter. I think that 'twixt the negroes of the South and the women at the North, all talking about rights, the white men will be in a fix pretty soon. But what's all this here talking about?
>
> That man over there says that women need to be helped into carriages, and lifted over ditches, and to have the best place everywhere. Nobody ever helps me into carriages, or over mud-puddles, or gives me any best place! And ain't I a woman? Look at me! Look at my arm! I have ploughed and planted, and

gathered into barns, and no man could head me! And ain't I a woman? I could work as much and eat as much as a man—when I could get it—and bear the lash as well! And ain't I a woman? I have borne thirteen children, and seen most all sold off to slavery, and when I cried out with my mother's grief, none but Jesus heard me! And ain't I a woman?

Then they talk about this thing in the head; what's this they call it? [member of audience whispers, "intellect"] That's it, honey. What's that got to do with women's rights or negroes' rights? If my cup won't hold but a pint, and yours holds a quart, wouldn't you be mean not to let me have my little half measure full?

Then that little man in black there, he says women can't have as much rights as men, 'cause Christ wasn't a woman! Where did your Christ come from? Where did your Christ come from? From God and a woman! Man had nothing to do with Him.

If the first woman God ever made was strong enough to turn the world upside down all alone, these women together ought to be able to turn it back, and get it right side up again! And now they is asking to do it, the men better let them.

Obliged to you for hearing me, and now old Sojourner ain't got nothing more to say.

Source: Aug, P. H. (1997). Ain't I a Woman? Modern History Sourcebook. Retrieved from sourcebooks.fordham.edu/mod/sojtruth-woman.asp

Comprehension Questions:

1. List five pieces of evidence Truth provides for why she should have equal rights with White men.

Activities:

1. Discuss with a small group: Is Truth's main point that women and men are the same? Or that women are superior to men? Or that men and women are different? Or is her main point something else? Find two quotations that support your argument, and present your work to the class.

Reflection: How have ideas about men and women changed since 1851? How have they stayed the same?

Resources:

National Women's History Museum. (n.d.). Sojourner Truth. Retrieved from www.nwhm.org/education-resources/biography/biographies/sojourner-truth/

LESSON 2.5

WHAT WAS THE SUPREME COURT'S RATIONALE FOR DENYING BLACK PEOPLE CITIZENSHIP?

Historical Figure: Roger Taney

Unit Question: What Does Equality Mean?

Event: *Scott v. Sandford*, 1856

Introduction: In 1776, the authors of the Declaration of Independence wrote, "All men are created equal." Do you think they meant *all* men? Why or why not?

Mini-Lecture:

- In 1853, an enslaved Black person named Dred Scott sued his owner, John Sandford, for his freedom.
- Scott had been born into slavery in Missouri but had been taken by his owner to Illinois, a state that outlawed slavery.
- When Scott returned to Missouri, he sued for his freedom, but was denied; his appeal went to the Supreme Court.
- Roger Taney was chief justice of the Supreme Court from 1836 to 1864.
- Our document comes from the Supreme Court's decision in the *Scott v. Sandford* case, which was written by Taney.
- The court decided in favor of Sandford, arguing that Scott had no grounds on which to sue anyone, because neither he nor any Black descendant of slaves was a citizen.

Vocabulary:

immunity: protection
subjection: being under the rule of others
pupilage: being a student, in a less powerful position
naturalize: to become a citizen
abode: home

instrument: document
traffic: trade
endowed: given
unalienable: not able to be taken away
institute: to create

Document: *Scott v. Sandford*, Supreme Court, 1856

> The question is simply this: can a negro whose ancestors were imported into this country and sold as slaves become a member of the political community formed and brought into existence by the Constitution of the United States, and as such become entitled to all the rights, and privileges, and immunities, guaranteed by that instrument to the citizen, one of which rights is the privilege of suing in a court of the United States in the cases specified in the Constitution? . . .
>
> The situation of this population was altogether unlike that of the Indian race. . . . although they [Native Americans] were uncivilized, they were yet a free and independent people, associated together in nations or tribes and governed by their own laws. . . . It is true that the course of events has brought the Indian tribes within the limits of the United States under subjection to the white race, and it has been found necessary, for their sake as well as our own, to regard them as in a state of pupilage, and to legislate to a certain extent over them and the territory they occupy. But they may, without doubt, like the subjects of any other foreign Government, be naturalized by the authority of Congress, and become citizens of a State, and of the United States, and if an individual should

leave his nation or tribe and take up his abode among the white population, he would be entitled to all the rights and privileges which would belong to an emigrant from any other foreign people.

. . . In the opinion of the court, the legislation and histories of the times, and the language used in the Declaration of Independence, show that neither the class of persons who had been imported as slaves nor their descendants, whether they had become free or not, were then acknowledged as a part of the people, nor intended to be included in the general words used in that memorable instrument. . . .

They [Black people] had for more than a century before been regarded as beings of an inferior order, and altogether unfit to associate with the white race either in social or political relations, and so far inferior that they had no rights which the white man was bound to respect, and that the negro might justly and lawfully be reduced to slavery for his benefit. He was bought and sold, and treated as an ordinary article of merchandise and traffic whenever a profit could be made by it. . . .

"We hold these truths to be self-evident: that all men are created equal; that they are endowed by their Creator with certain unalienable rights; that among them is life, liberty, and the pursuit of happiness; that to secure these rights, Governments are instituted, deriving their just powers from the consent of the governed."

The general words above quoted would seem to embrace the whole human family, and if they were used in a similar instrument at this day would be so understood. But it is too clear for dispute that the enslaved African race were not intended to be included.

Source: Justia. (n.d.). *Scott v. Sandford*. Retrieved from supreme.justia.com/cases/federal/us/60/393/case.html

Comprehension Questions:

1. According to Taney, why doesn't the promise of equal rights in the Declaration of Independence apply to Black people?
2. According to Taney, how could Native Americans become citizens of the United States?

Activities:

1. Create a Venn diagram that shows similarities and differences between Taney's views of Native Americans and of Black people.
2. How do you think Roger Sherman, from Lesson 2.2, would respond to Roger Taney's argument? Work with a partner to write a dialogue they might have, and act it out for the class.

Reflection: Do you think founding documents, including the Constitution and the Declaration of Independence, should be applied as the writers intended or as people today interpret them? Why?

Resources:

National Park Service. (2006). Dred Scott trial. Retrieved from nps.gov/jeff/learn/education/upload/dred4.pdf

LESSON 2.6
WHY DID JOHN BROWN THINK VIOLENCE WAS JUSTIFIED TO END SLAVERY?

Historical Figure: John Brown

Event: Attack on Harper's Ferry, 1859

Introduction: Would you break a law you thought was unjust? Why or why not?

Mini-Lecture:

- John Brown was a White abolitionist who was willing to use violence to end slavery.
- He had a plan to form an antislavery army, and he wanted to get guns for his soldiers.
- In 1859, he, along with 5 Black and 16 White people, attacked the federal arsenal (storage place for weapons) in Harper's Ferry, Virginia.
- The raid did not go as planned, and many of Brown's group, as well as bystanders, were killed in the fight.
- Brown was tried, convicted of treason (betraying his country), and executed.
- Our document is the speech he made at his trial.

Vocabulary:

design: purpose
incite: to provoke or motivate
insurrection: rebellion
candor: honesty
deem: to think

validity: truth
would that: to want
for the furtherance of: to contribute to
enactment: law

Document: Address to the Virginia Court, John Brown, 1859

> I have, may it please the Court, a few words to say. In the first place, I deny everything but what I have all along admitted, the design on my part to free the slaves. I intended certainly to have made a clean thing of that matter, as I did last winter, when I went into Missouri and there took slaves without the snapping of a gun on either side, moved them through the country, and finally left them in Canada. I designed to have done the same thing again, on a larger scale. That was all I intended. I never did intend murder, or treason, or the destruction of property, or to excite or incite slaves to rebellion, or to make insurrection.
>
> I have another objection; and that is, it is unjust that I should suffer such a penalty. Had I interfered in the manner which I admit, and which I admit

has been fairly proved (for I admire the truthfulness and candor of the greater portion of the witnesses who have testified in this case), had I so interfered in behalf of the rich, the powerful, the intelligent, the so-called great, or in behalf of any of their friends, either father, mother, brother, sister, wife, or children, or any of that class, and suffered and sacrificed what I have in this interference, it would have been all right; and every man in this court would have deemed it an act worthy of reward rather than punishment.

This court acknowledges, as I suppose, the validity of the law of God. I see a book kissed here which I suppose to be the Bible, or at least the New Testament. That teaches me that all things whatsoever I would that men should do to me, I should do even so to them. . . . I believe that to have interfered as I have done as I have always freely admitted I have done in behalf of His despised poor, was not wrong, but right. Now, if it is deemed necessary that I should forfeit my life for the furtherance of the ends of justice, and mingle my blood further with the blood of my children and with the blood of millions in this slave country whose rights are disregarded by wicked, cruel, and unjust enactments, I submit; so let it be done!

Source: The Gilder Lehman Institute of American History. (2016). Address of John Brown to the Virginia Court. Retrieved from www.gilderlehrman.org/sites/default/files/inline-pdfs/t-05508-051.pdf

Comprehension Questions:

1. According to Brown, what did he intend to do?
2. What does he think would have happened if he had broken the same laws, but in order to protect the rich and powerful?
3. What is Brown's argument for why he was right to break the law?

Activities:

1. In a letter he wrote on the morning of his execution, John Brown said that "the crimes of this guilty land will never be purged away but with blood." Divide the class in half and debate the following proposition: The only way to end slavery in the United States was through violence or war.

Reflection: Do you see John Brown as a hero, a villain, or something in between? Why?

Resources:

The Gilder Lehrman Institute of American History. (2016). Admiration and ambivalence: Frederick Douglass and John Brown. Retrieved from gilderlehrman.org/history-by-era/failure-compromise/essays/admiration-and-ambivalence-frederick-douglass-and-john-brow

PBS. (n.d.). John Brown. Retrieved from pbs.org/wgbh/aia/part4/4p1550.html

UNIT QUESTION: What Does Equality Mean?

LESSON 2.7

WHAT WAS THE SUPREME COURT'S REASONING FOR "SEPARATE BUT EQUAL" FACILITIES?

Historical Figure: Henry Billings Brown

Event: *Plessy v. Ferguson*, 1896

Introduction: Can laws create equality between different groups? Why or why not?

Mini-Lecture:

- Following the Civil War, during Reconstruction (1863–1877) Blacks and Whites in the South had many of the same legal rights; in the Jim Crow era that followed, the racist idea that Black people were inferior to White people was used as a rationale to resegregate the South.
- In 1890, Louisiana passed a law stating that railroads must provide segregated train cars for Blacks and Whites.
- A group of Black and multiracial citizens who thought the law was unfair convinced Homer Plessy to challenge it.
- Homer Plessy was seven-eighths White and one-eighth Black.
- Plessy bought a ticket for the "Whites Only" car, and he was arrested.
- The case went to the Supreme Court, which decided against Plessy and created the doctrine of "separate but equal" segregated facilities for Blacks and Whites.
- Henry Billings Brown, a justice on the Supreme Court from 1890 to 1906, wrote the majority opinion in this case, from which our document is taken.

Vocabulary:

act: law
statute: law
commingling: mixing
liable: likely
competency: powers
discretion: choice
usage: what people are used to
gauge: to measure

conveyance: transportation
obnoxious to: in conflict with
fallacy: mistake
construction: meaning
proposition: statement
affinities: preferences
mutual: joint
merits: good qualities

Document: *Plessy v. Ferguson*, Supreme Court, 1896

> This case turns upon the constitutionality of an act of the General Assembly of the State of Louisiana, passed in 1890, providing for separate railway carriages for the white and colored races. . . .
>
> The object of the [14th] amendment was undoubtedly to enforce the absolute equality of the two races before the law, but in the nature of things it could not have been intended to abolish distinctions based upon color, or to enforce social, as distinguished from political equality, or a commingling of the two races upon terms unsatisfactory to either. Laws permitting, and even

requiring, their separation in places where they are liable to be brought into contact do not necessarily imply the inferiority of either race to the other, and have been generally, if not universally, recognized as within the competency of the state legislatures in the exercise of their police power.

So far, then, as a conflict with the Fourteenth Amendment is concerned, the case reduces itself to the question whether the statute of Louisiana is a reasonable regulation, and with respect to this there must necessarily be a large discretion on the part of the legislature. In determining the question of reasonableness it is at liberty to act with reference to the established usages, customs and traditions of the people, and with a view to the promotion of their comfort, and the preservation of the public peace and good order.

Gauged by this standard, we cannot say that a law which authorizes or even requires the separation of the two races in public conveyances is unreasonable, or more obnoxious to the Fourteenth Amendment than the acts of Congress requiring separate schools for colored children in the District of Columbia, the constitutionality of which does not seem to have been questioned, or the corresponding acts of state legislatures.

We consider the underlying fallacy of the plaintiff's argument to consist in the assumption that the enforced separation of the two races stamps the colored race with a badge of inferiority. If this be so, it is not by reason of anything found in the act, but solely because the colored race chooses to put that construction upon it. . . . The argument also assumes that social prejudices may be overcome by legislation, and that equal rights cannot be secured to the negro except by an enforced commingling of the two races. We cannot accept this proposition. If the two races are to meet upon terms of social equality, it must be the result of natural affinities, a mutual appreciation of each other's merits and a voluntary consent of individuals. . . . If one race be inferior to the other socially, the Constitution of the United States cannot put them upon the same plane.

Source: Legal Information Institute. (n.d.). *Plessy v. Ferguson*. Retrieved from law.cornell.edu/supremecourt/text/163/537

Comprehension Questions:

1. According to Brown, what can the 14th Amendment do, and what can it *not* do?
2. What is Brown's definition of a "reasonable" law?

Activities:

1. Would John Brown (Lesson 2.6) agree with Henry Billings Brown that laws cannot create social equality between the races? Why or why not? Find a quotation from the document in Lesson 2.6 that supports your argument.
2. Henry Billings Brown argues that if separate train cars made Black people feel inferior, it was because they chose to feel that way. How do you think Homer Plessy would have responded? Write a note from Plessy to Billings Brown.

Unit Question: What Does Equality Mean?

3. In what ways do you think the separate facilities in the Jim Crow South were also unequal? With a partner, research this question and present your findings to the class.

Reflection: Which is more powerful, the Constitution itself or the Supreme Court's interpretation of it? Why?

Resources:

Medley, K. (2012). *We as Freemen: Plessy v. Ferguson*. Gretna, LA: Pelican.
Chafe, W. H. (2001). *Remembering Jim Crow: African Americans tell about life in the segregated South.* New York: The New Press.

LESSON 2.8
WHY DID ELIZABETH CADY STANTON BELIEVE WOMEN DESERVED THE SAME RIGHTS AS MEN?

Historical Figure: Elizabeth Cady Stanton

Event: Women's suffrage, 1920

Introduction: Rank the roles in your life in terms of their importance to you: (a) student, (b) brother or sister, (c) daughter or son, (d) friend, (e) citizen, (f) human, (g) parent or future parent, (h) other. Explain why you placed the roles in the order you did.

Mini-Lecture:

- Elizabeth Cady Stanton (1815–1902) was a women's rights activist.
- She was a White woman born to a wealthy family, and she had more formal education than most women of her time.
- She worked closely with activists, including Susan B. Anthony and Lucretia Mott.
- She was president of the National American Woman Suffrage Association (NAWSA), but she died before women won the right to vote in 1920.
- Our document is from a speech she gave as president of NAWSA.

Vocabulary:

Protestant: a form of Christianity that includes denominations like Baptist, Methodist, and Lutheran
arbiter: judge
faculties: abilities
fundamental: main
incidental: unimportant

sphere: area
subordinate: to give less importance to
self-sovereignty: power to make one's own decisions
endow: to give abilities to
perish: to die

Document: The Solitude of the Self, Elizabeth Cady Stanton, 1892

The point I wish plainly to bring before you on this occasion is the individuality of each human soul; our Protestant idea, the right of individual conscience and judgment—our republican idea, individual citizenship. In discussing the rights of woman, we are to consider, first, what belongs to her as an individual, in a world of her own, the arbiter of her own destiny. . . . Her rights under such circumstances are to use all her faculties for her own safety and happiness.

Secondly, if we consider her as a citizen, as a member of a great nation, she must have the same rights as all other members, according to the fundamental principles of our Government.

Thirdly, viewed as a woman, an equal factor in civilization, her rights and duties are still the same—individual happiness and development.

Fourthly, it is only the incidental relations of life, such as mother, wife, sister, daughter, that may involve some special duties and training. In the usual discussion in regard to woman's sphere, such a man as Herbert Spencer, Frederic Harrison, and Grant Allen uniformly subordinate her rights and duties as an individual, as a citizen, as a woman, to the necessities of these incidental relations, some of which a large class of woman may never assume.

In discussing the sphere of man, we do not decide his rights as an individual, as a citizen, as a man by his duties as a father, a husband, a brother, or a son, relations some of which he may never fill. Moreover he would be better fitted for these very relations and whatever special work he might choose to do to earn his bread by the complete development of all his faculties as an individual. . . .

The strongest reason why we ask for woman a voice in the government under which she lives; in the religion she is asked to believe; equality in social life, where she is the chief factor; a place in the trades and professions, where she may earn her bread, is because of her birthright to self-sovereignty; because, as an individual, she must rely on herself. No matter how much women prefer to lean, to be protected and supported, nor how much men desire to have them do so, they must make the voyage of life alone, and for safety in an emergency they must know something of the laws of navigation. To guide our own craft, we must be captain, pilot, engineer; with chart and compass to stand at the wheel; to match the wind and waves and know when to take in the sail, and to read the signs in the firmament over all. It matters not whether the solitary voyager is man or woman. . . .

Nature having endowed them equally, leaves them to their own skill and judgment in the hour of danger, and, if not equal to the occasion, alike they perish.

Source: PBS. (n.d.). The solitude of self. Retrieved from pbs.org/stantonanthony/resources/index.html?body=solitude_self.html

Comprehension Questions:

1. According to Stanton, what do male philosophers such as Spencer, Harrison, and Allen believe about women (in your own words)?
2. How do Stanton's views differ from these philosophers'?

Activities:

1. With a small group, discuss: Is Stanton's main point that women and men are the same? Or that women are superior to men? Or that men and women are different? Or is her main point something else? Find two quotations that support your argument, and present to the class.
2. How does Stanton's main point compare with Sojourner Truth's (Lesson 2.4)? What would they agree or disagree on? How might their different life experiences have shaped the points they made? Create a cartoon in which they meet, with thought bubbles and speech bubbles.

Reflection: Look back at the lists you made in the introduction. Did the female students rank their roles as daughters, sisters, and future parents higher than male students ranked their roles as brothers, sons, or future parents? If so, is it for the reasons Stanton described? If not, does it show a trend toward gender equality?

Resources:

Barnes, P. (Producer) & Burns, K. (Director) (1999). *Not for ourselves alone: The story of Elizabeth Cady Stanton and Susan B. Anthony*. USA: PBS.

LESSON 2.9

WHAT WAS THE SUPREME COURT'S ARGUMENT FOR EXCLUDING CHINESE PEOPLE FROM U.S. CITIZENSHIP?

Historical Figure: Horace Gray

Event: Chinese Exclusion Act, 1882

Introduction: Which of the following factors should the United States consider when deciding whether immigrants can enter the United States, and why? (a) nationality, (b) religion, (c) criminal history, (d) race or ethnicity, (e) gender, (f) level of education, (g) job skills, (h) height, (i) age, (j) wealth.

Mini-Lecture:

- Large-scale immigration of Chinese people to the United States began in the 1840s, when they came to work as gold miners, and later on the Transcontinental Railroad.
- Chinese workers were paid lower wages than Americans and had few health and safety protections.
- Some Americans resented the competition from Chinese workers and held the ethnocentric idea that Chinese culture was inferior to American culture.
- In 1882, the Chinese Exclusion Act stopped Chinese immigrants from entering the United States and forbid anyone of Chinese descent from becoming a U.S. citizen.
- In 1892, the Geary Act required all Chinese people to carry a residence permit or risk deportation. Chinese people were also banned from bearing witness in court.

- In 1893, three Chinese residents, Fong Yue Ting, Wong Quan, and Lee Joe, sued for the right to remain in the United States; they lost their case.
- Horace Gray was a Supreme Court justice from 1881 to 1902.
- He wrote the majority opinion from which our document is taken.

Vocabulary:

allege: to claim
collector of internal revenue: an official who takes fees from people
credible: trustworthy
Chinaman: term for a Chinese person that is now considered offensive
procure: to get

aforesaid: mentioned earlier
remanded: to be handed over to
deported: to be forced to leave a country
aliens: people from other countries
proposition: argument, claim
incident: privilege
jurisdiction: control

Document: *Fong Yue Ting, Wong Quan, and Lee Joe v. United States*, Supreme Court, 1893

In the third case the petition alleged, and the judge's order showed, the following state of facts: On April 11, 1893, the petitioner [Lee Joe] applied to the collector of internal revenue for a certificate of residence. The collector refused to give him a certificate, on the ground that the witnesses whom he produced to prove that he was entitled to the certificate were persons of the Chinese race, and not credible witnesses, and required of him to produce a witness other than a Chinaman to prove that he was entitled to the certificate, which he was unable to do, because there was no person other than one of the Chinese race who knew and could truthfully swear that he was lawfully within the United States on May 5, 1892, and then entitled to remain therein; and because of such unavoidable cause he was unable to produce a certificate of residence, and was now without one.

The petitioner [Lee Joe] was arrested by the marshal, and taken before the judge, and clearly established to the satisfaction of the judge that he was unable to procure a certificate of residence by reason of the unavoidable cause aforesaid; and also established to the judge's satisfaction, by the testimony of a Chinese resident of New York, that the petitioner was a resident of the United States at the time of the passage of the [Geary] act ; but, having failed to establish this fact clearly to the satisfaction of the court by at least one credible white witness, as required by the statute, the judge ordered the petitioner to be remanded to the custody of the marshal, and to be deported from the United States, as provided in the act.

Each petition alleged that the petitioner was arrested and detained without due process of law, and that section 6 of the act of May 5, 1892 [the Geary Act], was unconstitutional and void.

In the elaborate opinion delivered by Mr. Justice Field in behalf of the court it was said: "Those laborers are not citizens of the United States; they are aliens. That the government of the United States, through the action of the legislative department, can exclude aliens from its territory, is a proposition which we do not think open to controversy. Jurisdiction over its own territory to that extent is an incident of every independent nation. It is a part of its independence. If it could not exclude aliens, it would be to that extent subject to the control of another power."

Source: FindLaw. (2012). Fong Yue Ting, Wong Quan, and Lee Joe v. US, 149 U.S. 698 (Supreme Court Case, 1893). Retrieved from caselaw.lp.findlaw.com/cgi-bin/getcase.pl?court=us&vol=149&invol=698

Comprehension Questions:

1. Why didn't the collector of internal revenue give Lee Joe a certificate of residence?
2. Did the judge believe that Lee Joe had been living in the United States before 1892, when the Geary Act was passed? If not, why not? If so, why couldn't he stay in the United States?
3. How does the Supreme Court argue that the Geary Act is legal, appropriate, and constitutional?

Activities:

1. The Chinese Exclusion Act was the only time (before 2017) that a law forbid all members of a specific national group entry to the United States on the basis of their nationality. Why do you think Chinese people were singled out?
2. Divide the class in half and debate the following proposition: If the United States promises equality under the law and due process to all citizens, it must also treat people applying for citizenship or residency in the same way.

Reflection: Look back at the factors you did *not* think the United States should consider when admitting immigrants. Can you imagine a situation arising in the next 10 years in which those factors *would* be considered? Why or why not?

Resources:

Museum of Chinese in America. (2016). History of Chinese in America: An interactive timeline. Retrieved from mocanyc.org/learn/timeline

Stanford University. (2016). Chinese railroad workers in North America project. Retrieved from web.stanford.edu/group/chineserailroad/cgi-bin/wordpress/

LESSON 2.10

WHAT WAS THE KU KLUX KLAN'S ARGUMENT FOR WHITE SUPREMACY?

Historical Figure: Hiram W. Evans

Event: Peak popularity of the Klan, 1920s

Introduction: Close your eyes. When you hear the phrase "real American," what do you picture?

Mini-Lecture:

- The Ku Klux Klan was founded in 1886, when some White Southerners decided to resist the legal equality of Blacks and Whites that had been established during Reconstruction.
- The Klan claimed that White Christians were superior to people of other racial, ethnic, and religious backgrounds.
- The Klan secretly organized illegal activities, including intimidating and lynching Black people, other minority groups, and those who disagreed with them.
- The period 1920–1929 is known as the Roaring Twenties or the Jazz Age. This period is known for economic prosperity, new freedoms for women, and a surge in creativity among Black artists.
- At the same time, the Klan reached its peak popularity at 4 million members. Immigration of Southern and Eastern Europeans, which had peaked in the early 1900s, was restricted.
- Hiram W. Evans served as the Imperial Wizard (leader) of the Klan from 1922 to 1939.
- Our document comes from a book Evans wrote explaining the Klan's goals.

Vocabulary:

stock: ethnic background
mongrelized: of mixed parentage or background
Liberal: someone who favors tolerance of nontraditional ways of life
Nordic: with heritage from Northern Europe
jeers: mockery

revilings: hateful words
veneer: surface image
unalterably: unchangeably
plausible: reasonable
propagandists: people who put out biased information
subversive: dangerous

Document: The Klan's Fight for Americanism, Hiram W. Evans, 1926

> The Klan, therefore, has now come to speak for the great mass of Americans of the old pioneer stock. We believe that it does fairly and faithfully represent them, and our proof lies in their support. To understand the Klan, then, it is necessary to understand the character and the present mind of the mass of old-stock Americans. The mass, it must be remembered, as distinguished from the intellectually mongrelized "Liberals." These are, in the first place, a blend of various peoples of the so-called Nordic race, the race which, with all its faults, has given the world almost the whole of modern civilization. . . .
>
> The Nordic American today is a stranger in large parts of the land his father gave him. Moreover, he is a most unwelcome stranger, one much spit upon, and one to whom even the right to have his own opinions and to work for his own interests is now denied with jeers and revilings.
>
> They [Nordic Americans] decided that . . . an alien usually remains an alien no matter what is done to him, what veneer of education he gets, what oaths

Unit Question: What Does Equality Mean?

he takes, nor what public attitudes he adopts. They decided that the melting pot was a ghastly failure, and remembered that the very name was coined by a member of one of the races—the Jews—which most determinedly refuses to melt. They decided that in every way, as well as in politics, the alien in the vast majority of cases is unalterably fixed in his instincts, character, thought and interest by centuries of racial selection and development, that he thinks first for his own people, works only with and for them, cares entirely for their interests, considers himself always one of them, and never an American.

They [Nordic Americans] learned, though more slowly, that alien ideas are just as dangerous to us as the aliens themselves, no matter how plausible such ideas may sound. With most of the plain people this conclusion is based simply on the fact that the alien ideas do not work well for them. Others went deeper and came to understand that the differences in racial background, in breeding, instinct, character and emotional point of view are more important than logic. So ideas which may be perfectly healthy for an alien may also be poisonous for Americans.

Finally they [Nordic Americans] learned the great secret of the propagandists; that success in corrupting public opinion depends on putting out the subversive ideas without revealing their source. They came to suspect that "prejudice" against foreign ideas is really a protective device of nature against mental food that may be indigestible. They saw, finally, that the alien leaders in America act on this theory, and that there is a steady flood of alien ideas being spread over the country, always carefully disguised as American.

We [the Klan] are demanding, and we expect, to win, a return of power into the hands of the everyday, not highly cultured, not overly intellectualized, but entirely unspoiled and not de-Americanized, average citizen of the old stock.

Comprehension Questions:

1. How does Evans define a "real American"?
2. What evidence does Evans provide that the "melting pot" is a failure?
3. What does Evan see as the true reason for prejudice of "real" Americans against "aliens"?

Activities:

1. What is your own definition of a "real" American? Write it on one of the posters hung around the room, then do a gallery walk to view other students' definitions.
2. Based on what you know or can research about the Roaring Twenties or the Jazz Age, generate three reasons why the Klan reached its peak popularity during this era.
3. Do you agree with Evans that immigrants never consider themselves American? What evidence could you provide to support your claim?

Reflection: Did the person you pictured as a "real American" match Evans's description of a Northern European person? If so, why do you think your images matched? If not, why not?

Resources:

Southern Poverty Law Center. (2011). Ku Klux Klan: A history of racism and violence. Retrieved from splcenter.org/sites/default/files/Ku-Klux-Klan-A-History-of-Racism.pdf

History.com. (n.d.). The Roaring Twenties. Retrieved from history.com/topics/roaring-twenties

Wells-Barnett, I. B. (1895). *The Red Record: Tabulated statistics and alleged causes of lynching in the United States.* Retrieved from gutenberg.org/files/14977/14977-h/14977-h.htm

LESSON 2.11
How Did the Supreme Court Explain Its Decision to Overturn the "Separate but Equal" Doctrine?

Historical Figure: Thurgood Marshall

Event: *Brown v. Board of Education*, 1954

Introduction: Would you describe your school as racially and ethnically diverse? Why or why not?

Mini-Lecture:

- *Plessy v. Ferguson* had established the doctrine of "separate but equal" facilities for Blacks and Whites.
- In the 1950s, the National Association for the Advancement of Colored People (NAACP) began helping Black families to sue for the right to integrate schools.
- Oliver Brown sued the Board of Education of Topeka, Kansas, so that his children could attend the Whites-only school closer to their home than the segregated school, and the case went to the Supreme Court in 1954.
- The lawyer who led Brown's team was Thurgood Marshall, who would later become the first Black Supreme Court justice.
- Marshall argued that attending segregated schools was damaging to Black children; as evidence, he presented the results of a psychological experiment in which Black children preferred to play with White dolls.
- The Supreme Court decided in favor of Brown; our document comes from its unanimous decision.

Vocabulary:

pursuant: in accordance with
tangible: measurable or able to be touched
plaintiff: someone suing in a court case
detrimental: damaging

sanction: approval
retard: to slow down
amply: thoroughly
doctrine: framework on which to base legal decisions

UNIT QUESTION: What Does Equality Mean?

inherently: by definition   *disposition:* finding of the court

Document: *Brown v. Board of Education,* Supreme Court, 1954

> Segregation of white and Negro children in the public schools of a State solely on the basis of race, pursuant to state laws permitting or requiring such segregation, denies to Negro children the equal protection of the laws guaranteed by the Fourteenth Amendment—even though the physical facilities and other "tangible" factors of white and Negro schools may be equal. . . .
>
> Segregation of white and colored children in public schools has a detrimental effect upon the colored children. The impact is greater when it has the sanction of the law, for the policy of separating the races is usually interpreted as denoting the inferiority of the negro group. A sense of inferiority affects the motivation of a child to learn. Segregation with the sanction of law, therefore, has a tendency to [retard] the educational and mental development of negro children and to deprive them of some of the benefits they would receive in a racial[ly] integrated school system.
>
> Whatever may have been the extent of psychological knowledge at the time of Plessy v. Ferguson, this finding is amply supported by modern authority. Any language in Plessy v. Ferguson contrary to this finding is rejected.
>
> We conclude that, in the field of public education, the doctrine of "separate but equal" has no place. Separate educational facilities are inherently unequal. Therefore, we hold that the plaintiffs and others similarly situated for whom the actions have been brought are, by reason of the segregation complained of, deprived of the equal protection of the laws guaranteed by the Fourteenth Amendment. This disposition makes unnecessary any discussion whether such segregation also violates the Due Process Clause of the Fourteenth Amendment.
>
> *Source:* Legal Information Institute. (n.d.). *Brown v. Board of Education.* Retrieved from law.cornell.edu/supremecourt/text/347/483

Comprehension Questions:

1. Does the Supreme Court determine that the facilities in Whites-only school were superior to those in the school for Black children?
2. In your own words, what does the Supreme Court find was the problem with segregated schools?

Activities:

1. Look back at Lesson 2.7. Find a quotation that most directly contradicts the court's decision in *Brown v. Board of Education*.
2. What would Thurgood Marshall say to Justice Henry Billings Brown (Lesson 2.7, who wrote the majority opinion in the *Plessy v. Ferguson* case), about how ideas about equality had changed between 1896 and 1954? Work with a partner to write a dialogue between them, then act it out for the class.

Reflection: Researchers who have repeated the Clark doll test in the 21st century have found similar results: Black children prefer White dolls. Does this result indicate that the legal integration of schools has not had the desired effect? Why or why not?

Resources:

NAACP Legal Defense and Educational Fund. (n.d.). Brown at 60: The doll test. Retrieved from naacpldf.org/brown-at-60-the-doll-test

LESSON 2.12
How Did Malcolm X Think Racial Equality Could Be Achieved?

Historical Figure: Malcolm X

Event: Organization of Afro-American Unity founded, 1964

Introduction: Describe the conditions (if any) that would make you feel that you needed weapons to defend yourself.

Mini-Lecture:

- Malcolm X, an activist for the rights of Black people, was born in 1925 in Nebraska.
- When he was young, his home was burned by Klan members.
- He was convicted of stealing and went to prison at 20; there, he converted to Islam.
- He joined the Nation of Islam, an organization for Black Muslims that advocated for preservation of Black culture and rights through separation from White society; however, toward the end of his life, a trip to Mecca convinced him that people of all races could collaborate.
- Malcolm chose the surname "X" because he believed his father's surname came from his ancestors' slave masters.
- In 1964, he left the Nation of Islam and founded the Organization for Afro-American Unity; our document comes from a speech he gave announcing its creation.
- In 1965, Malcolm X was assassinated.

Vocabulary:

Salaam Alaikum: "Peace be with you" in Arabic, a Muslim greeting
charter: plan or mission
henceforth: in the future
submerge: to ignore
nonsectarian: not divided by religion

Document: By Any Means Necessary, Malcolm X, 1964

Salaam Alaikum, Mr. Moderator, our distinguished guests, brothers and sisters, our friends and our enemies, everybody who's here.

... So we have formed an organization known as the Organization of Afro American Unity which has the same aim and objective—to fight whoever gets in our way, to bring about the complete independence of people of African descent here in the Western Hemisphere, and first here in the United States, and bring about the freedom of these people by any means necessary. That's our motto.

[What follows is from the charter of the Organization of Afro-American Unity]: "Persuaded that the Charter of the United Nations, the Universal Declaration of Human Rights, the Constitution of the United States and the Bill of Rights are the principles in which we believe and that these documents if put into practice represent the essence of mankind's hopes and good intentions; Desirous that all Afro-American people and organizations should henceforth unite so that the welfare and well being of our people will be assured; We are resolved to reinforce the common bond of purpose between our people by submerging all of our differences and establishing a nonsectarian, constructive program for human rights";

We hereby present this charter. I–Establishment. The Organization of Afro American Unity shall include all people of African descent in the Western Hemisphere, as well as our brothers and sisters on the African continent." . . . In essence, what it is saying is instead of you and me running around here seeking allies in our struggle for freedom in the Irish neighborhood or the Jewish neighborhood or the Italian neighborhood, we need to seek some allies among people who look something like we do. It's time now for you and me to stop running away from the wolf right into the arms of the fox, looking for some kind of help. That's a drag. . . .

II–Self Defense: Since self preservation is the first law of nature, we assert the Afro American's right to self defense. The Constitution of the United States of America clearly affirms the right of every American citizen to bear arms. And as Americans, we will not give up a single right guaranteed under the Constitution. The history of unpunished violence against our people clearly indicates that we must be prepared to defend ourselves or we will continue to be a defenseless people at the mercy of a ruthless and violent racist mob.

Source: BlackPast.org. (2017). (1964) Malcolm X's speech at the founding rally of the Organization for Afro-American Unity. Retrieved from blackpast.org/1964-malcolm-x-s-speech-founding-rally-organization-afro-american-unity
Copyright 1970, 1992 by Betty Shabazz and Pathfinder Press. Reprinted by permission.

Comprehension Questions:

1. In Malcolm X's analogy in paragraph 4, who are the wolves and who are the foxes?
2. Infer why Malcolm X wouldn't just ask the police and government to protect Black people's rights.
3. According to Malcolm X, why do Black people need the right to bear arms?

Activities:

1. What do you think Malcolm X meant by "by any means necessary"? Justify your answer using a quote from the document.
2. Work with a partner to write and act out a dialogue between Thurgood Marshall (Lesson 2.11) and Malcolm X about how to bring positive change for Black people.

Reflection: Is there any cause you would fight for "by any means necessary"? If so, what is it? If not, why not?

Resources:

Bagwell, O. (Director), & Hampton, H. (Producer). Malcolm X: Make it plain. *American Experience.* USA: PBS.

UNIT CONCLUSION

This unit has illustrated how the American "we" has shifted over the past several hundred years, as racial and ethnic minority groups and women have fought for their rights as citizens. Teachers may make the connection back to the guiding question for the course, "What do we mean when we say 'we'?," so that students can reflect on how their views might have changed or been reinforced during the first two units. As this will be the second summit, students will be able to build on their experiences from the first. Teachers may have students look back on the first summit and consider how they could improve, either by reviewing their speeches or watching a recording of their performances.

The historical figures in this summit have been chosen in order to provide a balance of advocates for equality and those who resisted change or tried to reinforce the status quo. That means that some students will be representing the views of White supremacists, such as Hiram W. Evans, and apologists for discrimination, such as Roger Taney. Teachers should consider classroom climate and students' individual needs when assigning these roles, so that the summit remains a safe yet challenging event for all students.

CHAPTER 3

States' Rights and Federal Power

Unit Question: How Should Power Be Distributed Among Local, State, and Federal Governments?

Current Issue Question: Should states be allowed to set their own laws on who can vote?

Unit Introduction: In this unit, students will consider the division of powers between various levels of government. They will see that this question, which at first may seem dry, has animated some of the most fundamental conflicts in our nation's history, over the genesis of our government, the removal of Native Americans, the Civil War, and desegregation. They will learn about the tug-of-war between federal and state power in the Articles of Confederation and the Constitution, as well as Supreme Court precedents that guide us today. George Washington will justify his suppression of the Whiskey Rebellion, and Daniel Webster will argue against nullification of federal laws. Students will see how South Carolina used a state's rights argument to justify the racism that underpinned slavery. Dwight D. Eisenhower and Orval Faubus will show them what happens when military power is used to enforce federal law, and Sandra Day O'Connor will point out that state and federal authority is intended as a safeguard for individual rights.

Students will begin the unit by considering the current controversy over state voter ID laws. By now, students have plenty of practice having difficult conversations around race, but it is always helpful to reiterate Discussion Guidelines (see p. 18 and Appendix J). Teachers may also wish to make connections with voter ID laws in their own states, or with other current states' rights controversies.

LESSON 3.1

On What Basis Did the NAACP Argue That North Carolina Law Violated the Voting Rights Act?

Historical Figure: William J. Barber II

Event: The NAACP sues North Carolina's governor, 2015

Introduction: Sort the following questions into those that should be decided by states and those that should be decided by the federal government:

- Who should be allowed to vote?
- Who should be allowed to drive a car?
- Who should be required to go to school?
- Who should be allowed to own a gun?

Why did you classify the questions the way you did?

Mini-Lecture:

- The Constitution originally gave states the power to determine who could vote.
- Until the end of the Civil War, most states restricted voting privileges to White men.
- In 1870, the 15th Amendment was passed; it promised all citizens the right to vote regardless of race.
- In some southern states, Black people were prevented from voting through poll taxes (pay to vote) or literacy tests (e.g., recite the preamble of the Constitution) that were not applied to Whites.
- In 1965, the Voting Rights Act gave Congress special powers to ensure that southern states did not deny people the right to vote based on race.
- In 2013, the Supreme Court decided that it was no longer necessary for southern states to seek federal approval before changing voting regulations.
- In 2013, the North Carolina state legislature passed HB589, which introduced new restrictions that the legislature said were to reduce voter fraud (people casting votes illegally). Other people argued that this law was designed to make voting more difficult for African Americans, young people, and poor people.
- A group led by the North Carolina NAACP filed a lawsuit claiming that the bill violated national laws, including the Voting Rights Act, as well as the U.S. Constitution; our document comes from this case, which the NAACP won in 2016.
- Reverend William J. Barber II became president of the North Carolina NAACP in 2006.
- Patrick McCrory was the governor of North Carolina from 2013 to 2017.

Vocabulary:

illusory: not real, but seeming to be real
abridgement: limiting of
electoral: related to voting
electorate: voters
franchise: right to vote
onerous: difficult and complicated
discretion: power of judgment
precinct: part of a city or town

out-of-precinct voting: voting beyond limits of neighborhood where one lives
enjoin: to prohibit
provision: part of a law
disproportionate: affecting one group more than others
legislature: group that makes laws

credible legislative rationale: believable reason for making a law

depress: to reduce

Document: *North Carolina State Conference of the NAACP v. Patrick Lloyd McCrory*, North Carolina NAACP, 2015

> These cases seek to protect the voting rights of North Carolina citizens. . . . Because voting is the fundamental building block of political power, "[o]ther rights, even the most basic, are illusory if the right to vote is undermined." . . .
>
> Congress enacted Section 2 of the Voting Rights Act (VRA) to provide added protection to the fundamental right to vote. Section 2 announces a straightforward rule: regardless of the reasons why a state chooses to change a voting practice, the change is unlawful if it "results in a denial or abridgement of the right of any citizen of the United States to vote on account of race or color." . . . By the plain terms of the statute, such an abridgement occurs if a voting practice imposes electoral burdens that result in racial minorities having "less opportunity than other members of the electorate to participate in the political process." . . .
>
> During the waning hours of the 2013 legislative session, the General Assembly enacted House Bill 589 ("HB589"), which severely impairs access to the franchise of all North Carolinians—but especially African-American and young voters. Among other things, HB589 imposes onerous and strict voter ID requirements; eliminates same-day registration (SDR); eliminates out-of-precinct provisional voting; sharply reduces the availability of in-person early voting; eliminates the discretion previously given to localities to keep polls open for an extra hour on Election Day; expands poll observers and challengers; and eliminates the State's civic engagement programs that allowed 16- and 17-year-olds to pre-register to vote. . . .
>
> Indeed, at the time it enacted HB 589, the General Assembly had before it (or previously had been told) that African Americans used early voting, SDR, and out-of-precinct voting at far higher rates than whites. The evidence shows, moreover, that the elimination of these practices will interact with existing socioeconomic conditions to impose material burdens on African Americans' ability to vote. North Carolina has an unfortunate and judicially recognized history of racial discrimination, and the effects of that discrimination persist to this day: poverty rates for African Americans are far higher than poverty rates for whites; and educational attainment is significantly lower for African Americans than it is for whites. Under the statute and governing case law, these facts are enough to establish a Section 2 violation, and the Court should enjoin the challenged provisions on that statutory basis alone.
>
> . . . The law's disproportionate burdens on African Americans, the highly unusual and expedited manner in which HB 589 was enacted, the evidence that was before the legislature at the time, and the absence of any credible legislative rationale all show that the legislature enacted the statue (at least in part) to

depress minority voter turnout, in violation of the Fourteenth and Fifteenth Amendments. Even if the legislature lacked discriminatory intent, HB 589 would nonetheless be unlawful because it imposes substantial burdens on the right to vote that are not outweighed by any substantial state purpose.

Source: North Carolina State Conference of the NAACP. (2015). Plaintiffs' brief in support of motion for preliminary injunction. Retrieved from documentcloud.org/documents/1303109-nc-voter-rights-plaintiffs-brief.html

Comprehension Questions:

1. Which type of changes to voting practices does the Voting Rights Act outlaw?
2. Which voting practices does HB 589 outlaw that are disproportionately used by Black voters?
3. The NAACP argues that the law aimed to reduce turnout among Black voters. Infer why the state legislature would want to do that.

Activities:

1. For each of the voting practices you listed in Comprehension Question 2, provide at least one reason the practice would be used by people who are poorer and have less education.
2. Divide the class in half and debate this proposition: The North Carolina state legislature has the right to change North Carolina's voting laws, even if their actions result in lower turnout of Black and poor voters.

Reflection: Did this lesson cause you to change your view on whether states or the federal government should control who can vote? Why or why not?

Resources:

Zucchino, D. (2013, August 13). North Carolina faces ACLU, NAACP lawsuits over new voter ID law. *LA Times.* Retrieved from latimes.com/nation/nationnow/la-na-nn-north-carolina-voter-id-lawsuits-20130813-story.html

LESSON 3.2

What Was the Balance of Power Between the States and Congress in the Articles of Confederation?

Historical Figure: Patrick Henry

Event: Articles of Confederation, 1777

Introduction: Rank the powers a government should have in order of importance: (a) declare war, (b) collect taxes, (c) make laws, (d) control education, (e) run courts. Explain your choices.

UNIT QUESTION: How Should Power Be Distributed Among Local, State, and Federal Governments?

Mini-Lecture:

- The Articles of Confederation, from which our document is taken, was an agreement the 13 colonies made during the Revolutionary War, in which the United States gained independence from Britain.
- "Articles" are a legal document.
- "Confederation" is when a group of states or nations join together.
- Patrick Henry advocated independence from Britain and later served as governor of Virginia.
- Henry supported the Articles of Confederation because it allowed states to work together to defeat the British without giving up too many rights to a federal government.
- The Articles of Confederation was eventually replaced by the Constitution we have today.

Vocabulary:

these Presents: this document
delegate: representative
affixed: next to
perpetual: existing forever
stile: title
confederacy: group of states or nations working together
retain: to keep
sovereignty: control over itself
expressly: specifically
delegated: given
assembled: joined together
hereby: by signing below
severally: each

league: group
binding themselves: promising
offered to: threatened against
on account: because of
pretense: reason
whatever: at all
charges: costs
incurred: spent
defray: to pay for
treasury: pool of money
the several states: each state
lay: to set
levy: to collect

Document: Articles of Confederation, Articles I, II, III, VII, and IX, 1777.

To all to whom these Presents shall come, we the undersigned Delegates of the States affixed to our Names send greeting.

Articles of Confederation and perpetual Union between the states of New Hampshire, Massachusetts-bay Rhode Island and Providence Plantations, Connecticut, New York, New Jersey, Pennsylvania, Delaware, Maryland, Virginia, North Carolina, South Carolina and Georgia.

I. The Stile of this Confederacy shall be "The United States of America."

II. Each state retains its sovereignty, freedom, and independence, and every power, jurisdiction, and right, which is not by this Confederation expressly delegated to the United States, in Congress assembled.

III. The said States hereby severally enter into a firm league of friendship with each other, for their common defense, the security of their liberties, and their mutual and general welfare, binding themselves to assist each other, against all force offered to, or attacks made upon them, or any of them, on account of religion, sovereignty, trade, or any other pretense whatever. . . .

VIII. All charges of war, and all other expenses that shall be incurred for the common defense or general welfare, and allowed by the United States in Congress assembled, shall be defrayed out of a common treasury, which shall be supplied by the several States in proportion to the value of all land within each State. . . .

The taxes for paying that proportion shall be laid and levied by the authority and direction of the [state] legislatures of the several States within the time agreed upon by the United States in Congress assembled. . . .

IX. The united states in congress assembled, shall have the sole and exclusive right and power of determining on peace and war, . . . of sending and receiving ambassadors–entering into treaties and alliances.

Source: Avalon Project. (2008). Articles of Confederation. Retrieved from avalon.law.yale.edu/18th_century/artconf.asp

Comprehension Questions:

1. Of the powers listed in the introduction, which did Congress have?
2. How would Congress pay for the costs of war?

Activities:

1. What were the strengths and weaknesses of the Articles of Confederation? Work with a partner to make a T-chart.
2. Do you think the fact that the Revolutionary War was going on made the states more or less willing to help one another? Why?

Reflection: Patrick Henry supported the Articles of Confederation because he wanted states to have more power than the federal government. Give an example of something the federal government does today that Henry would think took too much power from states.

Resources:

Colonial Williamsburg Foundation. (2016). Patrick Henry. Retrieved from history.org/Almanack/people/bios/biohen.cfm?PHPSESSID=19af3aca2b6086426b88fe0608f0a9f0

LESSON 3.3

How Did the Constitution Compare with the Articles of Confederation?

Historical Figure: James Madison

Event: Constitution created, 1787

Introduction: What is one power you think states, instead of the federal government, should have, and why?

UNIT QUESTION: How Should Power Be Distributed Among Local, State, and Federal Governments?

Mini-Lecture:

- James Madison is known as the "architect of the Constitution" because of his lead role in writing it; he also served as president from 1809 to 1817.
- Madison wanted to balance the power of the federal government and states so that neither had too much control.
- A group of 55 men gathered in Philadelphia in 1787 at the Constitutional Convention in order to write the Constitution.
- The Constitution was ratified by all 13 states by 1790.
- Our document comes from Article I of the Constitution, and from the 10th Amendment, which was added in 1791.

Vocabulary:

duties, imposts, and excises: kinds of taxes
uniform: the same
regulate: to control
naturalization: process of becoming a citizen
coin: to create money
thereof: that is part of
coin: money
exclusive right: patent
tribunal: court
inferior to: less powerful than
Letters of Marque and Reprisal: documents allowing the government to take property of enemies

appropriation: when Congress takes money from the Treasury for a specific purpose
militia: army
execute: to enforce
suppress: to put down
insurrection: rebellion
repel: to defend against
carry into execution: to do
foregoing: listed above
vested by: given in
several: other
delegate: to give
prohibited: taken away
reserved to: kept for
respectively: individually

Document: Constitution, Article 1, Article 4 (1787), 10th Amendment (1791)

> Article I, Section 8 1. The Congress shall have Power To lay and collect Taxes, Duties, Imposts and Excises, to pay the Debts and provide for the common Defence and general Welfare of the United States; but all Duties, Imposts and Excises shall be uniform throughout the United States; 2. To borrow Money on the credit of the United States; 3. To regulate Commerce with foreign Nations, and among the several States, and with the Indian Tribes; 4. To establish an uniform Rule of Naturalization, and uniform Laws on the subject of Bankruptcies throughout the United States; 5. To coin Money, regulate the Value thereof, and of foreign Coin, and fix the Standard of Weights and Measures; 6. To provide for the Punishment of counterfeiting the Securities and current Coin of the United States; 7. To establish Post Offices and post Roads; 8. To promote the Progress of Science and useful Arts, by securing for limited Times to Authors

and Inventors the exclusive Right to their respective Writings and Discoveries; 9. To constitute Tribunals inferior to the supreme Court; 10. To define and punish Piracies and Felonies committed on the high Seas, and Offences against the Law of Nations; 11. To declare War, grant Letters of Marque and Reprisal, and make Rules concerning Captures on Land and Water; 12. To raise and support Armies, but no Appropriation of Money to that Use shall be for a longer Term than two Years; 13. To provide and maintain a Navy; 14. To make Rules for the Government and Regulation of the land and naval Forces; 15. To provide for calling forth the Militia to execute the Laws of the Union, suppress Insurrections and repel Invasions; . . . 17. To make all Laws which shall be necessary and proper for carrying into Execution the foregoing Powers, and all other Powers vested by this Constitution in the Government of the United States, or in any Department or Officer thereof.

Amendment X. The powers not delegated to the United States by the Constitution, nor prohibited by it to the States, are reserved to the States respectively, or to the people.

Source: Avalon Project. (2008). U.S. Constitution. Retrieved from avalon.law.yale.edu/18th_century/usconst.asp

Comprehension Questions:

1. Look back at the list of powers in the introduction of Lesson 3.2. Which of them does the Constitution give to Congress?
2. One clause of Article I, Section 8 is called the "Elastic Clause" because it can be used to stretch the powers of Congress. Infer which clause it is.
3. Because of the 10th Amendment, who gets powers, such as establishing a school system, that are not mentioned in the Constitution?

Activities:

1. Choose one of the powers listed in Article 1, Section 8. Work with a small group to create a cartoon or illustration showing what could go wrong if the states had that power instead of the federal government.
2. How do you think James Madison would have tried to convince people like Patrick Henry, who preferred more rights for states, to accept the Constitution? Write a letter from Madison to Henry.

Reflection: Which document do you think gives more appropriate powers to the states and the federal government, the Articles of Confederation or the Constitution? Why?

Resources:

Johnson, P. N. (Director), & Gasdik, N. J. (Producer). (1989). *A more perfect union: America becomes a nation*. USA: Brigham Young University.

UNIT QUESTION: How Should Power Be Distributed Among Local, State, and Federal Governments?

LESSON 3.4

How Did George Washington Explain His Decision to Suppress the Whiskey Rebellion?

Historical Figure: George Washington

Event: Whiskey Rebellion, 1791

Introduction: Which taxes do people today dislike most? Why?

Mini-Lecture:

- George Washington was president from 1789 to 1797.
- In order to pay debts from the Revolutionary War, the government needed to raise money, and it did so by collecting taxes.
- One of the taxes Congress passed while Washington was president was an "excise tax" on whiskey, which means that people had to pay a tax whenever they bought whiskey.
- This tax was unpopular especially in rural areas such as Western Pennsylvania, where people brewed their own whiskey and used it in place of money before U.S. dollars were widely used.
- A law was also passed rewarding people for turning in neighbors who might be buying or selling whiskey without paying the tax.
- Some people in Western Pennsylvania protested the tax and refused to pay it.
- George Washington eventually used the army to fight back against the rebels and force people to pay the tax.
- Our first document was written by a group of people who met in Pittsburgh in 1791 to discuss the tax on whiskey.
- Our second document is George Washington's response to the protests in 1792.

Vocabulary:

minutes: notes on what happened at a meeting
resolved: agreed
deservedly: for good reasons
obnoxious: upsetting
attend: to accompany
infringement: restriction
partial: unfair
liable to: likely to bring about
abuse: cheating
domestic manufacture: the action of people producing things in their own homes
vessel: bottle or container
ransack: to search
informer: tattletale

delinquency: bad behavior
precedent: example for the future
excise: tax on the sale of a good
sport with: to play with
gratify: to please
interested: biased
measure: action
whereas: because
unwarrantable: not allowable
proceedings: activities
obstruct: interfere with
revenue: tax
spirits: alcohol
pursuant to: in order to carry out
express: specific

contrary to: against
presents: documents
admonish: to scold
exhort: to urge
desist from: to stop
combinations and proceedings: actions

whatsoever having for object: with the purpose of
inasmuch as: because
put in execution: used
infractor: criminal
thereto: to that law

Documents:

1. Minutes of the meeting at Pittsburgh, unknown author, 1791

   Resolved, That the said law [taxing whiskey] is deservedly obnoxious to the feelings and interests of the people in general, as being attended with infringements on liberty, partial in its operations, attended with great expense in the collection, and liable to much abuse. It operates on a domestic manufacture, a manufacture not equal through the States. It is insulting to the feelings of the people to have their vessels marked [so they could be taxed], houses painted and ransacked, to be subject to informers, gaining by the occasional delinquency of others. It is a bad precedent tending to introduce the excise laws of Great Britain and of countries where the liberty, property and even the morals of the people are sported with, to gratify particular men in their ambitious and interested measures.

   Source: Pennsylvania Archives. (n.d.). Papers relating to what is known as the Whiskey Insurrection in Western Pennsylvania, 1794. Retrieved from fold3.com/document/3093996/

2. A Proclamation, George Washington, 1792

   Whereas certain violent and unwarrantable proceedings have lately taken place tending to obstruct the operation of the laws of the United States for raising a revenue upon spirits distilled within the same [United States], enacted pursuant to express authority delegated in the constitution of the United States; which proceedings are subversive of good order, contrary to the duty that every citizen owes to his country and to the laws, and of a nature dangerous to the very being of government:

   Now therefore I George Washington, President of the United States, do by these presents most earnestly admonish and exhort all persons whom it may concern, to refrain and desist from all unlawful combinations and proceedings whatsoever having for object or tending to obstruct the operation of the laws aforesaid; inasmuch as all lawful ways and means will be strictly put in execution for bringing to justice the infractors thereof and securing obedience thereto.

   Source: The Avalon Project. (2008). George Washington—Proclamation of September 15, 1792. Retrieved from avalon.law.yale.edu/18th_century/gwproc08.asp

UNIT QUESTION: How Should Power Be Distributed Among Local, State, and Federal Governments?

Comprehension Questions:

1. What was the main purpose of the authors of Document 1?
2. Choose a quotation in which the authors of Document 1 compare the tax to taxes from colonial times.
3. What reason does Washington give for why he should be able to collect taxes on whiskey?

Activities:

1. Divide the class in half and have Washington debate the people who met in Pittsburgh about whether the tax on whiskey was constitutional or not. Be sure to cite specific sections of the Constitution from Lesson 3.3.

Reflection: Do you think Washington was right to use the army to suppress the rebellion? Why or why not?

Resources:

The Gilder Lehman Institute for American History. (2016). The Whiskey Rebellion, 1794. Retrieved from gilderlehrman.org/history-by-era/early-republic/resources/whiskey-rebellion-1794

LESSON 3.5
HOW DID STATES' RIGHTS AND FEDERALIST INTERPRETATIONS OF THE CONSTITUTION DIFFER?

Historical Figure: John Marshall

Event: *McCulloch v. Maryland*, 1819

Introduction: Which of the following items are "necessary and proper" for human life? Choose only five from the list: (a) spiritual beliefs, (b) a loving family, (c) art and music, (d) a safe place to live, (e) friends who respect you, (f) good health, (g) food and water, (h) self-confidence, (i) freedom, (j) a fair government. Compare your list with a classmate's.

Mini-Lecture:

- In 1816, Congress opened a national bank, with branches in several cities around the country.
- Opening the bank was controversial, because the Constitution did not state that Congress could (or could not) open a bank.
- In 1818, the state of Maryland asked the national bank to pay taxes, just like any other business would.
- James McCulloch, the head of the Baltimore, Maryland, branch of the national bank, refused to pay the tax and sued the state of Maryland.
- McCulloch's lawyers argued that the federal government should not have to pay taxes to a state.

- Maryland's lawyers argued that the federal government did not have the right to open a national bank in the first place, but if the government did so, it should pay taxes.
- Our document comes from the Supreme Court's decision on the case, written by John Marshall, who was chief justice from 1801 to 1835.

Vocabulary:

cause: case
incorporate: to open
enumerated powers: powers of the federal government listed in Article I, Section 8 of the Constitution
minutely: in detail
incidental or implied: not directly stated but hinted at
foregoing: previously listed
supremacy: highest power
construe: to interpret
Elastic Clause: Article I, Section 8, Clause 18 of the Constitution, which grants Congress the ability to make laws that are "necessary and proper" for carrying out the rest of the "enumerated powers" (see Lesson 3.3)
abridge: to make smaller
annihilate: to destroy
legislature: U.S. Congress
means: way of working
intended: meant by the writers of the Constitution
purport: to intend
diminish: to make smaller
unconstitutional: not right according to the Constitution
void: not to be followed

Document: *McCulloch v. Maryland*, Supreme Court, 1819

> The first question made in the cause is—has Congress power to incorporate a bank? . . . Among the enumerated powers, we do not find that of establishing a bank or creating a corporation. But there is no phrase in the instrument which, like the Articles of Confederation, excludes incidental or implied powers and which requires that everything granted shall be expressly and minutely described. . . .
>
> To its enumeration of powers is added that of making "all laws which shall be necessary and proper for carrying into execution the foregoing powers, and all other powers vested by this Constitution in the Government of the United States or in any department thereof." . . .
>
> . . . The result is a conviction that the States have no power, by taxation or otherwise, to retard, impede, burden, or in any manner control the operations of the constitutional laws enacted by Congress to carry into execution the powers vested in the General Government. This is, we think, the unavoidable consequence of that supremacy which the Constitution has declared. . . .
>
> This ["necessary and proper"/Elastic] clause, as construed by the State of Maryland, would abridge, and almost annihilate, this useful and necessary right of the legislature to select its means. . . .
>
> We think so for the following reasons: 1st. The ["necessary and proper"/Elastic] clause is placed among the powers of Congress, not among the

limitations on those powers. 2d. Its terms purport to enlarge, not to diminish, the powers vested in the Government. It purports to be an additional power, not a restriction on those already granted. . . .

We [Supreme Court justices] are unanimously of opinion that the law passed by the Legislature of Maryland, imposing a tax on the Bank of the United States is unconstitutional and void.

Source: Justia. (n.d.). McCulloch v. Maryland 17 U.S. 316. Retrieved from supreme.justia.com/cases/federal/us/17/316/case.html

Comprehension Questions:

1. What reason does the Supreme Court give for why Congress can open a bank?
2. Choose a quotation that shows why the Supreme Court decided to let the Elastic Clause stretch the powers of the federal government.
3. Infer who won the case.

Activities:

1. Look back at the list of 17 powers in Article 1, Section 8 of the Constitution, which are included in Lesson 3.3. With a small group, pick one, then create an illustrated list of three actions that would be "necessary and proper" for Congress to take in order to carry out that duty.

Reflection: Why do you think the writers of the Constitution used a phrase like "necessary and proper," which people interpreted in such different ways?

Resources:

McBride, A. (2007). *McCulloch v. Maryland*. PBS. Retrieved from pbs.org/wnet/supremecourt/antebellum/landmark_mcculloch.html

LESSON 3.6
WHO IS RESPONSIBLE FOR PROTECTING NATIVE AMERICAN NATIONS: STATE OR FEDERAL GOVERNMENTS?

Historical Figure: John Ross

Event: *Cherokee Nation v. Georgia*, 1831

Introduction: Do you think of Native Americans as foreign to, or part of, the United States? Why?

Mini-Lecture:

- People of the Cherokee Nation had been living in what would become the southeastern United States for hundreds of years when the United States gained independence from Britain; the United States had signed treaties affirming the Cherokee's rights to the land.

- In the early 1800s, the state government of Georgia decided they wanted the Cherokee people to leave so they could use their land (see Lesson 2.3); they passed state laws taking away the Cherokee people's rights.
- The Cherokee Nation, led by a chief named John Ross, sued the state of Georgia in federal court. They wanted the federal government to treat them as a foreign nation and prevent Georgia from interfering with their rights.
- Our document comes from *Cherokee Nation v. Georgia*, in which the Supreme Court ruled that Indians were neither members of foreign nations nor U.S. citizens, so they could not sue in federal courts; John Marshall, from Lesson 3.5, wrote the opinion.
- A year later, in the case *Worcester v. Georgia*, the Supreme Court reversed its decision and claimed that the Cherokee were a foreign nation, and therefore the Indian Removal Act, which led to the Trail of Tears (see Lesson 2.3), was unconstitutional.
- President Andrew Jackson ignored the ruling and forced the Cherokee to leave Georgia anyway.

Vocabulary:

pray: to ask for
injunction: an order from a court saying something should or should not be done
annihilate: to destroy
in force: valid
indulge: to act according to
calculated: suited
successive: one after another
residue: what is left over
subsistence: survival
jurisdiction: the right of a court to make a decision about a care
foreign state: independent nation
counsel: lawyer
conclusively: without doubt

alien: foreigner
aggregate: group
peculiar: unique
cardinal: important
distinction: characteristic
denominate: to be called
pupilage: being in a state of learning from another group
ward: someone who cannot make decisions for him- or herself
bestow: to concentrate
tribunal: court
assert: to claim
apprehend: to understand
motion: a request made in court

Document: *Cherokee Nation v. Georgia*, 1831

This bill is brought by the Cherokee Nation, praying an injunction to restrain the state of Georgia from the execution of certain laws of that state, which as is alleged, go directly to annihilate the Cherokees as a political society, and to seize, for the use of Georgia, the lands of the nation which have been assured to them by the United States in solemn treaties repeatedly made and still in force.

If courts were permitted to indulge their sympathies, a case better calculated to excite them can scarcely be imagined. A people once numerous, powerful, and truly independent, found by our ancestors in the quiet and uncontrolled possession of an ample domain, gradually sinking beneath our superior policy, our arts, and our arms, have yielded their lands by successive treaties, each of which contains a solemn guarantee of the residue, until they retain no more of their formerly extensive territory than is deemed necessary to their comfortable subsistence. To preserve this remnant the present application is made.

Has this Court jurisdiction of the cause? . . .

Do the Cherokees constitute a foreign state in the sense of the Constitution?

The counsel have shown conclusively that they are not a state of the Union, and have insisted that individually they are aliens, not owing allegiance to the United States. An aggregate of aliens composing a state must, they say, be a foreign state. Each individual being foreign, the whole must be foreign.

. . . But the relation of the Indians to the United States is marked by peculiar and cardinal distinctions which exist nowhere else.

The Indian Territory is admitted to compose part of the United States. . . . They acknowledge themselves in their treaties to be under the protection of the United States. . . .

They may more correctly, perhaps, be denominated domestic dependent nations. . . . They are in a state of pupilage. Their relation to the United States resembles that of a ward to his guardian.

They look to our government for protection; rely upon its kindness and its power; appeal to it for relief to their wants; and address the President as their great father. . . .

These considerations go far to support the opinion that the framers of our Constitution had not the Indian tribes in view when they opened the courts of the Union to controversies between a state or the citizens thereof and foreign states.

The Court has bestowed its best attention on this question and, after mature deliberation, the majority is of opinion that an Indian tribe or nation within the United States is not a foreign state in the sense of the Constitution, and cannot maintain an action in the courts of the United States. . . .

If it be true that the Cherokee Nation have rights, this is not the tribunal in which those rights are to be asserted. If it be true that wrongs have been inflicted and that still greater are to be apprehended, this is not the tribunal which can redress the past or prevent the future.

The motion for an injunction is denied.

Source: Cherokee Nation. (2017). *Cherokee Nation v. State of Georgia.* Retrieved from cherokee.org/About-The-Nation/History/Trail-of-Tears/Cherokee-Nation-v-State-of-Georgia

Comprehension Questions:

1. What was the Cherokee's argument for why they were a foreign nation?
2. Why didn't the Supreme Court accept their argument?

Activities:

1. With a partner, create a flow chart showing cause-and-effect relationships between the following statements, showing the Supreme Court's reasoning: (a) The Cherokee Nation is not a foreign nation; (b) the State of Georgia can take away the Cherokee's rights; (c) the Cherokee people look to the federal government for protection; (d) the Cherokee Nation cannot file a suit in a federal court; (e) the federal government signed treaties with the Cherokee Nation; (f) the Cherokee are a domestic dependent nation; (g) the Cherokee live inside the United States. If you find a statement that cannot fit into the flow chart because the cause-effect relationship breaks down, circle it.
2. As a "domestic dependent nation," what privileges and rights do the Cherokee have when compared to the state of Georgia?

Reflection: What impact do you think the Supreme Court's decision had on the way Native American people live today?

Resources:

Cherokee Nation. (2017). History. Retrieved from cherokee.org/About-The-Nation/History

Cherokee Nation. (2017). Treaty of Holston, 1791. Retrieved from cherokee.org/About-The-Nation/History/Facts/Treaty-of-Holston-1791

LESSON 3.7

HOW DID DANIEL WEBSTER ARGUE THAT STATES COULDN'T NULLIFY FEDERAL LAWS?

Historical Figure: Daniel Webster

Event: Nullification crisis, 1832

Introduction: If students at your school had to choose a rule to "nullify," which one would it be? Why?

Mini-Lecture:

- In 1832, Congress passed a "tariff," or tax on imported products, such as cloth.
- This tax benefited factory owners in the North, but it caused economic hardship for people in the South, who bought more imported goods.
- As a result, southerners called this tax the "tariff of abominations," an "abomination" being something terrible.
- A South Carolina senator, Robert Hayne, made a speech to the Senate explaining that his state had "nullified" the tariff and they would not pay the tax.
- Massachusetts senator Daniel Webster gave a speech in response, from which our document is taken, in which he argued that South Carolina was wrong to nullify the tariff.
- President Andrew Jackson sent troops to South Carolina to make sure people paid the tariff.

UNIT QUESTION: How Should Power Be Distributed Among Local, State, and Federal Governments? 93

Vocabulary:

maintain: to claim
transcend: to go beyond
arrest: to stop
extent: amount
lodge: to keep
exclusively: only
exigency: urgency
annul: to nullify, to decide not to follow a law
palpably: noticeably
observable: obvious

contend: to argue
severally: on their own
assert: to take
four-and-twenty: 24
tariff: tax on imported goods
usurpation: something taken unfairly
duties: taxes
expedient: useful
provision: rule
absurdity: ridiculousness

Document: Reply to Robert Hayne, Daniel Webster, 1832

I understand the honorable gentleman from South Carolina [Robert Hayne] to maintain that it is a right of the State Legislatures to interfere whenever, in their judgment, this government transcends its constitutional limits, and to arrest the operation of its laws.

. . . I understand him to maintain that the ultimate power of judging of the constitutional extent of its own authority is not lodged exclusively in the general government, or any branch of it; but that, on the contrary, the States may lawfully decide for themselves, and each State for itself, whether, in a given case, the act of the general government transcends its power.

I understand him to insist that, if the exigency of the case, in the opinion of any State government, require it, such State government may, by its own sovereign authority, annul an act of the general government which it deems plainly and palpably unconstitutional.

This leads us to inquire into the origin of this government and the source of its power. . . . It is observable enough that the doctrine for which the honorable gentleman [Hayne] contends leads him to the necessity of maintaining, not only that this general government is the creature of the States, but that it is the creature of each of the States severally, so that each may assert the power for itself of determining whether it acts within the limits of its authority. It is the servant of four-and-twenty masters, of different wills and different purposes, and yet bound to obey all.

. . . In [South] Carolina, the tariff is a palpable, deliberate usurpation; Carolina, therefore, may nullify it, and refuse to pay the duties. In Pennsylvania it is both clearly constitutional and highly expedient; and there the duties are to be paid. And yet we live under a government of uniform laws, and under a Constitution, too, which contains an express provision, as it happens, that all duties shall be equal in all the States. Does not this approach absurdity?

> If there be no power to settle such questions, independent of either of the States, is not the whole Union a rope of sand? . . . Liberty and Union, now and forever, one and inseparable!
>
> Source: Byrd, R. C. (1994). *The Senate, 1789–1989: Classic speeches, 1830–1993*. Washington, DC: U.S. Government Printing Office.

Comprehension Questions:

1. What was Webster's main purpose in writing this document?
2. Choose a quotation that shows why Webster thinks Hayne's argument is wrong, then put it into your own words.

Activities:

1. Webster compares a Union in which states can nullify federal laws to a "rope of sand." What other metaphors can you think of to express his meaning?
2. "Liberty and Union, now and forever, one and inseparable!" is a "zinger," or memorable slogan, that Webster used to end his speech. With a partner, make a list of zingers that Hayne could use to respond in defense of states' rights, then share them with the class.

Reflection: Whose argument do you find more convincing, Webster's argument for federal power, or Hayne's for states' rights? Why?

Resources:

United States Senate. (n.d.). Robert Y. Hayne reply to Daniel Webster. Retrieved from senate.gov/artandhistory/history/common/generic/Speeches_HaynesReply.htm

LESSON 3.8

How Did the Southern States Explain Their Decision to Secede from the Union?

Historical Figure: Jefferson Davis

Event: Secession of South Carolina, 1860

Introduction: Should states have to follow federal laws they don't agree with? Why or why not?

Mini-Lecture:

- In 1860, Abraham Lincoln, who was known for opposing slavery, narrowly won the election for the presidency.
- Most Southern voters, many of whom were slave owners, opposed Lincoln.
- They were also upset that some Northern states that did not support slavery had not enforced Article IV, Section 2 of the Constitution (repeated in a law called the Fugitive Slave Act), which required that runaway slaves be returned to their owners (see Lesson 2.2).

UNIT QUESTION: How Should Power Be Distributed Among Local, State, and Federal Governments?

- As a result, South Carolina's state legislature gathered on December 20, 1860, and wrote a declaration announcing their reasons for seceding, or separating, from the Union.
- By the time Lincoln took office in March 1861, seven Southern states had seceded and formed the Confederate States of America, led by Jefferson Davis.
- In April 1861, the Civil War officially began when Confederate forces fired on Fort Sumter in South Carolina, which was held by the Union (Northern states led by Lincoln).

Vocabulary:

compact: contract, agreement
parties: groups
material: important
arbiter: judge
remitted: to be entitled to
render: to make
fugitive: runaway
comply: to follow a law
sectional: applying to one region

Convention: this gathering
Supreme Judge of the World: God
rectitude: rightness
dissolved: broken up
resumed: taken back
State: country
levy: to start
contract: to make

Document: Declaration of Immediate Causes, South Carolina legislature, 1860

> We maintain that in every compact between two or more parties, the obligation is mutual; that the failure of one of the contracting parties to perform a material part of the agreement, entirely releases the obligation of the other; and that where no arbiter is provided, each party is remitted to his own judgment to determine the fact of failure, with all its consequences.
>
> . . . We assert that fourteen of the States have deliberately refused, for years past, to fulfill their constitutional obligations, and we refer to their own Statutes for the proof. . . . The States of Maine, New Hampshire, Vermont, Massachusetts, Connecticut, Rhode Island, New York, Pennsylvania, Illinois, Indiana, Michigan, Wisconsin and Iowa, have enacted laws which either nullify the Acts of Congress or render useless any attempt to execute them. In many of these States the fugitive is discharged from service or labor claimed, and in none of them has the State Government complied with the stipulation made in the Constitution. . . .
>
> A geographical line has been drawn across the Union, and all the States north of that line have united in the election of a man [Abraham Lincoln] to the high office of President of the United States, whose opinions and purposes are hostile to slavery. He is to be entrusted with the administration of the common Government, because he has declared that that "Government cannot endure permanently half slave, half free," and that the public mind must rest in the belief that slavery is in the course of ultimate extinction.
>
> On the 4th day of March next, this party will take possession of the Government. It has announced that the South shall be excluded from the

common territory, that the judicial tribunals shall be made sectional, and that a war must be waged against slavery until it shall cease throughout the United States. The guarantees of the Constitution will then no longer exist; the equal rights of the States will be lost. The slaveholding States will no longer have the power of self-government, or self-protection, and the Federal Government will have become their enemy.

We, therefore, the People of South Carolina, by our delegates in Convention assembled, appealing to the Supreme Judge of the world for the rectitude of our intentions, have solemnly declared that the Union heretofore existing between this State and the other States of North America, is dissolved, and that the State of South Carolina has resumed her position among the nations of the world, as a separate and independent State; with full power to levy war, conclude peace, contract alliances, establish commerce, and to do all other acts and things which independent States may of right do.

Source: Teaching US History. (2009). Declaration of the Immediate Causes Which Induce and Justify the Secession of South Carolina. Retrieved from teachingushistory.org/pdfs/ImmCausesTranscription.pdf

Comprehension Questions:

1. What is the "compact" that the authors say is broken, and who do they think broke it?
2. What evidence do the authors present that the compact has been broken?

Activities:

1. The South Carolina legislature quotes Lincoln's views on slavery. How might Jefferson Davis have responded to Lincoln? Work with a partner to write a dialogue between Davis and Lincoln.
2. Although slave owners prevented most slaves from learning to read and write, write down what you think a slave might have said if he or she had a chance to respond to the authors of this declaration.
3. South Carolina argued that as a state, it was free to nullify federal laws. According to that reasoning, would Northern states mentioned be free to nullify the Fugitive Slave Act? Why or why not?

Reflection: Some history books say that the main cause of the Civil War was southern states governments' determination to assert their states' rights. Others say that the main cause was southern slaveowners' determination to continue the racist practice of slavery. After reading this document, what do you think?

Resources:

Spielberg, S. (Director), & Kennedy, K. (Producer). (2012). *Lincoln*. USA: Dreamworks.

UNIT QUESTION: How Should Power Be Distributed Among Local, State, and Federal Governments?

LESSON 3.9
WHY DID DWIGHT EISENHOWER ENFORCE DESEGREGATION?

Historical Figure: Dwight D. Eisenhower

Event: Little Rock Nine, 1957

Introduction: In what situations should the federal government use military power to enforce laws?

Mini-Lecture:

- In the *Brown v. Board of Education* case of 1954, the Supreme Court decided that segregated schools denied equal protection of the law to Black students.
- White leaders in some southern states announced that they would not enforce federal laws that desegregated schools; Orval Faubus of Arkansas was one such governor.
- Nine Black teenagers registered to attend the all-White Central High School, in Little Rock, Arkansas; they were called the "Little Rock Nine."
- On the first day of school, Governor Faubus ordered Arkansas National Guard troops to prevent students from entering Central High School.
- A large, angry group of White people gathered to protest desegregation.
- President Eisenhower took control of the Arkansas National Guard and ordered Faubus to allow the students into the school under the protection of the 101st Airborne Division of the U.S. Army; our document comes from a speech he made explaining his decision.
- The Little Rock Nine did attend Central High School, but they continued to face discrimination.

Vocabulary:

mob: large group of angry people
facilities: buildings
compulsory: required
bearing: impact
enforcement: making sure people follow laws

decree: instruction
deliberate: careful
mob rule: control by a group of people who do not have legal powers and may use violence
relieve: to replace

Document: Desegregation address, Dwight Eisenhower, 1957

> This morning the mob again gathered in front of the Central High School of Little Rock, obviously for the purpose of again preventing the carrying out of the [Supreme] Court's order relating to the admission of Negro children to that school. . . .
>
> As you know, the Supreme Court of the United States has decided that separate public educational facilities for the races are inherently unequal and therefore compulsory school segregation laws are unconstitutional.

Our personal opinions about the decision have no bearing on the matter of enforcement; the responsibility and authority of the Supreme Court to interpret the Constitution are very clear. Local Federal Courts were instructed by the Supreme Court to issue such orders and decrees as might be necessary to achieve admission to public schools without regard to race—and with all deliberate speed.

... The interest of the nation in the proper fulfillment of the law's requirements cannot yield to opposition and demonstrations by some few persons. Mob rule cannot be allowed to override the decisions of our courts. Now, let me make it very clear that Federal troops are not being used to relieve local and state authorities of their primary duty to preserve the peace and order of the community. Nor are the troops there for the purpose of taking over the responsibility of the School Board and the other responsible local officials in running Central High School. The running of our school system and the maintenance of peace and order in each of our States are strictly local affairs and the Federal Government does not interfere except in a very few special cases and when requested by one of the several States. In the present case the troops are there, pursuant to law, solely for the purpose of preventing interference with the orders of the Court.

Source: Lawson, S. F., & Payne, C. (1998). Dwight D. Eisenhower's Radio and Television Address to the American People on the Situation in Little Rock. In *Debating the Civil Rights Movement, 1945–1968* (pp. 60–64). Lanham, MD: Rowman & Littlefield.

Comprehension Questions:

1. To which decision of the Supreme Court is Eisenhower referring, and what did the case decide (see Lesson 2.11)?
2. According to Eisenhower, what is the purpose of the federal troops in Little Rock?

Activities:

1. Based on this speech, can you figure out Eisenhower's personal feelings about segregation? Choose one quotation that provides evidence for your answer.
2. What alternatives did Eisenhower have to sending federal troops to Little Rock? With a small group, come up with a list of alternatives, then explain why you think he didn't choose those alternatives.

Reflection: Do you think Eisenhower was right to use the military to enforce federal law in this case? Why or why not?

Resources:

Beals, M. P. (2001). *Warriors don't cry*. New York, NY: Simon Pulse.

Unit Question: How Should Power Be Distributed Among Local, State, and Federal Governments?

LESSON 3.10
How Did Orval Faubus Argue for Segregation as a "State's Right"?

Historical Figure: Orval Faubus

Event: Little Rock Nine, 1957

Introduction: Why do you think so many White people in Arkansas opposed the integration of schools?

Mini-Lecture:

- In 1958, Arkansas governor Orval Faubus closed all public high schools in Little Rock rather than allow them to be integrated.
- Later that year, the majority of Little Rock voters chose for the schools to remain closed.
- Our document comes from a speech Governor Faubus made after announcing that the schools would close.
- In 1959, Little Rock public schools reopened and slowly began to integrate.

Vocabulary:

autocracy: government that controls people's lives	*expend:* to spend
intolerable: terrible	*compel:* to require
exhausted: lost	*shirk:* to avoid
in essence: basically	*effect:* to do
	attain: to gain

Document: Speech on School Integration, Orval Faubus, 1958

> Last year, I stated during the September crisis that I was not elected Governor of Arkansas to surrender all our rights as citizens to an all-powerful federal autocracy.... It is my responsibility, and it is my purpose and determination, to defend the constitutional rights of the people of Arkansas to the full extent of my ability....
>
> It was with a heavy heart that I found it necessary to sign the bills of the Extraordinary Session of the General Assembly and to close the High Schools in the City of Little Rock. I took this action only after the last hope of relief from an intolerable situation had been exhausted. The Supreme Court shut its eyes to all the facts, and in essence said—integration at any price, even if it means the destruction of our school system, our educational processes, and the risk of disorder and violence that could result in the loss of life—perhaps yours....
>
> First. The federal government has no authority to require any state to operate public schools. Second. The federal government has no authority to tell a state government for what purposes it may levy taxes, or how the tax money may be expended.... Once again I am compelled to point out to the

people of this city, this state, this nation, and the world, if you please, that our objective has been to maintain the peace and good order of the community. As long as there is a legal way, as I have outlined, to maintain the peace and good order and a suitable educational system, I will not shirk from my duty and responsibility. . . .

Some people dread, shrink from, and grow weary of the struggle in which we are now engaged. I grow weary, also, but is there any choice? Once integration is effected totally and completely, will the peace and harmony you desire be attained? If we are to judge by the results elsewhere, anywhere, once total, or near total integration is effected, the peace, the quiet, the harmony, the pride in our schools, and even the good relations that existed heretofore between the races here, will be gone forever.

Source: Special Collections Department, University of Arkansas Libraries. (2008). Gov. Orval E. Faubus speech lesson plan. Retrieved from libinfo.uark.edu/specialcollections/research/lessonplans/FaubusSpeechLessonPlan.pdf

Comprehension Questions:

1. Whom is Faubus addressing, and why is he making the speech at this time?
2. According to Faubus, how is the federal government overstepping its rights?
3. According to Faubus, what will happen if schools are integrated?

Activities:

1. Segregationists like Faubus often said that segregation was necessary to keep "good relations . . . between the races." Do you think that he and others really thought that race relations under segregation were good, or was this just an excuse to prevent change? Explain.
2. Look back at Lesson 3.3 to refresh your memory about the enumerated powers in the Constitution. Divide the class in half and stage a debate between Faubus and Eisenhower (Lesson 3.9) in which each of them uses the Constitution to defend his actions.

Reflection: Who do you think had a stronger constitutional argument for their actions, Faubus or Eisenhower? Who had a stronger moral argument?

Resources:

Hampton, H. (Producer). *Eyes on the prize: America's civil rights movement.* USA: PBS.

LESSON 3.11

DOES THE STATE OR FEDERAL GOVERNMENT PROTECT INDIVIDUALS FROM ENVIRONMENTAL HARM?

Historical Figure: Sandra Day O'Connor

Event: *New York v. United States,* 1992

Unit Question: How Should Power Be Distributed Among Local, State, and Federal Governments?

Introduction: Who should make the decision about the disposal of environmental pollutants that might endanger human health: state, federal, or local governments? Why?

Mini-Lecture:

- When nuclear energy is made, radioactive waste is left over that can be dangerous to human health.
- It is difficult to build facilities to dispose of this waste, because most people don't want it near their homes.
- In 1985, Congress passed a law that allowed it, instead of the states, to decide where these facilities would be located.
- New York State cooperated with this law, but when Congress decided to place radioactive waste disposal sites in Allegany and Cortland, the residents of those areas objected.
- In response to public pressure, New York sued the United States, claiming the law was unconstitutional because it violated their state's right to make decisions about businesses within the state; New York won the case.
- Our document is from the Supreme Court's decision in *New York v. United States*, which was written by Sandra Day O'Connor.
- O'Connor was on the Supreme Court from 1981 to 2006; she was the first woman to be appointed.

Vocabulary:

infringement: violation
enactment: passage
abstract: theoretical, not practical
entity: thing
incentive: motivation or reward
accountable: responsible

sovereign: individual or group with power to make decisions
expedient: convenient
judiciary: court system
extraconstitutional: unconstitutional
gravity: seriousness

Document: *New York v. United States*, Supreme Court, 1992

> How can a federal statute be found an unconstitutional infringement of state sovereignty when state officials consented to the statute's enactment? The answer follows from an understanding of the fundamental purpose served by our Government's federal structure. The Constitution does not protect the sovereignty of States for the benefit of the States or state governments as abstract political entities, or even for the benefit of the public officials governing the States. To the contrary, the Constitution divides authority between federal and state governments for the protection of individuals. . . .
>
> State officials thus cannot consent to the enlargement of the powers of Congress beyond those enumerated in the Constitution. Indeed, the facts of these cases raise the possibility that powerful incentives might lead both federal and state officials to view departures from the federal structure to be in

their personal interests. Most citizens recognize the need for radioactive waste disposal sites, but few want sites near their homes. As a result, while it would be well within the authority of either federal or state officials to choose where the disposal sites will be, it is likely to be in the political interest of each individual official to avoid being held accountable to the voters for the choice of location. If a federal official is faced with the alternatives of choosing a location or directing the States to do it, the official may well prefer the latter, as a means of shifting responsibility for the eventual decision. If a state official is faced with the same set of alternatives—choosing a location or having Congress direct the choice of a location—the state official may also prefer the latter, as it may permit the avoidance of personal responsibility. . . .

. . . The Constitution protects us from our own best intentions: It divides power among sovereigns and among branches of government precisely so that we may resist the temptation to concentrate power in one location as an expedient solution to the crisis of the day. The shortage of disposal sites for radioactive waste is a pressing national problem, but a judiciary that licensed extraconstitutional government with each issue of comparable gravity would, in the long run, be far worse.

Source: Justia. (n.d.). *New York v. United States.* Retrieved from supreme.justia.com/cases/federal/us/505/144/case.html

Comprehension Questions:

1. According to O'Connor, why does the Constitution separate state and federal powers?
2. According to O'Connor, why might both state and federal officials want to avoid deciding where the radioactive waste disposal site would be located?

Activities:

1. Divide the class in half and debate the following proposition: Because pollution of the air and water (caused, for instance, by radioactive waste) has the potential to move across state lines, the federal government, not individual states, should regulate businesses that create pollution.
2. Imagine you are a citizen who lived in Cortland, New York, where the radioactive waste disposal site was located. Write a letter to O'Connor explaining your reaction to the decision in *New York v. United States.*

Reflection: Most of the time, we think of state and federal governments as competing for power. Yet O'Connor points out that deciding the location of radioactive waste facilities may be a power that neither federal nor state officials want. Can you think of other powers in this category?

Resources:

Union of Concerned Scientists. (n.d.). Nuclear waste. Retrieved from ucsusa.org/nuclear-power/nuclear-waste#.WQOrUlJSV3U

UNIT CONCLUSION

In this unit, students have gained a sense of the balance of power that exists in our federalist structure of government. They have seen how the Constitution's ambiguity allows for a give-and-take between state and federal control, and they will have realized that these questions can have a deeply personal impact on people's lives, from which schools they can attend, to whether they are allowed to remain on their land, to whether they are able to vote.

Students may be noticing patterns in how states' rights arguments have been used to justify the status quo, while the federal government has often pushed states to accept social change. They may make connections to the political spectrum they learned about in Unit 1 by noticing that conservatives favor a less powerful federal government, as well as the preservation of tradition. However, it is important to point out that both liberals and conservatives have used states' rights arguments (for instance, liberals did so on same-sex marriage before federal law supported it). Furthermore, the fact that conservative forces of the past resisted abolition and desegregation does not necessarily mean that conservatives today would hold those positions. Noting these points may ease the tension that can build up when students try to apply what they are learning to the current political situation in a way that lacks nuance.

Students will be on track for a smoother summit, having had two experiences already. Again, teachers will want to consider students' identities and feelings when deciding who should represent figures such as Jefferson Davis and Orval Faubus. Teachers may also notice that some students gravitate toward representing less controversial figures, such as Sandra Day O'Connor; whether they should be encouraged to step out of their comfort zones or keep within them for the time being will depend on the teacher's judgment.

CHAPTER 4

Government, Business, and Workers

Unit Question: What Role Should Government and Businesses Play in Promoting Citizens' Well-Being?

Current Issue Question: How should the government promote a strong economy?

Unit Introduction: In this unit, students will consider the overlap of economic, social, and political concerns. This exploration begins with a reminder that many of the people with whose labor our continent's economic prosperity was built were not "workers," but Native American and African slaves; W. E. B. Du Bois will show students that the process of integrating freed slaves into the economy was anything but smooth. Students will learn about labor rights activists such as Sarah Bagley and Cesar Chavez, as well as entrepreneurs like Henry Ford and Andrew Carnegie. They will see the different approaches the federal government has taken to the economy, from Franklin D. Roosevelt's and Lyndon Johnson's federal antipoverty programs to Ronald Reagan's business-centric approach. The vivid photographic and literary works of Jacob Riis and Upton Sinclair will illustrate the economic hardships that many of our historical figures were trying to ameliorate.

This unit may raise new controversies for students. Depending on their socioeconomic status (SES) and political affiliations, they may identify more with the socialist and liberal voices in this unit or with the conservative voices of private enterprise. While students' race, ethnicity, and gender are more visible characteristics, students may not know one another's SES. Teachers may want to introduce these topics to students with care to avoid making any student feel ashamed of his or her background.

Our current issue leads students to a document from Donald Trump, whose presidency has led to some of the most polarized approval ratings in history. While students and families will probably have strong opinions on the 45th president, teachers may wish to keep the focus on how Trump's economic policies fit into the historic patterns established by the rest of the unit—or, if they have the energy to engage difficult conversations, they could connect Trump's positions on other issues to the topics students have covered earlier in the course.

UNIT QUESTION: What Role Should Government and Business Play in Promoting Citizens' Well-Being?

LESSON 4.1

How Did Donald Trump Think the Government Should Promote a Strong Economy?

Historical Figure: Donald J. Trump

Event: Donald Trump elected, 2016

Introduction: Name five things the government could do to improve the economy.

Mini-Lecture:

- In 2017, Donald Trump took office as the 45th president.
- Before he took office, Donald Trump was a businessperson who was president of the Trump Organization.
- Our document is from the Trump administration's website, in a section explaining his plans for promoting economic growth.

Vocabulary:

recession: period of slow economic growth
national debt: the money that a country has borrowed from other countries, organizations, or banks
pro-growth: promoting economic growth
tax bracket: a range of incomes that is taxed at a certain rate
tax code: rules from the government about who should pay taxes and how much they should pay

tax rate: the percentage of income that a person or business pays in taxes
onerous: burdensome
entrepreneur: person starting or running his or her own business
regulation: rule
moratorium: a temporary end to a certain practice
trade deal: an agreement between countries about the rules that govern trade among them
renegotiate: to change an agreement

Document: Bringing Back Jobs and Growth, Donald Trump administration, 2017

> Since the recession of 2008, American workers and businesses have suffered through the slowest economic recovery since World War II. The U.S. lost nearly 300,000 manufacturing jobs during this period, while the share of Americans in the work force plummeted to lows not seen since the 1970s, the national debt doubled, and [the] middle class got smaller. To get the economy back on track, President Trump has outlined a bold plan to create 25 million new American jobs in the next decade and return to 4 percent annual economic growth.
>
> The plan starts with pro-growth tax reform to help American workers and businesses keep more of their hard-earned dollars. The President's plan will lower rates for Americans in every tax bracket, simplify the tax code, and reduce the U.S. corporate tax rate, which is one of the highest in the world. Fixing a tax

code that is outdated, overly complex, and too onerous will unleash America's economy, creating millions of new jobs and boosting economic growth.

As a lifelong job-creator and businessman, the President also knows how important it is to get Washington out of the way of America's small businesses, entrepreneurs, and workers. In 2015 alone, federal regulations cost the American economy more than $2 trillion. That is why the President has proposed a moratorium on new federal regulations and is ordering the heads of federal agencies and departments to identify job-killing regulations that should be repealed.

With decades of deal-making experience, the President also understands how critical it is to negotiate the best possible trade deals for the United States. By renegotiating existing trade deals, and taking a tough stance on future ones, we will ensure that trade agreements bring good-paying jobs to our shores and support American manufacturing, the backbone of our economy. The President plans to show America's trading partners that we mean business by ensuring consequences for countries that engage in illegal or unfair trade practices that hurt American workers.

By standing side-by-side with America's workers and businesses, the President's policies will unleash economic growth, create 25 million new jobs, and help Make America Great Again.

Source: The White House. (2017). Bringing back jobs and growth. Retrieved from whitehouse.gov/bringing-back-jobs-and-growth

Comprehension Questions:

1. Name three problems Trump describes with the economy, then in your own words explain the steps he plans to take to fix the problems.

Activities:

1. For each of Trump's three plans, work with a small group to list several positive effects that could result and several negative effects that could result.
2. Which do you think are more likely to occur: the positive effects or the negative effects? Discuss with your group, then determine what evidence you would need to support your prediction.

Reflection: Did any of your recommendations for promoting economic growth overlap with Trump's? Which of his plans do you think is most likely to be successful? Least likely to be successful? Why?

Resources:

Obama White House Archive. (2017). Economic rescue, recovery, and rebuilding on a new foundation. Retrieved from obamawhitehouse.archives.gov/the-record/economy

UNIT QUESTION: What Role Should Government and Business Play in Promoting Citizens' Well-Being?

LESSON 4.2
WHAT WERE CHRISTOPHER COLUMBUS'S ECONOMIC AND SOCIAL GOALS?

Historical Figure: Christopher Columbus

Event: Columbus lands in the Americas, 1492

Introduction: List what you know about Christopher Columbus's reasons for sailing to the Americas.

Mini-Lecture:

- In 1492, Christopher Columbus (c. 1451–1506) sailed from Europe to an island he called Hispaniola (today Haiti and the Dominican Republic), on a mission from the Spanish king and queen to find gold, take over land, and convert native people to Christianity.
- On the island lived as many as 3 million Arawak/Taíno people.
- Spanish forces colonized (took over) the land, and enslaved and killed many Arawak people; many others died of diseases that the Europeans brought with them.
- By 1650, the Spanish found there were no Arawak people left on Hispaniola; however, because Arawak women were forced to bear the children of European men, people in that area today may have Arawak ancestors.
- Our document comes from the journal Columbus kept of his voyage.

Vocabulary:

skein: ball
in fine: finally
fair: average
ascertain: to find out
stature: height
inclination: desire

simple: without knowledge
your Highnesses: term used to refer to royalty—in this case, the king and queen of Spain
subjugate: to take control over people's lives

Document: Log, Christopher Columbus, 1492

> Friday, 12th of October: . . . I . . . that we might form great friendship, for I knew that they were a people who could be more easily freed and converted to our holy faith by love than by force, gave to some of them red caps, and glass beads to put around their necks, and many other things of little value, which gave them great pleasure, and made them so much our friends that it was a marvel to see. They afterwards came to the ship's boats where we were, swimming and bringing us parrots, cotton threads in skeins, darts, and many other things; and we exchanged them for other things that we gave them, such as glass beads and bells. In fine, they took all, and gave what they had with good will. It appeared to me to be a race of people very poor in everything. They go as naked as when their mothers bore them. . . . They neither carry nor know of arms, for I showed

them swords, and they took them by the blade and cut themselves though ignorance. . . . They are all of fair stature and size, with good faces, and well made. . . . They should be good servants and intelligent, for I observed that they quickly took in what was said to them, and I believe they would easily be made Christians, as it appeared to me that they had no religion.

Saturday, October 13: . . . I was attentive, and took trouble to ascertain if there was gold. I saw that some of them had a small piece fastened in a hole they have in the nose, and by signs I was able to make out that to the south, or going from the island to the south, there was a king who had great cups full, and who possessed a great quantity. I tried to get them to go there, but afterwards I saw that they had no inclination. . . .

Sunday, October 14: . . . At dawn I . . . went along the coast of the island to the [north by northeast], to see the other side. . . . Presently I saw two or three, and the people all came to the shore, calling out and giving thanks to God. Some of them brought us water, others came with food. . . . We understood that they asked us if we had come from heaven. . . . I saw a piece of land which appeared like an island, although it is not one, and on it there were six houses. It might be converted into an island in two days, though I do not see that it would be necessary, for these people are very simple as regards the use of arms, as your Highnesses will see from that seven that I caused to be taken, to bring home and learn our language and return; unless your Highnesses should order them all to be brought to Castile [Spain], or to be kept as captives on the same island; for with fifty men they can all be subjugated and made to do what is required of them.

Source: Wisconsin Historical Society. (2003). Journal of the first voyage of Columbus. Retrieved from americanjourneys.org/pdf/AJ-062.pdf

Comprehension Questions:

1. Why did Columbus give the Arawak people caps and beads?
2. Why did Columbus think the Arawaks would make good servants?

Activities:

1. For each of the quotes below, work with a partner to find another that either corroborates or contradicts it:
   a. "I knew that they were a people who could be more easily freed and converted to our holy faith by love than by force."
   b. "It appeared to me to be a race of people very poor in everything."
   c. "It appeared to me that they had no religion."

Reflection: Columbus identifies several different goals in his log. Which do you think was most important to him? Why?

Resources:

Zinn, H. (2003). Columbus, the Indians, and human progress. In *A people's history of the United States* (chap. 1). New York: HarperCollins.

LESSON 4.3
WHY DID JOHN CALHOUN DEFINE SLAVERY AS A "POSITIVE GOOD"?

Historical Figure: John C. Calhoun

Event: Britain outlaws slave trade, 1807

Introduction: Do you think most slaveowners knew that slavery was morally wrong, but practiced it anyway because it was in their economic interest? Or do you think they believed slavery was morally right? Explain your answer.

Mini-Lecture:

- In 1807, Britain outlawed the trans-Atlantic slave trade and pressured other countries, including the United States, to do the same.
- The abolition of the slave trade in Britain caused slaveowners in other countries to believe that slavery might be outlawed in their countries too.
- Some slaveowners, like John C. Calhoun, who wrote our document, tried to defend on both moral and economic grounds the racism that underpinned slavery.
- Calhoun served as vice president from 1825 to 1832, and he was a senator for South Carolina in the 1830s and 1840s.

Vocabulary:

attain: to reach
borne out: proven
allotted: given
innumerable: many
gross: ignorant
artful: tricky
fiscal: financial
contrivance: trick

exacted from: required of
infirmity: weakness
superintending: thoughtful and responsible
forlorn: sad
pauper: poor person
exempt: to protect

Document: Slavery as a Positive Good, John C. Calhoun, 1837

> I appeal to facts. Never before has the black race of Central Africa, from the dawn of history to the present day, attained a condition so civilized and so improved, not only physically, but morally and intellectually [as it has under slavery]. But I take higher ground. I hold that in the present state of civilization, where two races of different origin, and distinguished by color, and other physical differences, as well as intellectual, are brought together, the relation now existing in the slaveholding States between the two, is, instead of an evil, a good—a positive good. . . .
>
> I hold then, that there never has yet existed a wealthy and civilized society in which one portion of the community did not, in point of fact, live on the labor of the other. Broad and general as is this assertion, it is fully borne out by

history. This is not the proper occasion, but, if it were, it would not be difficult to trace the various devices by which the wealth of all civilized communities has been so unequally divided, and to show by what means so small a share has been allotted to those by whose labor it was produced, and so large a share given to the non-producing classes. The devices are almost innumerable, from the brute force and gross superstition of ancient times, to the subtle and artful fiscal contrivances of modern.

I may say with truth, that in few countries so much is left to the share of the laborer, and so little exacted from him [the slave], or where there is more kind attention paid to him in sickness or infirmities of age. Compare his condition with the tenants of the poor houses in the more civilized portions of Europe—look at the sick, and the old and infirm slave, on one hand, in the midst of his family and friends, under the kind superintending care of his master and mistress, and compare it with the forlorn and wretched condition of the pauper in the poorhouse.

The condition of society in the South exempts us from the disorders and dangers resulting from this conflict; and which explains why it is that the political condition of the slaveholding States has been so much more stable and quiet than that of the North.

Source: Ashbrook Center. (2016). Slavery as a positive good. Retrieved from teachingamericanhistory.org/library/document/slavery-a-positive-good/

Comprehension Questions:

1. According to Calhoun, what do all civilized societies have in common?
2. According to Calhoun, how do slaves benefit from slavery?

Activities:

1. Work with a partner to choose one of the claims Calhoun makes, then list three pieces of evidence he would need to support it. Then list three pieces of evidence that abolitionists could use to refute his claim.
2. When slaves were abused, who was more responsible: the government (which allowed slavery), or the masters (who mistreated the slaves)? Why?

Reflection: How would you personally respond to Calhoun if you could go back in time?

Resources:

New York Public Library. (2012). The abolition of the slave trade. Retrieved from abolition.nypl.org/home/

UNIT QUESTION: What Role Should Government and Business Play in Promoting Citizens' Well-Being?

LESSON 4.4
WHY DID THE LOWELL MILL WOMEN GO ON STRIKE?

Historical Figure: Sarah Bagley

Event: Lowell mill women strike, 1834

Introduction: How many hours per day and days per week do most adults you know work? Are there any jobs that require people to work more than the regular number of hours?

Mini-Lecture:

- In the early 19th century, many factories opened in the northeastern United States.
- In Lowell, Massachusetts, there was a textile mill where mostly female workers wove cloth.
- Sarah Bagley (1806–1888) was an activist for labor rights and women's rights.
- Bagley worked in a textile mill in Lowell, and she helped organize a union (a group to protect workers' rights).
- Our document is based on Bagley's testimony in the Massachusetts legislature, where she asked for better conditions for workers.

Vocabulary:

petition: request by a group of people made to the government, a business, or an individual
hastening: moving quickly
privation: hardship
by the piece: work paid according to the amount produced

operative: worker
millinery: the business of making hats
cultivate: to develop
pecuniary: financial
kept: served as a teacher

Document: Investigation of Labor Conditions, Massachusetts House Document no. 50, 1845

> The first petition which was referred to your committee, came from the city of Lowell, and was signed by Mr. John Quincy Adams Thayer, and eight hundred and fifty others, "peaceable, industrious, hard working men and women of Lowell." The petitioners declare that they are confined "from thirteen to fourteen hours per day in unhealthy apartments," and are thereby "hastening through pain, disease and privation, down to a premature grave." They therefore ask the Legislature "to pass a law providing that ten hours shall constitute a day's work," and that no corporation or private citizen "shall be allowed except in cases of emergency, to employ one set of hands more than ten hours per day." . . .

The whole number of names on the several petitions is 2,139, of which 1,151 are from Lowell. A very large proportion of the Lowell petitioners are females. . . .

On the 13th of February, the Committee held a session to hear the petitioners from the city of Lowell. Six of the female and three of the male petitioners were present, and gave in their testimony.

Miss Sarah G. Bagley said she had worked in the Lowell Mills eight years and a half, six years and a half on the Hamilton Corporation, and two years on the Middlesex. She is a weaver, and works by the piece. She worked in the mills three years before her health began to fail. She is a native of New Hampshire, and went home six weeks during the summer. Last year she was out of the mill a third of the time. She thinks the health of the operatives is not so good as the health of females who do house-work or millinery business. The chief evil, so far as health is concerned, is the shortness of time allowed for meals. The next evil is the length of time employed—not giving them time to cultivate their minds. She spoke of the high moral and intellectual character of the girls. That many were engaged as teachers in the Sunday schools. That many attended the lectures of the Lowell Institute; and she thought, if more time was allowed, that more lectures would be given and more girls attend. She thought that the girls generally were favorable to the ten hour system. She had presented a petition, same as the one before the Committee, to 132 girls, most of whom said that they would prefer to work but ten hours. In a pecuniary point of view, it would be better, as their health would be improved. They would have more time for sewing. Their intellectual, moral and religious habits would also be benefited by the change. Miss Bagley said, in addition to her labor in the mills, she had kept evening school during the winter months, for four years, and thought that this extra labor must have injured her health.

Source: Commons, J. (Ed.). (1910). *A documentary history of American industrial society.* Cleveland, OH: Arthur H. Clark.

Comprehension Questions:

1. How many hours a day did the mill workers work, and how many hours did they want to work?
2. According to Bagley, what negative effects did long working hours have?

Activities:

1. Imagine that you are the owner of the mill where Bagley worked. If you were called upon to testify, what would you say? Prepare your testimony and perform it for the class.
2. Because of activists like Bagley, the government made a law that most workers can't be required to work more than 40 hours per week without overtime pay. Do you think it is right for the government to regulate work hours, or should businesses make their own decisions? Why?

UNIT QUESTION: What Role Should Government and Business Play in Promoting Citizens' Well-Being?

Reflection: What changes, if any, should be made to conditions or hours of workers today?

Resources:

AFL-CIO. (2016). Lowell mill women create first union of working women. Retrieved from aflcio.org/Issues/Civil-and-Workplace-Rights/Working-Women/Working-Women-in-Union-History/Lowell-Mill-Women-Create-First-Union-of-Working-Women

LESSON 4.5
HOW DID W. E. B. DU BOIS THINK THAT THE GOVERNMENT SUCCEEDED AND FAILED IN HELPING FORMER SLAVES?

Historical Figure: W. E. B. Du Bois

Event: Reconstruction, 1865–1877

Introduction: What kind of work do you think former slaves did after they were freed?

Mini-Lecture:

- When the Civil War ended, the federal government stepped in to manage former Confederate states. This period, from 1865 to 1877, is called Reconstruction.
- During Reconstruction, the government tried to integrate former slaves, or "freedmen," into society through an agency called the Freedmen's Bureau.
- W. E. B. Du Bois (1868–1963) was one of the first Black sociologists to write about the Reconstruction; he also helped found the NAACP.
- Our document comes from his book *The Souls of Black Folk*.

Vocabulary:

guised: disguised
singular: unique
plain: clear
dimensions: size
spasmodically: inconsistently
perchance: by chance
squander: to waste
demoralizing: discouraging
epitomize: to present the best possible example
dole: charity

benevolent: kind
proprietorship: ownership of land
paternalistic: treating people like children
philanthropist: donor
agent: official
inherent: unavoidable
legacy: effect
heritage: inheritance
servile caste: a group of people who serve others

Document: *The Souls of Black Folk*, W. E. B. Du Bois, 1903

The problem of the twentieth century is the problem of the color-line,—the relation of the darker to the lighter races of men in Asia and Africa, in America and the islands of the sea. It was a phase of this problem that caused the Civil War. . . . No sooner had Northern armies touched Southern soil than this old question, newly guised, sprang from the earth,—What shall be done with Negroes? . . . .

It is the aim of this essay to study the period of history from 1861 to 1872 so far as it relates to the American Negro. In effect, this tale of the dawn of Freedom is an account of that government of men called the Freedmen's Bureau,—one of the most singular and interesting of the attempts made by a great nation to grapple with vast problems of race and social condition.

. . . And daily, too, it seemed more plain that this [the task of the Freedmen's Bureau] was no ordinary matter of temporary relief, but a national crisis; for here loomed a labor problem of vast dimensions. Masses of Negroes stood idle, or, if they worked spasmodically, were never sure of pay; and if perchance they received pay, squandered the new thing thoughtlessly. In these and other ways were camp-life [in camps established after the Civil War] and the new liberty demoralizing the freedmen.

. . . The work of the Freedmen's Bureau, which, summed up in brief, may be epitomized thus: For some fifteen million dollars, beside the sums spent before 1865, and the dole of benevolent societies, this Bureau set going a system of free labor, established a beginning of peasant proprietorship, secured the recognition of black freedmen before courts of law, and founded the free common school in the South. On the other hand, it failed to begin the establishment of good-will between ex-masters and freedmen, to guard its work wholly from paternalistic methods which discouraged self-reliance, and to carry out to any considerable extent its implied promises to furnish the freedmen with land. Its successes were the result of hard work, supplemented by the aid of philanthropists and the eager striving of black men. Its failures were the result of bad local agents, the inherent difficulties of the work, and national neglect.

. . . The legacy of the Freedmen's Bureau is the heavy heritage of this generation. . . . For this much all men know: despite compromise, war, and struggle, the Negro is not free. . . . In the most cultured sections and cities of the South the Negroes are a segregated servile caste, with restricted rights and privileges. Before the courts, both in law and custom, they stand on a different and peculiar basis. Taxation without representation is the rule of their political life. And the result of all this is, and in nature must have been, lawlessness and crime. That is the large legacy of the Freedmen's Bureau, the work it did not do because it could not.

Source: Project Gutenberg. (2008). W. E. B. Du Bois—Of our spiritual strivings. In *The souls of Black folk* (chap. 1). Retrieved from gutenberg.org/files/408/408-h/408-h.htm

Comprehension Questions:

1. According to Du Bois, what were the causes and effects (both positive and negative) of the Freedmen's Bureau being established?
2. What is Du Bois's evidence that the Freedmen's Bureau did not succeed?

UNIT QUESTION: What Role Should Government and Business Play in Promoting Citizens' Well-Being?

Activities:

1. Work with a partner to write and act out a dialogue between John C. Calhoun (Lesson 4.3) and W. E. B. Du Bois about what the government should do to help Black people.
2. Du Bois claimed in 1903 that "the problem of the twentieth century is the problem of the color-line," meaning that race relations would be difficult throughout the 1900s. Do you agree with his statement, or do you think other lines (economic, gender, etc.) were more important? Provide evidence to support your claim.

Reflection: Do you think the federal government's plans to help disadvantaged people (for example, the Freedmen's Bureau) usually succeed? Why or why not?

Resources:

Smith, L. M. (Producer, Director). Reconstruction. *American Experience*. USA: PBS.

LESSON 4.6
WHAT WAS ANDREW CARNEGIE'S ARGUMENT FOR SOCIAL DARWINISM?

Historical Figure: Andrew Carnegie

Event: Gilded Age, 1877–1900

Introduction: Why do you think some people are poor and some are rich?

Mini-Lecture:

- The time between the end of Reconstruction and the beginning of the 20th century is known as the Gilded Age, because some businesspeople became very rich, while poor people remained poor.
- One of the wealthiest businesspeople was Andrew Carnegie, who was born to a poor family but accumulated millions of dollars in the railroad and steel business.
- He donated money to causes he supported; in 1911, he founded the Carnegie Corporation, which supports libraries, education, and research.
- He believed in social Darwinism, which applied the theory of evolution or "survival of the fittest" to human society by arguing that people who became rich in capitalist societies were superior to those who were poor.
- Our document comes from his essay "The Gospel of Wealth," in which he explains his theories about economics and society.

Vocabulary:

administration: management
retainer: servant
salutary: admirable
capital and labor: owners and workers
disposition: tendency

hoard: to keep more than one needs
the state: the government
graduated tax: tax structure requiring rich people to pay a greater percentage of their income than poor people do

unostentatious: modest, not showing off   *gospel:* guiding principle or doctrine
shun: to avoid

Document: The Gospel of Wealth, Andrew Carnegie, 1889

The problem of our age is the proper administration of wealth, so that the ties of brotherhood may still bind together the rich and poor in harmonious relationship. The conditions of human life have not only been changed, but revolutionized, within the past few hundred years. In former days there was little difference between the dwelling, dress, food, and environment of the chief and those of his retainers. . . . The contrast between the palace of the millionaire and the cottage of the laborer with us to-day measures the change which has come with civilization. . . .

The price we pay for this salutary change is, no doubt, great. . . . Under the law of competition, the employer of thousands is forced into the strictest economies, among which the rates paid to labor figure prominently, and often there is friction between the employer and the employed, between capital and labor, between rich and poor.

. . . While the law [of competition] may be sometimes hard for the individual, it is best for the race, because it insures the survival of the fittest in every department. We accept and welcome therefore, as conditions to which we must accommodate ourselves, great inequality of environment, the concentration of business, industrial and commercial, in the hands of a few, and the law of competition between these, as being not only beneficial, but essential for the future progress of the race. . . .

The growing disposition to tax more and more heavily large estates left at death is a cheering indication of the growth of a salutary change in public opinion. The State of Pennsylvania now takes—subject to some exceptions—one-tenth of the property left by its citizens. The budget presented in the British Parliament the other day proposes to increase the death-duties; and, most significant of all, the new tax is to be a graduated one. Of all forms of taxation, this seems the wisest. Men who continue hoarding great sums all their lives, the proper use of which for public ends would work good to the community, should be made to feel that the community, in the form of the state, cannot thus be deprived of its proper share. . . .

This, then, is held to be the duty of the man of Wealth: First, to set an example of modest, unostentatious living, shunning display or extravagance; to provide moderately for the legitimate wants of those dependent upon him; and after doing so to consider all surplus revenues which come to him simply as trust funds, which he is called upon to administer, and strictly bound as a matter of duty to administer in the manner which, in his judgment, is best calculated to produce the most beneficial results for the community—the man of wealth thus becoming the mere agent and trustee for his poorer brethren, bringing to their service his superior wisdom, experience and ability to administer, doing for them better than they would or could do for themselves. . . .

Such, in my opinion, is the true Gospel concerning Wealth, obedience to which is destined some day to solve the problem of the Rich and the Poor, and to bring "Peace on earth, among men Good-Will."

Source: Carnegie Corporation. (n.d.). The gospel of wealth. Retrieved from carnegie.org/media/filer_public/9d/1b/ 9d1b670b-681c-48e2-a607-48ea5282c891/ccny_essay_1889_gospel.pdf

Comprehension Questions:

1. According to Carnegie, what are the causes and effects of the increasing gap between rich and poor?
2. What kind of taxation plan does Carnegie favor?
3. What does Carnegie think rich people should do with their money?

Activities:

1. What advice would Carnegie give Donald Trump (Lesson 4.1) about how much the government should tax rich people? Write a letter from Carnegie to Trump.
2. Imagine you are a poor person who lived in Carnegie's time. How would you respond to his ideas? Work with a partner to create a cartoon with thought and speech bubbles.

Reflection: If you were extremely wealthy, what would you do with your money? Why?

Resources:

PBS. (1997). Andrew Carnegie. *The American experience.* USA: PBS.

LESSON 4.7

How Did the "Other Half" Live in Jacob Riis's Photos?

Historical Figure: Jacob Riis

Event: Progressive Era, 1890–1920

Introduction: What are the most unsafe or unsanitary houses or apartments that you have seen, heard about, or experienced?

Mini-Lecture:

- In the late 19th and early 20th century, journalists known as "muckrakers" tried to bring the public's attention to social and economic problems.
- Jacob Riis was a muckraking journalist who took photographs of and wrote about poor immigrants living in tenements (crowded apartment buildings) in New York City.
- Our document consists of photographs from his book *How the Other Half Lives,* in which he argued that the government should make laws to create safer and more sanitary living conditions for urban poor people.

- His book helped to begin the Progressive Era, a period in which social reformers and politicians tried to solve the problems created by industrialization (people working in factories) and urbanization (people moving to cities).
- Progressives such as Jacob Riis disagreed with social Darwinism and believed the government should create equal opportunities for poor people.

Document: *How the Other Half Lives*, Jacob Riis, 1890

Figure 4.1. Scene in Tenement, Jacob Riis, 1890

Figure 4.2. One of Four Pedlars Who Slept in the Cellar of 11 Ludlow St. Rear, Jacob Riis, 1890

UNIT QUESTION: What Role Should Government and Business Play in Promoting Citizens' Well-Being? 119

Figure 4.3. "The Bend," Jacob Riis, 1890

Figure 4.4. "Five Cent a Spot," Unauthorized Lodging in a Bayard Street Tenement, 1890

Comprehension Questions:

1. About how old are the people in Figure 4.1? How can you tell?
2. "Pedlar" is an alternate spelling of "peddler." What does a peddler do?
3. The building in Figure 4.3 is missing something that many tall buildings have today. What is it?
4. How many people can you count in Figure 4.4?

Activities:

1. Work with a partner to write a dialogue between Riis and Andrew Carnegie (Lesson 4.6) about why there is a gap between rich and poor, then act it out for the class.
2. The Gilded Age and the Progressive Era overlapped. What changes happened in the Gilded Age that may have caused the Progressive Era to begin? What kind of era would you predict came next, and why?

Reflection: If Riis traveled through time to the present, what places or people do you think he would photograph to show how the "other half" lives now?

Resources:

Riis, J. (1890). *How the other half lives: Studies among the tenements of New York.* New York, NY: Charles Scribner's Sons.

George Washington University. (n.d.). The Progressive Era. Retrieved from www2.gwu.edu/~erpapers/teachinger/glossary/progressive-era.cfm

LESSON 4.8

How Did Upton Sinclair Want to Change the Meatpacking Industry?

Historical Figure: Upton Sinclair

Event: Pure Food and Drug Act, 1906

Introduction: Do you have confidence that the food you eat is clean, safe, and healthy? Why or why not?

Mini-Lecture:

- Upton Sinclair (1878–1968) was a muckraking journalist and author active during the Progressive Era.
- He was a socialist: He believed that the government should facilitate people sharing wealth instead of allowing rich people to accumulate it.
- Our document comes from his novel *The Jungle*, in which he describes the hardships faced by immigrants who worked in Chicago's meatpacking factories.
- Sinclair wanted to build sympathy for workers, but his book was more effective at motivating concerns about food safety.
- Shortly after *The Jungle* was published, Congress passed the Pure Food and Drug Act, which created the Food and Drug Administration (FDA) to regulate consumer products.

Vocabulary:

pickle-room: place where meat is soaked in brine for canning
scarce a one: almost none
tuberculosis: a disease of the lungs
quarter: a section of a dead cow
rheumatism: a disease in which joints and muscles swell

fertilizer: a material put on the soil to make plants grow

vat: large container

exhibit: to show

Document: *The Jungle*, Upton Sinclair, 1906

There were the men in the pickle-rooms, for instance, where old Antanas had gotten his death; scarce a one of these that had not some spot of horror on his person. Let a man so much as scrape his finger pushing a truck in the pickle-rooms, and he might have a sore that would put him out of the world; all the joints in his fingers might be eaten by the acid, one by one. Of the butchers and floorsmen, the beef-boners and trimmers, and all those who used knives, you could scarcely find a person who had the use of his thumb; time and time again the base of it had been slashed, till it was a mere lump of flesh against which the man pressed the knife to hold it. The hands of these men would be criss-crossed with cuts, until you could no longer pretend to count them or to trace them. They would have no nails,—they had worn them off pulling hides; their knuckles were swollen so that their fingers spread out like a fan. There were men who worked in the cooking-rooms, in the midst of steam and sickening odors, by artificial light; in these rooms the germs of tuberculosis might live for two years, but the supply was renewed every hour. There were the beef-luggers, who carried two-hundred-pound quarters into the refrigerator-cars; a fearful kind of work, that began at four o'clock in the morning, and that wore out the most powerful men in a few years. There were those who worked in the chilling-rooms, and whose special disease was rheumatism; the time-limit that a man could work in the chilling-rooms was said to be five years. There were the woolpluckers, whose hands went to pieces even sooner than the hands of the pickle-men; for the pelts of the sheep had to be painted with acid to loosen the wool, and then the pluckers had to pull out this wool with their bare hands, till the acid had eaten their fingers off. There were those who made the tins for the canned-meat; and their hands, too, were a maze of cuts, and each cut represented a chance for blood-poisoning. Some worked at the stamping machines, and it was very seldom that one could work long there at the pace that was set, and not give out and forget himself, and have a part of his hand chopped off. There were the "hoisters," as they were called, whose task it was to press the lever which lifted the dead cattle off the floor. They ran along upon a rafter, peering down through the damp and the steam; and as old Durham's architects had not built the killing-room for the convenience of the hoisters, at every few feet they would have to stoop under a beam, say four feet above the one they ran on; which got them into the habit of stooping, so that in a few years they would be walking like chimpanzees. Worst of any, however, were the fertilizer-men, and those who served in the cooking-rooms. These people could not be shown to the visitor,—for the odor of a fertilizer-man would scare any ordinary visitor at a hundred yards, and as for the other men, who worked in tank-rooms full of steam, and in some of which there were open vats near the level of the floor, their peculiar trouble was that they fell into the vats; and when they were fished out, there was never enough of them left to be worth exhibiting,—sometimes they would be overlooked for days, till all but the bones of them had gone out to the world as Durham's Pure Leaf Lard!

Comprehension Questions:

1. For each of the occupations Sinclair describes, list one danger involved.

Activities:

1. After the Pure Food and Drug Act was passed, Sinclair said, "I aimed at the public's heart and by accident hit its stomach." What did he mean?
2. Discuss with a small group: Who do you think was best able to fix the dangerous conditions Sinclair described—the factory owners, the government, the workers themselves, muckraking journalists, or society as a whole? Why? Create a poster illustrating one action each group could take.

Reflection: Which workers today may still face dangerous conditions? How might this be changed?

Resources:

Younge, G. (2006, August 4). Blood, sweat, and fears. *The Guardian*. Retrieved from theguardian.com/books/2006/aug/05/featuresreviews.guardianreview24

Office of Art and Archives. (n.d.). The Pure Food and Drug Act. Retrieved from history.house.gov/HistoricalHighlight/Detail/15032393280?ret=True

LESSON 4.9

WHAT WAS HENRY FORD'S PLAN FOR ENDING POVERTY?

Historical Figure: Henry Ford

Event: Assembly line invented, 1913

Introduction: If you owned a factory, how much would you pay workers per day? Why?

Mini-Lecture:

- Henry Ford (1863–1947) was an inventor and businessperson who founded the Ford Motor Company.
- In 1913, he pioneered the use of the assembly line, which made the production of cars more efficient.
- His business model involved producing goods most people could afford, and paying workers higher than usual wages.
- Ford discriminated against some groups; for instance, he did not hire Jewish workers.
- Our document comes from Ford's autobiography, in which he explains how he ran his car company.

UNIT QUESTION: What Role Should Government and Business Play in Promoting Citizens' Well-Being?

Vocabulary:

disservice: harm
prosperous: wealthy

initiative: motivation and hard work
ingenuity: cleverness and originality

Document: *My Life and Work*, Henry Ford, 1922

Laws can do very little. Law never does anything constructive. It can never be more than a policeman, and so it is a waste of time to look to our state capitals or to Washington to do that which law was not designed to do. As long as we look to legislation to cure poverty or to abolish special privilege we are going to see poverty spread and special privilege grow. We have had enough of looking to Washington and we have had enough of legislators—not so much, however, in this as in other countries—promising laws to do that which laws cannot do. . . .

There is no reason why a man who is willing to work should not be able to work and to receive the full value of his work. There is equally no reason why a man who can but will not work should not receive the full value of his services to the community. He should most certainly be permitted to take away from the community an equivalent of what he contributes to it. If he contributes nothing he should take away nothing. He should have the freedom of starvation. We are not getting anywhere when we insist that every man ought to have more than he deserves to have—just because some do get more than they deserve to have. There can be no greater absurdity and no greater disservice to humanity in general than to insist that all men are equal.

. . . We announced and put into operation in January, 1914, a kind of profit-sharing plan in which the minimum wage for any class of work and under certain conditions was five dollars a day. At the same time we reduced the working day to eight hours—it had been nine—and the week to forty-eight hours. This was entirely a voluntary act. All of our wage rates have been voluntary. It was to our way of thinking an act of social justice, and in the last analysis we did it for our own satisfaction of mind. . . . There was, however, no charity in any way involved. That was not generally understood. Many employers thought we were just making the announcement because we were prosperous and wanted advertising and they condemned us because we were upsetting standards—violating the custom of paying a man the smallest amount he would take. There is nothing to such standards and customs. They have to be wiped out. Some day they will be. Otherwise, we cannot abolish poverty. We made the change not merely because we wanted to pay higher wages and thought we could pay them. We wanted to pay these wages so that the business would be on a lasting foundation. We were not distributing anything—we were building for the future. A low wage business is always insecure. . . .

Modern industry is gradually lifting the worker and the world. We only need to know more about planning and methods. The best results can and will be brought about by individual initiative and ingenuity—by intelligent individual leadership. The government, because it is essentially negative, cannot give positive aid to any really constructive programme. It can give negative aid—by removing obstructions [blocks] to progress and by ceasing to be a burden upon the community.

Source: Project Gutenberg. (2008). Henry Ford—Introduction. In *My life and work*. Retrieved from gutenberg.org/cache/epub/7213/pg7213-images.html

Comprehension Questions:

1. According to Ford, why did he raise wages?
2. According to Ford, how is the government's role different from the role of businesses in helping workers?

Activities:

1. Imagine an encounter between Sarah Bagley (Lesson 4.4) and Ford on the role of businesses and government in helping workers. Work with a partner to create a cartoon with speech and thought bubbles.
2. Was Ford a social Darwinist? Find a quotation that supports your claim.

Reflection: Ford disagrees with the statement "All men are equal." What do you think?

Resources:

The Henry Ford. (2016). Assembly line. Retrieved from thehenryford.org/collections-and-research/digital-collections/expert-sets/7139

PBS. (2013). Henry Ford. *American Experience*. USA: PBS.

LESSON 4.10

WHAT WERE THE AIMS OF THE NEW DEAL?

Historical Figure: Franklin D. Roosevelt

Event: Great Depression, 1929–1939

Introduction: The stock market has crashed. Millions of people are unemployed. Poverty is skyrocketing. You are president. What do you do?

Mini-Lecture:

- The Great Depression was a serious economic crisis that followed the stock market crash of 1929.
- By 1932, 20% of the U.S. population was unemployed, and over half were living in poverty.
- Franklin D. Roosevelt was president from 1933 to 1945.
- When Roosevelt ran for president in 1932, he created a plan called the New Deal, in order to promote economic recovery.

UNIT QUESTION: What Role Should Government and Business Play in Promoting Citizens' Well-Being?

- As part of the New Deal, Roosevelt created social safety net programs, including unemployment insurance and Social Security, and initiated public works programs to employ people.
- Our document comes from one of his campaign speeches.

Vocabulary:

favored: lucky

public works: projects that are financed by government through tax revenues for the benefit of people—for example, building roads

stimulate: to increase

issuance: giving out

bond: a debt security that the government sells in order to finance its spending

marginal land: land not good for farming

reforestation: planting trees in areas where they had been cut down

cut-over land: land where trees have been cut down

soil erosion: wearing away of the top, fertile layer of soil

timber famine: lack of trees that can be cut down and used

soundness: security

constitute: to define oneself

prophet: someone who tells about the future

call to arms: a strong invitation to participate in an important project

crusade: a campaign to support a political, social, or religious cause

Document: The New Deal, Franklin D. Roosevelt, 1932

There are two ways of viewing the Government's duty in matters affecting economic and social life. The first sees to it that a favored few are helped and hopes that some of their prosperity will leak through, sift through, to labor, to the farmer, to the small business man. . . . But it is not and never will be the theory of the Democratic Party. . . .

Now it is inevitable . . . that the main issue of this campaign should revolve about the clear fact of our economic condition, a depression so deep that it is without precedent in modern history. . . .

For three long years I have been going up and down this country preaching that Government—Federal and State and local—costs too much. I shall not stop that preaching. As an immediate program of action we must abolish useless offices. We must eliminate unnecessary functions of Government. . . . We must merge, we must consolidate subdivisions of Government, and, like the private citizen, give up luxuries which we can no longer afford. . . .

I have favored the use of certain types of public works as a further emergency means of stimulating employment and the issuance of bonds to pay for such public works, but I have pointed out that no economic end is served if we merely build without building for a necessary purpose. . . .

Just as one example, we know that a very hopeful and immediate means of relief, both for the unemployed and for agriculture, will come from a wide plan of the converting of many millions of acres of marginal and unused land into timberland through reforestation. There are tens of millions of acres east of the Mississippi River alone in abandoned farms, in cut-over land, now growing up in worthless brush. . . . We face a future of soil erosion and timber famine. It is clear that economic foresight and immediate employment march hand in hand in the call for the reforestation of these vast areas.

In so doing, employment can be given to a million men. That is the kind of public work that is self-sustaining. . . .

My program, of which I can only touch on these points, is based upon this simple moral principle: the welfare and the soundness of a Nation depend first upon what the great mass of the people wish and need; and second, whether or not they are getting it. . . . Yes, when—not if—when we get the chance, the Federal Government will assume bold leadership in distress relief.

. . . I pledge you, I pledge myself, to a new deal for the American people. Let us all here assembled constitute ourselves prophets of a new order of competence and of courage. This is more than a political campaign; it is a call to arms. Give me your help, not to win votes alone, but to win in this crusade to restore America to its own people.

Source: Pepperdine University. (2016). Presidential nomination address. Retrieved from publicpolicy.pepperdine.edu/academics/research/faculty-research/new-deal/roosevelt-speeches/fr070232.htm

Comprehension Questions:

1. How does Roosevelt define the role of the government?
2. List three benefits Roosevelt claims will result from reforestation.

Activities:

1. Work with a partner to write and act out a dialogue between Roosevelt and Henry Ford (Lesson 4.9) about the role government and business should play in the economy.
2. Work with a small group to research the Civilian Conservation Corps (CCC), Roosevelt's "tree planting army," or another New Deal program, and evaluate whether it achieved its goals. Share what you learned with your classmates.

Reflection: How similar was your plan to this lesson's introduction to the New Deal? What would you criticize or praise about Roosevelt's response to the Great Depression?

Resources:

Pepperdine University. (2016). Hoover-Roosevelt exchanges. Retrieved from publicpolicy.pepperdine.edu/academics/research/faculty-research/new-deal/hoover-roosevelt/

The History Place. (2012). Dorothea Lange. Retrieved from historyplace.com/unitedstates/lange/

PBS. (2009). The Civilian Conservation Corps. *The American experience.* USA: PBS.

UNIT QUESTION: What Role Should Government and Business Play in Promoting Citizens' Well-Being?

LESSON 4.11
WHY DID LYNDON JOHNSON LAUNCH A WAR ON POVERTY?

Historical Figure: Lyndon Johnson

Event: War on Poverty begins, 1964

Introduction: What evidence do you see around you or in the media of poverty in the United States today?

Mini-Lecture:

- Lyndon B. Johnson was president from 1963 to 1969.
- In 1964, he launched an effort called the "War on Poverty," which created government programs aimed at helping poor people.
- Johnson said he wanted to create a "Great Society" in which everyone had equal opportunities.
- Johnson was inspired by a book by sociologist Michael Harrington, called *The Other America*, which documented poverty in the United States.
- As part of this effort, Johnson created health insurance programs for the poor (Medicaid) and elderly (Medicare); the Head Start program, which offers free preschool to poor children; and the Food Stamp program, which helps poor people buy food.
- Our document is from his State of the Union speech in 1964; presidents give this type of speech each year describing their accomplishments and goals.

Vocabulary:

unconditional: total
suffice: to be successful enough
squalor: unsanitary conditions
slum: poor neighborhood with inadequate housing
sharecropper: a farmer who pays rent to a landowner in the form of crops
boom town: an area with rapid economic growth
depressed: economically disadvantaged

Document: State of the Union address, Lyndon B. Johnson, 1964

> Unfortunately, many Americans live on the outskirts of hope—some because of their poverty, and some because of their color, and all too many because of both. Our task is to help replace their despair with opportunity.
>
> This administration today, here and now, declares unconditional war on poverty in America. I urge this Congress and all Americans to join with me in that effort.
>
> It will not be a short or easy struggle, no single weapon or strategy will suffice, but we shall not rest until that war is won. The richest Nation on earth can afford to win it. We cannot afford to lose it. One thousand dollars invested in salvaging an unemployable youth today can return $40,000 or more in his lifetime.

. . . The war against poverty will not be won here in Washington. It must be won in the field, in every private home, in every public office, from the courthouse to the White House.

The program I shall propose will emphasize this cooperative approach to help that one-fifth of all American families with incomes too small to even meet their basic needs.

Our chief weapons in a more pinpointed attack will be better schools, and better health, and better homes, and better training, and better job opportunities to help more Americans, especially young Americans, escape from squalor and misery and unemployment rolls where other citizens help to carry them.

Very often a lack of jobs and money is not the cause of poverty, but the symptom. The cause may lie deeper—in our failure to give our fellow citizens a fair chance to develop their own capacities, in a lack of education and training, in a lack of medical care and housing, in a lack of decent communities in which to live and bring up their children.

But whatever the cause, our joint Federal-local effort must pursue poverty, pursue it wherever it exists—in city slums and small towns, in sharecropper shacks or in migrant worker camps, on Indian Reservations, among whites as well as Negroes, among the young as well as the aged, in the boom towns and in the depressed areas.

Our aim is not only to relieve the symptom of poverty, but to cure it and, above all, to prevent it.

Source: University of Groningen. (2012). Lyndon Baines Johnson, State of the Union 1964. Retrieved from let.rug.nl/usa/presidents/lyndon-baines-johnson/state-of-the-union-1964.php

Comprehension Questions:

1. What is Johnson's explanation for why people are poor?
2. What is Johnson's plan for curing and preventing poverty?

Activities:

1. Work with a partner to write and act out a dialogue between Johnson and Andrew Carnegie (Lesson 4.6) about the causes of poverty.
2. Explain the similarities and differences between the New Deal and the War on Poverty.

Reflection: Do you believe poverty can be ended? Why or why not?

Resources:

Harrington, M. (1993). *The other America: Poverty in the United States.* New York, NY: Simon and Schuster. (Originally published 1962)

Lowry, A. (2014, January 4). Fifty years later, War on Poverty is a mixed bag. *The New York Times.* Retrieved from nytimes.com/2014/01/05/business/50-years-later-war-on-poverty-is-a-mixed-bag.html

UNIT QUESTION: What Role Should Government and Business Play in Promoting Citizens' Well-Being?

LESSON 4.12
WHY DID CESAR CHAVEZ BELIEVE FARMWORKERS SHOULD UNIONIZE?

Historical Figure: Cesar Chavez

Event: Delano grape strike, 1965–1970

Introduction: If your working conditions were not healthy or safe, what would you do?

Mini-Lecture:

- Cesar Chavez (1927–1993) was a Mexican American migrant farmworker who became a labor rights activist.
- Many farmworkers, like Chavez's family, had immigrated from Mexico or other South American countries.
- Along with Dolores Huerta, Chavez co-founded United Farm Workers (UFW), a union of people who planted and harvested crops.
- Chavez led "collective bargaining," a process by which workers negotiate with business owners for safer and healthier conditions and for higher wages.
- In 1965, Chavez and the UFW organized a strike (refusal to work) among people who picked grapes in Delano, California; they also asked consumers to boycott (not buy) grapes in order to support them. In 1970, the workers reached an agreement with the owners of grape farms.
- Our document comes from a speech Chavez gave in 1984.

Vocabulary:

excrement: waste
infant mortality: the percentage of children who die before they are one year old
implement: tool
collective bargaining: negotiation between a union and an employer over pay, working conditions, or other issues

rhetoric: fancy words
boycott: agreement not to buy a product, in order to achieve a political or social goal
pesticide: chemical used to kill insects

Document: Address to the Commonwealth Club of California, Cesar Chavez, 1984

> Today, thousands of farm workers live under savage conditions—beneath trees and amid garbage and human excrement—near tomato fields in San Diego County, tomato fields which use the most modern farm technology. Vicious rats gnaw on them as they sleep. They walk miles to buy food at inflated prices. And they carry in water from irrigation pumps.
>
> Child labor is still common in many farm areas. As much as 30 percent of Northern California's garlic harvesters are under-aged children. Kids as young as six years old have voted in state-conducted union elections since they qualified as workers. Some 800,000 under-aged children work with their families harvesting crops across America. Babies born to migrant workers suffer

25 percent higher infant mortality than the rest of the population. Malnutrition among migrant worker children is 10 times higher than the national rate. Farm workers' average life expectancy is still 49 years—compared to 73 years for the average American.

All my life, I have been driven by one dream, one goal, one vision: To overthrow a farm labor system in this nation which treats farm workers as if they were not important human beings. Farm workers are not agricultural implements. They are not beasts of burden—to be used and discarded. . . .

Those who attack our union often say, "It's not really a union. It's something else: A social movement. A civil rights movement. It's something dangerous." They're half right. The United Farm Workers is first and foremost a union. A union like any other. . . . We attacked . . . injustice, not by complaining; not by seeking hand-outs; not by becoming soldiers in the War on Poverty. We organized! Farm workers acknowledged we had allowed ourselves to become victims in a democratic society—a society where majority rule and collective bargaining are supposed to be more than academic theories or political rhetoric. And by addressing this historical problem, we created confidence and pride and hope in an entire people's ability to create the future. . . .

During the early- and mid-'70s, millions of Americans supported our boycotts. After 1975, we redirected our efforts from the boycott to organizing and winning elections under the law. The law helped farm workers make progress in overcoming poverty and injustice. At companies where farm workers are protected by union contracts, we have made progress in overcoming child labor, in overcoming miserable wages and working conditions, in overcoming sexual harassment of women workers, in overcoming dangerous pesticides which poison our people and poison the food we all eat.

© 2017 The Cesar Chavez Foundation, www.chavezfoundation.org

Source: Cesar Chavez Foundation. (2012). 1984 Address by Cesar Chavez to the Commonwealth Club of California. Retrieved from chavezfoundation.org/_cms.php?mode=view&b_code=0010080000000000&b_no=16&page=1&field=&key=&n=7

Comprehension Questions:

1. Name three problems for farm workers that Chavez describes.
2. What is Chavez asking of the government? Of businesses? Of the public?

Activities:

1. Of the people we've studied in this unit, who might consider the UFW "dangerous," and why?
2. What are the similarities and differences between Chavez's goals and Sarah Bagley's (Lesson 4.4)? Work with a partner to create a Venn diagram.

UNIT QUESTION: What Role Should Government and Business Play in Promoting Citizens' Well-Being?

Reflection: Of the tactics Chavez mentions (organizing boycotts, working for changes to the law, and negotiating with farm owners), which do you think would be most effective in securing workers' rights, and why?

Resources:

Pawel, M. (n.d.). The union of their dreams: Primary sources. Retrieved from unionoftheirdreams.com/Primary_Sources.php

United Farm Workers. (2016). History. Retrieved from ufw.org/research/history/

LESSON 4.13
WHAT WAS REAGANOMICS?

Historical Figure: Ronald Reagan

Event: Reaganomics launched, 1981

Introduction: Would you prefer a large, powerful federal government that provided many services (education, roads, social safety net), or a small, limited federal government that provided few services? What are the advantages and disadvantages of each?

Mini-Lecture:

- Ronald Reagan was president from 1981 to 1989.
- In 1981, there was a recession, or period of slow economic growth, during which unemployment and inflation increased.
- Reagan had just been elected, and his plan to improve the economy involved cutting government spending on social safety net programs and lowering tax rates, especially on businesses and wealthy people.
- This plan was known as Reaganomics. It was also called supply-side economics (give consumers a greater supply of goods at lower prices by cutting taxes on businesses that produce those goods), or "trickle-down" economics (money should trickle down from the rich to the poor without government redistributing it), similar to the "leak-through" approach that was criticized by Franklin Roosevelt (Lesson 4.10).
- Our document is from a speech Reagan gave soon after he took office.

Vocabulary:

deficit: the amount of government spending that is greater than the money a government has

interest: a percentage of a loan that is paid each month or year for the privilege of delayed repayment of the loan

national debt: money borrowed by a country

Federal budget: the amount of money the government spends

regulation: a law

revenue: money a government uses for public needs

cost-of-living pay raises: increases in salary to keep up with the prices of everyday items

inflation: increase in prices, or decrease in the value of money

progressive tax: tax structure in which the percentage of your income you pay in taxes increases with the amount of income you earn

tax bracket: a range of incomes that is taxed at a certain rate

standard of living: the degree of wealth and comfort people have

Document: Address to the Nation on the Economy, Ronald Reagan, 1981

> I'm speaking to you tonight to give you a report on the state of our Nation's economy. I regret to say that we're in the worst economic mess since the Great Depression. . . .
>
> The Federal budget is out of control, and we face runaway deficits of almost $80 billion for this budget year that ends September 30th. That deficit is larger than the entire Federal budget in 1957, and so is the almost $80 billion we will pay in interest this year on the national debt.
>
> Twenty years ago, in 1960, our Federal Government payroll was less than $13 billion. Today it is $75 billion. During these 20 years our population has only increased by 23.3 percent. The Federal budget has gone up 528 percent. . . .
>
> Regulations adopted by government with the best of intentions have added $666 to the cost of an automobile. It is estimated that altogether regulations of every kind, on shopkeepers, farmers, and major industries, add $100 billion or more to the cost of the goods and services we buy. And then another $20 billion is spent by government handling the paperwork created by those regulations. . . .
>
> Now, we all had a hand in looking to government for benefits as if government had some source of revenue other than our earnings. Many if not most of the things we thought of or that government offered to us seemed attractive.
>
> In the years following the Second World War it was easy, for a while at least, to overlook the price tag. . . . Some government programs seemed so worthwhile that borrowing to fund them didn't bother us. . . .
>
> Some say shift the tax burden to business and industry, but business doesn't pay taxes. Oh, don't get the wrong idea. Business is being taxed, so much so that we're being priced out of the world market. But business must pass its costs of operations—and that includes taxes—on to the customer in the price of the product. Only people pay taxes, all the taxes. Government just uses business in a kind of sneaky way to help collect the taxes. They're hidden in the price; we aren't aware of how much tax we actually pay. . . .
>
> All of you who are working know that even with cost-of-living pay raises, you can't keep up with inflation. In our progressive tax system, as you increase the number of dollars you earn, you find yourself moved up into higher tax

brackets, paying a higher tax rate just for trying to hold your own. The result? Your standard of living is going down. . . .

Now, at the same time we're doing this, we must go forward with a tax relief package. I shall ask for a 10-percent reduction across the board in personal income tax rates for each of the next 3 years.

Source: The New York Times. (1981, February 6). Transcript of Reagan's address reporting on the state of the nation's economy. Retrieved from nytimes.com/1981/02/06/us/transcript-of-reagan-address-reporting-on-the-state-of-the-nation-s.html?pagewanted=all

Comprehension Questions:

1. According to Reagan, what are the causes and effects of the "economic mess"?
2. What is Reagan's criticism of the tax system, and how does he want to change it?

Activities:

1. Draw a flow chart showing how money was moving in the economy, according to Reagan. Then draw another chart showing how Reagan wanted money to move. Include the federal government, businesses, rich people, middle-class people, and poor people.
2. Work with a partner to write and act out a dialogue between Lyndon B. Johnson (Lesson 4.11) and Reagan about the impact of the War on Poverty.

Reflection: What might Reagan think of Donald Trump's plan for the economy (Lesson 4.1)?

Resources:

Alexander, C. (1981, September 21). Reaganomics: Making it work. *Time* magazine. Retrieved from content.time.com/time/subscriber/article/0,33009,953082,00.html
UShistory.org. (2016). Reaganomics. Retrieved from ushistory.org/us/59b.asp

UNIT CONCLUSION

In this unit, students have considered arguments for government-supported social safety net programs and for approaches to economic prosperity based on the success of businesses. They have also caught glimpses of how race and gender may intertwine with poverty. They may be considering for the first time why economic inequality exists, as well as locating the roots of this divide in the colonial encounter and slavery. Again, they are likely making connections to contemporary politics and the liberal-conservative divide. It can be helpful to remind students that many people—both the historical figures they study and they themselves—may not fit neatly into one or the other political box. It is also good to remind them that many of the historical figures we studied identified similar goals (such as ending poverty), even if their views on how to achieve those goals were diametrically opposed. These reminders may help students find common ground with one another. The Current Issue Letter (Appendix H) can also provide a satisfying venue for students to express their own views.

This summit is an interesting one, as the historical figures represented are quite polarized in their views. Representing views that many people today find offensive, such as those of John C. Calhoun and Andrew Carnegie, can be a challenge for students. The last section of the summit, in which students can speak for themselves and distance themselves from the views of those they represented, is important in this regard.

CHAPTER 5

Foreign Policy

UNIT QUESTION: **Under What Circumstances Should the United States Intervene in World Events?**

Current Issue Question: How should the United States react to the civil war in Syria?

Unit Introduction: In this unit, students will gain an overview of how the United States has interacted with the rest of the world. Proponents of isolationism or neutrality, such as George Washington and Woodrow Wilson, are juxtaposed with interventionists, including Franklin Roosevelt and Bill Clinton. Eleanor Roosevelt will ask students to consider the United States' role in international organizations, and Martin Luther King Jr. will bring to light the effects of war on U.S. society. Secret documents from the Nixon administration will reveal that the United States took covert action to depose leaders in Latin America. The Monroe Doctrine and the Truman Doctrine will reveal the rationale for many of these foreign policy decisions. George Bush's call to the War on Terror sets the stage for our contemporary era.

The current issue is the U.S. bombing of Syria in 2017. As with other current issues, teachers may wish to replace or supplement the material with documents that reflect more recent developments. If students have military connections, if they have relatives in the Middle East or other war zones, or if they are refugees themselves, this issue (as well as others in the unit) may be emotional for them to discuss. Teachers will want to be sensitive to their needs and alert parents and administrators about the topics under discussion.

LESSON 5.1
HOW DID DONALD TRUMP EXPLAIN HIS DECISION TO BOMB SYRIA?

Historical Figure: Donald Trump

Event: United States bombs Syria, 2017

Introduction: What do you know about the lives of people in war zones? How did you learn it?

Mini-Lecture:

- In 2011, a civil war broke out in Syria between forces led by dictator Bashar al-Assad and rebels who wanted more freedom and democracy; as of 2017, almost 500,000 people had been killed, and 12 million displaced from their homes, with millions fleeing abroad as refugees.
- President Obama instructed the U.S. military to provide training to the rebels and said that the use of chemical weapons would be a "red line" that would require U.S. intervention.
- In 2013, Assad apparently used chemical weapons against Syrian rebels and civilians, but the United States did not intervene.
- The situation is complicated because ISIS/ISIL (Islamic State of Iraq and Syria/Islamic State of Iraq and the Levant), a terrorist group that formed in 2014 and that has inspired attacks in the United States and elsewhere, is fighting both Assad's forces and the rebels.
- In 2017, Assad apparently used chemical weapons again.
- Donald Trump, who had become president earlier that year, ordered the military to bomb the airfield from which the chemical attack may have been launched.
- Trump had made campaign promises not to get involved in Syria; his inaugural address promised an "America first" policy. However, he planned to increase military spending.
- Our document comes from a speech Trump gave explaining the attack.

Vocabulary:

dictator: a ruler who has absolute power

nerve agent: a chemical that damages people's nerves, leading to injury or death

Document: Statement on Syria, Donald Trump, 2017

> My fellow Americans: On Tuesday, Syrian dictator Bashar al-Assad launched a horrible chemical weapons attack on innocent civilians. Using a deadly nerve agent, Assad choked out the lives of helpless men, women, and children. It was a slow and brutal death for so many. Even beautiful babies were cruelly murdered in this very barbaric attack. No child of God should ever suffer such horror.
>
> Tonight, I ordered a targeted military strike on the airfield in Syria from where the chemical attack was launched. It is in this vital national security interest of the United States to prevent and deter the spread and use of deadly chemical weapons. There can be no dispute that Syria used banned chemical weapons, violated its obligations under the Chemical Weapons Convention, and ignored the urging of the U.N. Security Council.

Years of previous attempts at changing Assad's behavior have all failed, and failed very dramatically. As a result, the refugee crisis continues to deepen and the region continues to destabilize, threatening the United States and its allies.

Tonight, I call on all civilized nations to join us in seeking to end the slaughter and bloodshed in Syria, and also to end terrorism of all kinds and all types. We ask for God's wisdom as we face the challenge of our very troubled world. We pray for the lives of the wounded and for the souls of those who have passed. And we hope that as long as America stands for justice, then peace and harmony will, in the end, prevail.

Goodnight. And God bless America and the entire world. Thank you.

Source: White House. (2017). Statement by President Trump on Syria. Retrieved from whitehouse.gov/the-press-office/2017/04/06/statement-president-trump-syria

Comprehension Questions:

1. According to Trump, what are two negative outcomes that could have resulted if the United States had not bombed Syria?

Activities:

1. Analyze these three sentences from Trump's 2017 inaugural address. For each sentence below, find one sentence from our document that corroborates or contradicts it:
   a. "We will seek friendship and goodwill with the nations of the world—but we do so with the understanding that it is the right of all nations to put their own interests first."
   b. "We do not seek to impose our way of life on anyone, but rather to let it shine as an example for everyone to follow."
   c. "We will reinforce old alliances and form new ones—and unite the civilized world against radical Islamic terrorism, which we will eradicate completely from the face of the Earth."
2. With a small group, create a list of the pros and cons of Trump's actions; do some research on the Syrian civil war and on the consequences of the bombing. Then decide together whether the pros outweigh the cons, or vice versa.

Reflection: Would you guess that most Syrian Americans supported or opposed Trump's actions? What factors might determine their support or opposition?

Resources:

Al Jazeera. (2017) Syria's civil war explained from the beginning. Retrieved from aljazeera.com/news/2016/05/syria-civil-war-explained-160505084119966.html

CNN. (January 21, 2017). Inaugural address: Trump's full speech. Retrieved from cnn.com/2017/01/20/politics/trump-inaugural-address/

LESSON 5.2

WHY DID GEORGE WASHINGTON BELIEVE THE UNITED STATES SHOULD STAY NEUTRAL?

Historical Figure: George Washington

Event: Proclamation of Neutrality, 1793

Introduction: When conflicts arise between your friends or family members, do you usually stay neutral or take a side? Why?

Mini-Lecture:

- George Washington was president from 1789 to 1797.
- In 1793, war broke out between France and Britain.
- Secretary of State Thomas Jefferson thought the United States should side with France because it had signed a treaty promising to defend the country.
- Others, such as Washington's adviser Alexander Hamilton, thought the United States should side with Britain because of the countries' close ties in the past, because the French king with whom they'd signed the treaty had been deposed and killed during the French Revolution, and because the United States was not financially or militarily prepared for another war.
- Our document is the proclamation Washington made announcing that the United States would stay neutral in the conflict.

Vocabulary:

impartial: neutral
belligerent: in conflict
these presents: this document
disposition: intention
exhort: to urge
contravene: to contradict

forfeiture: giving up property or money because of committing a crime
abet: to help
contraband: goods that are illegal to trade
usage: customs
cognizance: knowledge

Document: Proclamation of Neutrality, George Washington, 1793

> Whereas it appears that a state of war exists between Austria, Prussia, Sardinia, Great Britain, and the United Netherlands, of the one part, and France on the other; and the duty and interest of the United States require, that they should with sincerity and good faith adopt and pursue a conduct friendly and impartial toward the belligerent Powers;
>
> I have therefore thought fit by these presents to declare the disposition of the United States to observe the conduct aforesaid towards those Powers respectfully; and to exhort and warn the citizens of the United States carefully to avoid all acts and proceedings whatsoever, which may in any manner tend to contravene such disposition.
>
> And I do hereby also make known, that whatsoever of the citizens of the United States shall render himself liable to punishment or forfeiture under the

law of nations, by committing, aiding, or abetting hostilities against any of the said Powers, or by carrying to any of them those articles which are deemed contraband by the modern usage of nations, will not receive the protection of the United States, against such punishment or forfeiture; and further, that I have given instructions to those officers, to whom it belongs, to cause prosecutions to be instituted against all persons, who shall, within the cognizance of the courts of the United States, violate the law of nations, with respect to the Powers at war, or any of them.

> *Source:* Lillian Goldman Law Library. (2008). The Proclamation of Neutrality, 1793. Retrieved from avalon.law.yale.edu/18th_century/neutra93.asp

Comprehension Questions:

1. Who is Washington addressing in this proclamation? Name at least three groups of people.
2. What will happen to U.S. citizens who help France or Britain in the war?

Activities:

1. Work in groups of three to write and act out a discussion among Jefferson, Hamilton, and Washington about how the United States should react to the war between Britain and France.

Reflection: Do you think Washington made a wise decision? Why or why not?

Resources:

Liberty Fund. (2017). Alexander Hamilton: The Pacifus-Helvidius debates of 1793–1794. Retrieved from oll.libertyfund.org/titles/hamilton-the-pacificus-helvidius-debates-of-1793-1794

Various Artists. (2015). Cabinet Battle #2—Hamilton. *Hamilton: An American Musical.* USA: Atlantic.

LESSON 5.3

How Did the Monroe Doctrine Change U.S. Foreign Policy?

Historical Figure: James Monroe

Event: Monroe Doctrine, 1823

Introduction: Do you feel that events in Latin America and Canada affect the United States more than, less than, or the same amount as events in Europe, Asia, and Africa? Why?

Mini-Lecture:

- James Monroe was president from 1817 to 1825.
- During that time, Spain's colonies in Latin America were fighting for independence.

- Monroe did not want European powers to interfere with or colonize areas in the United States' "sphere of influence"—the Western Hemisphere (including North and South America).
- However, Monroe did not want to intervene in wars in Europe.
- Our document comes from one of his messages to Congress, which became known as the "Monroe Doctrine," and which expressed his views on foreign policy.

Vocabulary:

intercourse: involvement
derive: to take from
origin: founding
comport with: to be consistent with
menaced: put in danger
hemisphere: half the world
candor: honesty

amicable: friendly
dependency: territory that is controlled by another country
interposition: interference
manifestation: proof
indifference: lack of caring
subdue: to control

Document: Monroe Doctrine, James Monroe, 1823

As a principle in which the rights and interests of the United States are involved, that the American continents, by the free and independent condition which they have assumed and maintain, are henceforth not to be considered as subjects for future colonization by any European powers . . .

Of events in [Europe], with which we have so much intercourse and from which we derive our origin, we have always been anxious and interested spectators. The citizens of the United States cherish sentiments the most friendly in favor of the liberty and happiness of their fellow-men on that side of the Atlantic. In the wars of the European powers in matters relating to themselves we have never taken any part, nor does it comport with our policy to do so. It is only when our rights are invaded or seriously menaced that we resent injuries or make preparation for our defense. With the movements in this hemisphere we are of necessity more immediately connected, and by causes which must be obvious to all enlightened and impartial observers.

. . . We owe it, therefore, to candor and to the amicable relations existing between the United States and those [European] powers to declare that we should consider any attempt on their part to extend their [political] system to any portion of this hemisphere as dangerous to our peace and safety. With the existing colonies or dependencies of any European power we have not interfered and shall not interfere. But with the Governments who have declared their independence and maintain it, and whose independence we have, on great consideration and on just principles, acknowledged, we could not view any interposition for the purpose of oppressing them, or controlling in any other manner their destiny, by any European power in any other light than as the manifestation of an unfriendly disposition toward the United States. . . .

> It is impossible that the allied powers [of Europe] should extend their political system to any portion of either continent [North or South America] without endangering our peace and happiness; nor can anyone believe that our southern brethren, if left to themselves, would adopt it of their own accord. It is equally impossible, therefore, that we should behold such interposition in any form with indifference. If we look to the comparative strength and resources of Spain and those new Governments [in Latin America], and their distance from each other, it must be obvious that she can never subdue them. It is still the true policy of the United States to leave the parties to themselves, in hope that other powers will pursue the same course.
>
> *Source:* Lillian Goldman Law Library. (2008). Monroe Doctrine. Retrieved from avalon.law.yale.edu/19th_century/monroe.asp

Comprehension Questions:

1. In what case would the United States intervene in a war in Europe?
2. Why doesn't Monroe think Europe should try to control independent countries in Latin America?

Activities:

1. Monroe asks Europe not to try to control independent Latin American countries. Does he think the United States has a right to do so? Choose a quotation that supports your answer.
2. Work with a partner to create a Venn diagram showing the similarities and differences between George Washington's foreign policy (Lesson 5.2) and James Monroe's.

Reflection: Is the Monroe Doctrine a good basis for foreign policy today? Why or why not?

Resources:

National Endowment for the Humanities. (n.d.). The Monroe Doctrine. Retrieved from edsitement.neh.gov/lesson-plan/monroe-doctrine-whose-doctrine-was-it#sect-extending

---

LESSON 5.4

HOW WAS THE IDEA OF MANIFEST DESTINY USED TO JUSTIFY TAKING OVER FOREIGN LANDS?

Historical Figure: James K. Polk

Event: Mexican-American War, 1846–1848

Introduction: What do you know about how the United States gained the territory that now includes Texas, New Mexico, Arizona, Utah, and California?

Mini-Lecture:

- James K. Polk was president from 1845 to 1849.
- He believed in the idea of Manifest Destiny: that God intended for the United States to expand across North America.
- Mexico owned the territory that would later become Texas, New Mexico, Arizona, Utah, and California.
- Polk wanted to buy this land, but Mexico refused. He sent U.S. troops into a disputed area in Texas, and when Mexican forces attacked them, Polk asked Congress to declare war.
- The United States won the war and took the territory.
- Our document is a painting that shows "American Progress," a female figure who represents Manifest Destiny.

Vocabulary:

manifest: obvious

destiny: fate, God's plan

Document: *American Progress*, John Gast, 1872

Figure 5.1. *American Progress*, John Gast, 1872; Chromolithograph by George Crofutt, circa 1873

Source: Courtesy of the Library of Congress Prints and Photographs Division

Comprehension Questions:

1. What two items is American Progress carrying?
2. Who is running away from American Progress, and who is accompanying her?

Activities:

1. Work with a small group to create a different image of American Progress, from the point of view of Mexican people and Native Americans.

Reflection: Why do you think Polk was so confident that the United States was destined to expand across North America?

Resources:

Zinn, H. (2003). We take nothing by conquest, thank God. In *A people's history of the United States* (chap. 8). New York, NY: HarperCollins.

LESSON 5.5

WHY DID MARK TWAIN OPPOSE U.S. COLONIZATION OF THE PHILIPPINES?

Historical Figure: Mark Twain

Event: Spanish-American War, 1898

Introduction: Which do you think has happened more often in history: the United States has used its power over other countries to (a) help them become stable democracies or (b) gain resources for itself? Give an example.

Mini-Lecture:

- In the late 19th century, Spain controlled colonies that included Cuba, Puerto Rico, the Philippines, and Guam.
- Cuba was fighting for independence from Spain, and the United States decided to support Cuba by declaring war on Spain.
- The United States won the war in 1898, and the Treaty of Paris gave it control of Spain's former colonies; Cuba became independent, but the United States decided to colonize the Philippines.
- Mark Twain (1835–1910) was an author of books, including *Huckleberry Finn*, and he also joined the Anti-Imperialist League.
- Imperialism is when one country exerts military, economic, or political control over another; anti-imperialists are against such policies.
- Our document is from an interview with Twain that was printed in the *New York Herald* newspaper.

Vocabulary:

tiresome: boring

subjugate: to take power over

Document: On American Imperialism, Mark Twain, 1898

> I left these shores, at Vancouver, a red-hot imperialist. I wanted the American eagle to go screaming into the Pacific. It seemed tiresome and tame for it to content itself with the Rockies. Why not spread its wings over the Philippines, I asked myself? And I thought it would be a real good thing to do. I said to myself, here are a people who have suffered for three centuries. We can make them as free as ourselves, give them a government and country of their own, put a miniature of the American constitution afloat in the Pacific, start a brand new republic to take its place among the free nations of the world. It seemed to me a great task to which [we] had addressed ourselves.
>
> But I have thought some more, since then, and I have read carefully the Treaty of Paris, and I have seen that we do not intend to free, but to subjugate the people of the Philippines. We have gone there to conquer, not to redeem. It should, it seems to me, be our pleasure and duty to make those people free, and let them deal with their own domestic questions in their own way. And so I am an anti-imperialist. I am opposed to having the eagle put its talons on any other land.
>
> *Source:* Library of Congress. (2011). The world of 1898: The Spanish-American War: Mark Twain. Retrieved from loc.gov/rr/hispanic/1898/twain.html

Comprehension Questions:

1. Why did Twain think at first that it was a good idea for the United States to colonize the Philippines?
2. Put Twain's definition of anti-imperialism in your own words.

Activities:

1. Work with a partner to think of three pieces of evidence that Twain could use to support the conclusions in his second paragraph. Then do some research to see if you can find such pieces of evidence.
2. Was the United States' decision to declare war on Spain in line with the Monroe Doctrine (Lesson 5.3)? Why or why not?

Reflection: Do you agree more with the reasoning in Twain's first paragraph or the second? Why?

Resources:

Library of Congress. (2011). The world of 1898: The Spanish-American War. Retrieved from loc.gov/rr/hispanic/1898/intro.html

Mandel, K. (Producer), & Miller, D. A. (Director). (1999). *The crucible of empire: The Spanish-American War.* USA: Great Film Projects.

UNIT QUESTION: Under What Circumstances Should the United States Intervene in World Events?

LESSON 5.6

HOW DID WOODROW WILSON TRY TO CONVINCE AMERICANS TO STAY NEUTRAL IN WORLD WAR I?

Historical Figure: Woodrow Wilson

Event: United States in World War I, 1917–1919

Introduction: If a country your ancestors came from was involved in a war outside the United States, would you take that country's side? Why or why not?

Mini-Lecture:

- Woodrow Wilson was president from 1913 to 1921.
- World War I broke out in 1914 in Europe, between the Allied Powers (Russia, France, and Britain) and the Central Powers (Germany and Austria-Hungary).
- The United States did not take sides at first, but tried to keep trading with both sides while negotiating a peace agreement.
- Our document is from a message Wilson gave to the American people urging them to stay neutral.
- Germany began sinking American ships in 1915, and in 1917 the Germans secretly invited Mexico to join the Central Powers, promising Mexico territory in the United States that the United States had captured in the Mexican-American War of 1846–1848 (see Lesson 5.4).
- Wilson decided the United States could no longer stay neutral and entered the war on the side of the Allied powers, who won the war in 1918.
- After the United States entered the war, Wilson established the Committee on Public Information, which tried to get Americans to support the war by spreading anti-German propaganda; posters portrayed Germans as gorillas and warned Americans that "German agents are everywhere."

Vocabulary:

exert: to cause
momentous: important
allay: to calm
fatal: damaging
mediation: help for people in conflict to come to an agreement

partisan: biased person
peculiar: special
poise: calm
counsels: advice
covet: to want

Document: Appeal for Neutrality, Woodrow Wilson, 1914

> My fellow countrymen: I suppose that every thoughtful man in America has asked himself, during these last troubled weeks, what influence the European war may exert upon the United States, and I take the liberty of addressing a few words to you in order to point out that it is entirely within our own choice what its effects upon us will be and to urge very earnestly upon you the sort of speech and conduct which will best safeguard the Nation against distress and disaster.

... Every man who really loves America will act and speak in the true spirit of neutrality, which is the spirit of impartiality and fairness and friendliness to all concerned. The spirit of the Nation in this critical matter will be determined largely by what individuals and society and those gathered in public meetings do and say, upon what newspapers and magazines contain, upon what ministers utter in their pulpits and men proclaim as their opinions on the street.

The people of the United States are drawn from many nations, and chiefly from the nations now at war. It is natural and inevitable that there should be the utmost variety of sympathy and desire among them with regard to the issues and circumstances of the conflict. Some will wish one nation, others another, to succeed in the momentous struggle. It will be easy to excite passion and difficult to allay it. . . . Such divisions amongst us would be fatal to our peace of mind and might seriously stand in the way of the proper performance of our duty as the one great nation at peace, the one people holding itself ready to play a part of impartial mediation and speak the counsels of peace and accommodation not as a partisan, but as a friend. . . .

My thought is of America. I am speaking, I feel sure, the earnest wish and purpose of every thoughtful American that this great country of ours, which is, of course, the first in our thoughts and in our hearts, should show herself in this time of peculiar trial a Nation fit beyond others to exhibit the fine poise of undisturbed judgment, the dignity of self-control, the efficiency of dispassionate action; a Nation that neither sits in judgment upon others nor is disturbed in her own counsels and which keeps herself fit and free to do what is honest and disinterested and truly serviceable for the peace of the world. Shall we not resolve to put upon ourselves the restraints which will bring to our people the happiness and the great and lasting influence for peace we covet for them?

Source: Rector and Visitors Center of the University of Virginia. (2017). Message on Neutrality. Retrieved from millercenter.org/president/wilson/speeches/speech-3791

Comprehension Questions:

1. What does Wilson ask of the American people?
2. Explain two negative consequences Wilson predicts if U.S. citizens were to take sides in World War I.

Activities:

1. Why do you think Wilson urged Americans to stay neutral in 1914, but created the Committee on Public Information to make anti-German propaganda in 1917?
2. Work with a partner to create a cartoon with thought and speech bubbles, showing a conversation between a German American and a British American discussing President Wilson's message.

Reflection: Do you agree with the timing of Wilson's decision to get involved in World War I? Why or why not?

UNIT QUESTION: Under What Circumstances Should the United States Intervene in World Events?

Resources:

National World War I Museum and Memorial. (2017). Interactive WWI timeline. Retrieved from theworldwar.org/explore/interactive-wwi-timeline

PBS. (2001). Gallery: Poster art of World War I. Retrieved from pbs.org/wgbh//amex/wilson/gallery/posters.html

LESSON 5.7
HOW DID FRANKLIN D. ROOSEVELT EXPLAIN HIS DECISION TO INVOLVE THE UNITED STATES IN WORLD WAR II?

Historical Figure: Franklin D. Roosevelt

Event: United States in World War II, 1941–1945

Introduction: What events might cause the United States to enter a world war?

Mini-Lecture:

- Franklin D. Roosevelt was president from 1933 to 1945.
- In 1939, World War II broke out when German leader Adolf Hitler invaded Poland. Britain and France joined with Poland to form the Allied powers, while Japan and Italy joined Germany to form the Axis powers.
- Roosevelt believed that U.S. entry into the war was inevitable, and he prepared by building up the United States' military.
- The United States was technically neutral, but Japanese leaders resented that the United States was selling weapons to the Allies.
- In 1941, Japan bombed Pearl Harbor, a military base in Hawaii, killing more than 2400 people.
- Our document comes from the speech Roosevelt gave the day after the attack, which marked U.S. entry into World War II.
- The Allies won World War II in 1945.

Vocabulary:

infamy: fame for negative reasons
solicitation: invitation
intervening: in between
implications: hidden meaning

premeditated: planned in advance
onslaught: wide-ranging attack
uttermost: greatest degree possible
dastardly: terrible

Document: Day of Infamy, Franklin D. Roosevelt, 1941

> Mr. Vice President, Mr. Speaker, Members of the Senate, and of the House of Representatives: Yesterday, December 7th, 1941—a date which will live in infamy—the United States of America was suddenly and deliberately attacked by naval and air forces of the Empire of Japan. The United States was at peace with that nation and, at the solicitation of Japan, was still in conversation with its government and its emperor looking toward the maintenance of peace in the Pacific.

Indeed, one hour after Japanese air squadrons had commenced bombing in the American island of Oahu, the Japanese ambassador to the United States and his colleague delivered to our Secretary of State a formal reply to a recent American message. And while this reply stated that it seemed useless to continue the existing diplomatic negotiations, it contained no threat or hint of war or of armed attack. It will be recorded that the distance of Hawaii from Japan makes it obvious that the attack was deliberately planned many days or even weeks ago. During the intervening time, the Japanese government has deliberately sought to deceive the United States by false statements and expressions of hope for continued peace. The attack yesterday on the Hawaiian islands has caused severe damage to American naval and military forces. I regret to tell you that very many American lives have been lost. In addition, American ships have been reported torpedoed on the high seas between San Francisco and Honolulu.

Yesterday, the Japanese government also launched an attack against Malaya. Last night, Japanese forces attacked Hong Kong. Last night, Japanese forces attacked Guam. Last night, Japanese forces attacked the Philippine Islands. Last night, the Japanese attacked Wake Island. And this morning, the Japanese attacked Midway Island.

Japan has, therefore, undertaken a surprise offensive extending throughout the Pacific area. The facts of yesterday and today speak for themselves. The people of the United States have already formed their opinions and well understand the implications to the very life and safety of our nation. As commander in chief of the Army and Navy, I have directed that all measures be taken for our defense. But always will our whole nation remember the character of the onslaught against us.

No matter how long it may take us to overcome this premeditated invasion, the American people in their righteous might will win through to absolute victory.

I believe that I interpret the will of the Congress and of the people when I assert that we will not only defend ourselves to the uttermost, but will make it very certain that this form of treachery shall never again endanger us. Hostilities exist. There is no blinking at the fact that our people, our territory, and our interests are in grave danger. With confidence in our armed forces, with the unbounding determination of our people, we will gain the inevitable triumph– so help us God. I ask that the Congress declare that since the unprovoked and dastardly attack by Japan on Sunday, December 7th, 1941, a state of war has existed between the United States and the Japanese empire.

Source: About.com. (2012). Day of Infamy Speech. Retrieved from history1900s.about.com/od/franklindroosevelt/a/Day-Of-Infamy-Speech.htm

Comprehension Questions:

1. What is Roosevelt's evidence that the attack was premeditated?
2. Locate on a map the places that were attacked by Japan.

Activities:

1. Compare Woodrow Wilson's leadership during World War I (Lesson 5.6) to Roosevelt's during World War II. What were the similarities and differences?
2. Work with a partner to write and act out a dialogue between George Washington (Lesson 5.2) and Roosevelt about the decision to enter World War II.

Reflection: What event do you think could spark World War III? How do you think world war might be prevented?

Resources:

National Endowment for the Humanities. (n.d.). The road to Pearl Harbor. Retrieved from edsitement.neh.gov/curriculum-unit/road-pearl-harbor-united-states-and-east-asia-1915-1941#sect-thelessons

LESSON 5.8

How Did Eleanor Roosevelt Explain the Purpose of the United Nations?

Historical Figure: Eleanor Roosevelt

Event: Creation of the United Nations, 1945

Introduction: Are there rights that people in all countries have? If so, what are they? If not, why not?

Mini-Lecture:

- The United Nations (UN) was formed in 1945 to promote international cooperation and peace.
- The United States, Britain, the Soviet Union, and China were the founding members, and most countries in the world are members today.
- Eleanor Roosevelt served as the United States' representative to the UN's Commission on Human Rights from 1947 to 1953.
- She was the wife of President Franklin D. Roosevelt.
- During that time, she contributed to the drafting of the Universal Declaration of Human Rights, which the UN encourages member countries to follow.
- Our document comes from a speech she gave promoting the Universal Declaration of Human Rights.

Vocabulary:

charter: mission statement of an organization
premise: idea
humanitarian: concerning the welfare of people

abstention: not voting yes or no
bourgeois: capitalist middle class
arbitrary: without good reason

Document: The Struggle for Human Rights, Eleanor Roosevelt, 1948

I have come this evening to talk with you on one of the greatest issues of our time—that is the preservation of human freedom. . . . I have chosen to discuss it in the early days of the General Assembly because the issue of human liberty is decisive for the settlement of outstanding political differences and for the future of the United Nations.

The decisive importance of this issue was fully recognized by the founders of the United Nations at San Francisco. . . . In the preamble to the Charter the keynote is set when it declares: "We the people of the United Nations determined . . . to reaffirm faith in fundamental human rights, in the dignity and worth of the human person, in the equal rights of men and women and of nations large and small, and . . . to promote social progress and better standards of life in larger freedom." This reflects the basic premise of the Charter that the peace and security of mankind are dependent on mutual respect for the rights and freedoms of all.

One of the purposes of the United Nations is declared in article 1 to be: "to achieve international cooperation in solving international problems of an economic, social, cultural, or humanitarian character, and in promoting and encouraging respect for human rights and for fundamental freedoms for all without distinction as to race, sex, language, or religion." . . .

The Declaration has come from the Human Rights Commission with unanimous acceptance except for four abstentions—the U.S.S.R., Yugoslavia, Ukraine, and Byelorussia. The reason for this is a fundamental difference in the conception of human rights as they exist in these states and in certain other Member States in the United Nations. . . .

The U.S.S.R. Representatives assert that they already have achieved many things which we, in what they call the "bourgeois democracies" cannot achieve because their government controls the accomplishment of these things. Our government seems powerless to them because, in the last analysis, it is controlled by the people. They would not put it that way—they would say that the people in the U.S.S.R. control their government by allowing their government to have certain absolute rights. We, on the other hand, feel that certain rights can never be granted to the government, but must be kept in the hands of the people. . . .

The place to discuss the issue of human rights is in the forum of the United Nations. The United Nations has been set up as the common meeting ground for nations, where we can consider together our mutual problems and take advantage of our differences in experience. It is inherent in our firm attachment to democracy and freedom that we stand always ready to use the fundamental democratic procedures of honest discussion and negotiation. It is now as always our hope that despite the wide differences in approach we face in the world today, we can with mutual good faith in the principles of the United Nations Charter, arrive at a common basis of understanding.... As one of the Delegates from the United States I pray Almighty God that we may win another victory here for the rights and freedoms of all men.

Source: George Washington University. (n.d.). The struggle for human rights. Retrieved from www2.gwu.edu/~erpapers/documents/speeches/doc026617.cfm

Comprehension Questions:

1. According to Roosevelt, how do the United States and the USSR (Soviet Union) define human rights differently?
2. What does Roosevelt think is the best way to secure freedom around the world?

Activities:

1. According to this document, is the United States obligated to intervene if another country is violating human rights? Choose a quote that supports your answer.
2. Of the historical figures discussed so far in this unit, who would support the goals of the United Nations? Who might not? Work with a small group to create a list supported by quotations from the documents.

Reflection: Can countries that interpret rights differently, as the United States and the Soviet Union did, work together to protect rights? Why or why not?

Resources:

United Nations. (n.d.). History of the United Nations. Retrieved from un.org/en/sections/history/history-united-nations/

LESSON 5.9

How Did the Truman Doctrine Change U.S. Foreign Policy?

Historical Figure: Harry Truman

Event: Truman Doctrine, 1947

Introduction: What do you know about communism? Where did you learn it?

Mini-Lecture:

- Harry Truman was president from 1945 to 1953.
- He was president during the end of World War II and the beginning of the Cold War, which was a rivalry between capitalist countries that were led by the United States, and communist countries, led by the Soviet Union.
- The United States, and many other capitalist countries, had democratic political systems.

- While communist theory calls for workers to control the government, in practice, communist countries, including the Soviet Union, had dictators such as Joseph Stalin.
- Our document comes from a speech Truman made to Congress in 1947, expressing his concerns about the spread of communism around the world.
- The following year, Truman used his doctrine to argue that the United States should give money to anticommunist forces in Turkey and Greece.

Vocabulary:

coercion: being forced to do something
totalitarian: having control of all aspects of citizens' lives through government
Yalta Agreement: arrangement carried out in 1945 through which Britain, the United States, and the Soviet Union agreed to give independence to the people they planned to liberate from Nazi Germany
fixed: in which the outcome is secretly determined in advance
subjugation: bringing people under control without respecting their rights
static: unchanging
status quo: the way things are currently
subterfuge: trickery
infiltration: entering secretly

Document: Truman Doctrine, Harry Truman, 1947

> One of the primary objectives of the foreign policy of the United States is the creation of conditions in which we and other nations will be able to work out a way of life free from coercion. This was a fundamental issue in the war with Germany and Japan. Our victory was won over countries which sought to impose their will, and their way of life, upon other nations.
>
> The peoples of a number of countries of the world have recently had totalitarian regimes forced upon them against their will. The Government of the United States has made frequent protests against coercion and intimidation, in violation of the Yalta Agreement, in Poland, Rumania, and Bulgaria. . . .
>
> At the present moment in world history nearly every nation must choose between alternative ways of life. The choice is too often not a free one. One way of life is based upon the will of the majority, and is distinguished by free institutions, representative government, free elections, guarantees of individual liberty, freedom of speech and religion, and freedom from political oppression. The second way of life is based upon the will of a minority forcibly imposed upon the majority. It relies upon terror and oppression, a controlled press and radio, fixed elections, and the suppression of personal freedoms.
>
> I believe that it must be the policy of the United States to support free peoples who are resisting attempted subjugation by armed minorities or by outside pressures. I believe that we must assist free peoples to work out their own destinies in their own way. I believe that our help should be primarily through economic and financial aid which is essential to economic stability and orderly political processes.

UNIT QUESTION: Under What Circumstances Should the United States Intervene in World Events?

> The world is not static, and the status quo is not sacred. But we cannot allow changes in the status quo in violation of the Charter of the United Nations by such methods as coercion, or by such subterfuges as political infiltration. In helping free and independent nations to maintain their freedom, the United States will be giving effect to the principles of the Charter of the United Nations.
>
> *Source:* American Rhetoric. (2016). The Truman Doctrine. Retrieved from americanrhetoric.com/speeches/harrystrumantrumandoctrine.html

Comprehension Questions:

1. What are the two ways of life that Truman describes in the third paragraph?
2. According to Truman, why should the United States help countries that are fighting against communism?

Activities:

1. Work with a partner to write and act out a dialogue in which Truman explains to James Monroe (Lesson 5.3) why he updated the United States' approach to foreign policy.
2. Truman argues that the United States should help countries freely choose their form of government. What would he say to people in a country that freely chose communism?

Reflection: What do you think Joseph Stalin, the leader of the Soviet Union in 1949, told Russian people about the difference between communism and democracy? What do you think students in Russia today are taught about that topic?

Resources:

Harry S. Truman Library and Museum. (n.d.). Home page. Retrieved from trumanlibrary.org/index.php

Romagnolo, D. J. (2000). Speech delivered by J. V. Stalin. Retrieved from marx2mao.com/Stalin/SS46.html

LESSON 5.10

WHY DID MARTIN LUTHER KING JR. OPPOSE THE VIETNAM WAR?

Historical Figure: Martin Luther King Jr.

Event: Civil rights movement, 1954–1968

Introduction: What effects, both positive and negative, could U.S. involvement in wars abroad have on U.S. citizens?

Mini-Lecture:

- Reverend Dr. Martin Luther King Jr. (1929–1968) was an activist for the rights of Black people and poor people.

- He was active during the civil rights movement (1954–1968), a struggle led by Black people with the goal of achieving equal rights with White people.
- The Vietnam War (1955–1975) took place in Southeast Asia and centered on the conflict between communist North Vietnamese forces, supported by the Soviet Union, and South Vietnamese forces, supported by the United States and other capitalist countries. It is considered part of the Cold War.
- About 60,000 U.S. soldiers died in the Vietnam War, and between 1.5 and 3.5 million Vietnamese, Laotian, and Cambodian people died.
- Our document comes from a speech King gave against the Vietnam War in 1967, a year before he was assassinated.

Vocabulary:

futile: pointless
Dante: an Italian writer who described levels of hell
neutrality: not taking a side
facile: simple
rehabilitation: building back up
demonic: evil

devastating: destroying
irony: contradiction between reality and what you would expect
solidarity: working together
manipulation: tricking people into doing something that hurts them

Document: Why I Am Opposed to the War in Vietnam, Martin Luther King Jr., 1967

Now, let me make it clear in the beginning, that I see this war as an unjust, evil, and futile war. I preach to you today on the war in Vietnam because my conscience leaves me with no other choice. The time has come for America to hear the truth about this tragic war. . . .

Now, I've chosen to preach about the war in Vietnam because I agree with Dante, that the hottest places in hell are reserved for those who in a period of moral crisis maintain their neutrality. There comes a time when silence becomes betrayal. . . .

There is at the outset a very obvious and almost facile connection between the war in Vietnam and the struggle I and others have been waging in America. A few years ago there was a shining moment in that struggle. It seemed that there was a real promise of hope for the poor, both black and white, through the Poverty Program. There were experiments, hopes, and new beginnings. Then came the build-up in Vietnam. And I watched the program broken as if it was some idle political plaything of a society gone mad on war. And I knew that America would never invest the necessary funds or energies in rehabilitation of its poor so long as adventures like Vietnam continued to draw men and skills and money, like some demonic, destructive suction tube. And you may not know it, my friends, but it is estimated that we spend $500,000 to kill each enemy soldier, while we spend only fifty-three dollars for each person classified as poor, and much of that fifty-three dollars goes for salaries to people who are not poor. So I was increasingly compelled to see the war as an enemy of the poor, and attack it as such.

Perhaps the more tragic recognition of reality took place when it became clear to me that the war was doing far more than devastating the hope of the poor at home. It was sending their sons, and their brothers, and their husbands to fight and die in extraordinarily high proportion relative to the rest of the population. We were taking the black young men who had been crippled by society and sending them eight thousand miles away to guarantee liberties in Southeast Asia which they had not found in Southwest Georgia and East Harlem. So we have been repeatedly faced with a cruel irony of watching Negro and white boys on TV screens as they kill and die together for a nation that has been unable to seat them together in the same school room. So we watch them in brutal solidarity, burning the huts of a poor village. But we realize that they would hardly live on the same block in Chicago or Atlanta. Now, I could not be silent in the face of such cruel manipulation of the poor.

Source: Library, University of California. (2006).
Martin Luther King, "Why I am opposed to the war in Vietnam."
Retrieved from lib.berkeley.edu/MRC/pacificaviet/riversidetranscript.html
Reprinted by arrangement with The Heirs to the Estate of Martin Luther King Jr.,
c/o Writers House as agent for the proprietor in New York, NY.
© Dr. Martin Luther King Jr. © Renewed 1995 Coretta Scott King.

Comprehension Questions:

1. Name two ways that the Vietnam War affected poor people in the United States, according to King.
2. In your own words, what is the irony that King identifies?

Activities:

1. How did King and Woodrow Wilson (Lesson 5.6) see neutrality differently? Choose quotations from each document to illustrate your point.
2. Work with a partner to write and act out a dialogue between Harry Truman (Lesson 5.9) and King about the spread of communism.

Reflection: Look back at your responses from the introduction. What negative effects did you and King identify in common? Would you add any from his list to yours? Would you point out to him positive effects the Vietnam War might have had on U.S. citizens?

Resources:

The King Center. (n.d.). King editorials. Retrieved from kingencyclopedia.stanford.edu/kingweb/liberation_curriculum/pdfs/vietnameditorials.pdf

LESSON 5.11

ON WHAT BASIS DID HENRY KISSINGER ADVISE RICHARD NIXON TO OPPOSE CHILEAN PRESIDENT SALVADOR ALLENDE?

Historical Figure: Henry Kissinger

Event: Military coup in Chile, 1973

Introduction: What should the U.S. president do if another country elects a leader who is hostile to the United States? Think of three possibilities and choose the best one.

Mini-Lecture:

- Salvador Allende was elected president of Chile in 1970.
- Allende called himself a socialist (he believed that the government should facilitate people sharing wealth instead of rich people accumulating it) and a Marxist (he followed the teachings of Karl Marx, who wanted to establish a society without socioeconomic classes).
- Allende was elected during the Cold War, when some people believed in the "domino theory"—that if communists or socialists gained power in countries like Chile or Vietnam, those ideas would spread throughout the region and challenge the power of capitalist countries, including the United States.
- Henry Kissinger was secretary of state from 1973 to 1977, and at the time Allende was elected, Kissinger was the national security adviser to President Richard Nixon.
- Our document comes from a "secret/sensitive" memorandum that Kissinger wrote to Nixon in 1970.
- In 1973, the U.S. Central Intelligence Agency secretly supported a military coup against Allende, which allowed dictator Augusto Pinochet to depose Allende and take power and rule until 1990.

Vocabulary:

consolidation: the process by which a leader makes his or her power secure
adverse: negative
self-determination: the right of a nation or group to make decisions for themselves
non-intervention: foreign policy of not interfering in the domestic affairs of another country unless national security is at risk

Modus Vivendi Strategy: plan of peaceful coexistence
patent: obvious
overt: done openly
punitive: intended to punish
embargo: ban on trade
marshal: to gain
covertly: secretly

UNIT QUESTION: Under What Circumstances Should the United States Intervene in World Events?

Document: Memorandum for the President, National Security Council meeting, November 6, Chile; Henry Kissinger, 1970

A. DIMENSIONS OF THE PROBLEM

The election of Allende as President of Chile poses for us one of the most serious challenges ever faced in this hemisphere. . . .

Allende is a tough, dedicated Marxist. He comes to power with a profound anti-US bias. . . .

The consolidation of Allende in power in Chile, therefore, would pose some very serious threats to our interests and position in the hemisphere, and would affect developments in our relations to them elsewhere in the world: . . .

While events in Chile post these potentially very adverse consequences for us, they are taking a form which makes them extremely difficult for us to deal with or offset, and which in fact poses some very painful dilemmas for us:
a. Allende was elected legally, the first Marxist government ever to come to power by free elections. . . .
b. We are strongly on record in support of self-determination and respect for free election; you are firmly on record for non-intervention in the internal affairs of this hemisphere and of accepting nations "as they are." . . .

C. OUR CHOICES . . .

1. The Modus Vivendi Strategy:
This school of thought . . . argues that . . . the best thing we can do in these circumstances is maintain our relationship and our presence in Chile so that over the long haul we may be able to foster and influence domestic trends favorable to our interests. . . .

2. The Hostile Approach:
DOD [Department of Defense], CIA [Central Intelligence Agency], and some State [Department] people, on the other hand, argue that it is patent that Allende is our enemy, that he will move to counter us just as soon and as strongly as he feels he can; . . . we should try to prevent him from consolidating [power] now when he is at his weakest. . . .

Within this approach there are in turn two schools of thought:
a. Overt Hostility.
This view argues that we should not delay in putting pressure on Allende and therefore should not wait to react to his moves with counter-punches. . . . This approach therefore would call for (1) initiating punitive measures, such as terminating aid or economic embargo; (2) making every effort to rally international support of this position; and (3) declaring and publicizing our concern and hostility.
b. Non-overt Pressure, Cold, Correct Approach.
This approach concurs in the view that pressure should be placed on Allende now and that we should oppose him. . . . It argues that an image of the US initiating punitive measures will permit Allende to marshal domestic support

and international sympathy on the one hand, and make it difficult for us to obtain international cooperation on the other. . . . This approach therefore calls for essentially the same range of pressures as the previous one, but would use them quietly and covertly; on the surface our posture would be correct, but cold.

D. ASSESSMENTS

[. . .] I recommend, therefore that you make a decision that we will oppose Allende as strongly as we can and do all that we can to keep him from consolidating power, taking care to package those efforts in a style that gives us the appearance of reacting to his moves.

Source: NSA Archive, George Washington University. (2016). Retrieved from Memorandum for the President, NSC Meeting, November 6, Chile. nsarchive.gwu.edu/NSAEBB/NSAEBB437/docs/Doc%204%20-%20 Kissinger%20to%20Nixon%20re%20Nov%206%20NSC%20meeting.pdf

Comprehension Questions:

1. Who is the "you" in this document, and who is the "I"?
2. According to Kissinger, why does Allende's election pose a problem for the United States?
3. What solution does Kissinger propose?

Activities:

1. Divide the class into three groups. Work with a group of your classmates to argue for one of the three strategies outlined in this document—modus vivendi, overt hostility, or non-overt pressure.
2. Which historical figure whom we've studied in this unit could give Nixon the best advice on how to deal with Allende's election, and why? What advice would he or she give? Write a letter from that person to Nixon, offering advice.

Reflection: Was the United States' decision to secretly support a coup against Allende wise? Morally right?

Resources:

Jarecki, E. (Director). (2002). *The trials of Henry Kissinger*. USA: First Run Features.

Allende, S. (n.d.). Salvador Allende: First speech to the Chilean Parliament after his election. Retrieved from marxists.org/archive/allende/1970/september/20.htm

LESSON 5.12

How Did Bill Clinton Explain His Decision to Intervene in the Genocide of Bosnian Muslims?

Historical Figure: Bill Clinton

Event: Dayton Peace Accords, 1995

UNIT QUESTION: Under What Circumstances Should the United States Intervene in World Events?

Introduction: Do you think the United States should intervene only when it is to the United States' advantage, or also when innocent people in another country are being killed? Why?

Mini-Lecture:

- Bill Clinton was president from 1993 to 2001.
- In 1993, a civil war broke out between several ethnic groups in Bosnia-Herzegovina: the Bosnians, the Croats, and the Serbs.
- Bosnian Muslims and Catholic Croats accused Orthodox Christian Serbs of carrying out "ethnic cleansing," or genocide (killing a large group based on ethnicity, nation, or religion), against them.
- In 1995, Serbs carried out massacres in "safe areas" the UN peacekeeping troops had set up for Bosnians and Croats.
- The United States and other members of the North Atlantic Treaty Organization (NATO) became involved to stop the conflict.
- Clinton helped broker peace accords in Dayton, Ohio.
- Our document comes from a speech Clinton made explaining the role the United States would take in implementing the peace plan.

Vocabulary:

vital: important
unparalleled: better than others
strategic: related to military, financial, or political goals

Document: On Bosnia, Bill Clinton, 1995

> Last week, the warring factions in Bosnia reached a peace agreement as a result of our efforts in Dayton, Ohio, and the support of our European and Russian partners. Tonight I want to speak with you about implementing the Bosnian peace agreement and why our values and interests as Americans require that we participate.
>
> Let me say at the outset America's role will not be about fighting a war. It will be about helping the people of Bosnia to secure their own peace agreement. Our mission will be limited, focused, and under the command of an American general.
>
> In fulfilling this mission, we will have the chance to help stop the killing of innocent civilians, especially children, and at the same time, to bring stability to central Europe, a region of the world that is vital to our national interests. It is the right thing to do.
>
> From our birth, America has always been more than just a place. America has embodied an idea that has become the ideal for billions of people throughout the world. Our founders said it best: America is about life, liberty and the pursuit of happiness.

In this century especially, America has done more than simply stand for these ideals. We have acted on them and sacrificed for them. Our people fought two world wars so that freedom could triumph over tyranny. After World War I, we pulled back from the world, leaving a vacuum that was filled by the forces of hatred. After World War II, we continued to lead the world. We made the commitments that kept the peace, that helped to spread democracy, that created unparalleled prosperity and that brought victory in the Cold War. . . .

Now that doesn't mean that we can solve every problem. My duty as president is to match the demands for American leadership to our strategic interests and to our ability to make a difference. America cannot and must not be the world's policeman. We cannot stop all war for all time but we can stop some wars. We cannot save all women and all children but we can save many of them. We can't do everything but we must do what we can. There are times and places where our leadership can mean the difference between peace and war and where we can defend our fundamental values as a people and serve our most basic strategic interests.

Source: CNN. (1995, November 27). Transcript of President Clinton's speech on Bosnia. Retrieved from cnn.com/US/9511/bosnia_speech/speech.html

Comprehension Questions:

1. According to Clinton, why did the United States become involved in the war in Bosnia?
2. Describe in your own words the role Clinton thinks the United States should take in the world.

Activities:

1. Write a letter from Mark Twain (Lesson 5.5) to Clinton praising or criticizing his decision to intervene in Bosnia.
2. If Eleanor Roosevelt (Lesson 5.8) heard Clinton's speech, would she be pleased with the role the UN had taken in defending human rights? Why or why not?
3. Find Bosnia-Herzegovina on a map. Why would that part of the world be strategically important for the United States?

Reflection: Should Clinton have intervened in Bosnia earlier? When he did? Or not at all? Discuss your reasoning.

Resources:

Facing History. (2016). Aftermath: Bosnia's long road to peace. Retrieved from facinghistory.org/war-only-half-story/bosnias-long-road-peace

Office of the Historian. (n.d) The war in Bosnia, 1992–1995. Retrieved from history.state.gov/milestones/1993-2000/bosnia

Unit Question: Under What Circumstances Should the United States Intervene in World Events?

LESSON 5.13
What Was George W. Bush's Strategy in the War on Terror?

Historical Figure: George W. Bush

Event: War on Terror begins, 2001

Introduction: What do you know about Islam? Where did you learn it?

Mini-Lecture:

- George W. Bush was president from 2001 to 2009.
- On September 11, 2001, the terrorist group al-Qaeda attacked several sites in the United States, killing almost 3,000 people.
- The leader of al-Qaida (also spelled al-Qaeda), Osama bin Laden, was thought to be hiding in Afghanistan.
- The Afghan government (the Taliban) did not cooperate with U.S. authorities to find bin Laden, and the United States launched a war on Afghanistan that (officially) lasted from 2001 to 2014.
- From 2003 to 2011, the United States carried out a war on Iraq, which was alleged to have connections to al-Qaida and to have "weapons of mass destruction" that could be used in a terrorist attack. These weapons were never found, and evidence of them was later called into question.
- U.S. forces located and killed bin Laden in Pakistan in 2011.
- Our document is from the speech Bush gave several days after the September 11 attacks.

Vocabulary:

affiliated: connected
fringe: unpopular
pervert: to distort
cleric: religious authority

diplomacy: trying to solve problems through negotiation
covert: secret

Document: The War on Terror, George W. Bush, 2001

> On September 11th, enemies of freedom committed an act of war against our country. . . . Americans have many questions tonight. Americans are asking, who attacked our country? The evidence we have gathered all points to a collection of loosely affiliated terrorist organizations known as Al Qaida. . . . The terrorists practice a fringe form of Islamic extremism that has been rejected by Muslim scholars and the vast majority of Muslim clerics, a fringe movement that perverts the peaceful teachings of Islam. The terrorists' directive commands them to kill Christians and Jews, to kill all Americans, and make no distinctions among military and civilians, including women and children. . . .

The leadership of Al Qaida has great influence in Afghanistan and supports the Taliban regime in controlling most of that country. In Afghanistan, we see Al Qaida's vision for the world. Afghanistan's people have been brutalized. Many are starving, and many have fled. Women are not allowed to attend school. You can be jailed for owning a television. Religion can be practiced only as their leaders dictate. A man can be jailed in Afghanistan if his beard is not long enough. . . .

Our war on terror begins with Al Qaida, but it does not end there. It will not end until every terrorist group of global reach has been found, stopped, and defeated.

. . . Americans are asking, how will we fight and win this war? We will direct every resource at our command, every means of diplomacy, every tool of intelligence, every instrument of law enforcement, every financial influence, and every necessary weapon of war, to the disruption and to the defeat of the global terror network.

Our response involves far more than instant retaliation and isolated strikes. Americans should not expect one battle but a lengthy campaign, unlike any other we have ever seen. It may include dramatic strikes, visible on TV, and covert operations, secret even in success. We will starve terrorists of funding, turn them one against another, drive them from place to place, until there is no refuge or no rest. And we will pursue nations that provide aid or safe haven to terrorism. Every nation, in every region, now has a decision to make. Either you are with us, or you are with the terrorists. From this day forward, any nation that continues to harbor or support terrorism will be regarded by the United States as a hostile regime.

Source: Cable News Network. (2003). Transcript of President Bush's address. Retrieved from edition.cnn.com/2001/US/09/20/gen.bush.transcript/

Comprehension Questions:

1. According to Bush, how are the tactics and targets in the War on Terror different from those in previous wars?

Activities:

1. Work with a partner to create a Venn diagram showing the similarities and differences between Roosevelt's Day of Infamy speech (Lesson 5.7) and Bush's speech.
2. Bush takes a strong stand when he says, "Either you are with us, or you are with the terrorists." Think of a different message he could have addressed to neutral countries, and then guess why he did not do so.

Reflection: U.S. presidents have used different words to refer to al-Qaida and similar terrorist organizations like ISIS. Bush called them "Islamic extremists," whereas President Obama just called them "extremists," because Obama didn't think it was fair to associate them with Islam when most Muslims don't support them. Donald Trump calls them "radical Islamic terrorists." What do you think they should be called, and why?

Resources:

Carroll, L., & Sanders, S. (2015, February 22). Punditfact: Why Obama won't label ISIS "Islamic extremists." *Politifact*. Retrieved from politifact.com/truth-o-meter/article/2015/feb/22/punditfact-why-obama-wont-label-isis-islamic-extre/

Schulten, K. (2010, July 6). The wars in Afghanistan and Iraq: Teaching resources and essential questions. *The New York Times*. Retrieved from learning.blogs.nytimes.com/2010/07/06/the-wars-in-afghanistan-and-iraq-teaching-resources-and-essential-questions/

WGBH Educational Foundation. (2003). Terrorism: What's in a word? Retrieved from pbs.org/wgbh/globalconnections/mideast/educators/militant/lesson1.html

UNIT CONCLUSION

In this unit, students have become aware of the complexity of foreign affairs and the ways in which a country's "national interests" shift over time. They may be proud of the United States' role in averting genocide or protecting democracy, or they may be disillusioned by what they have learned about the social and economic cost of war. It is important to support students at all points on this spectrum from idealism to cynicism, and to encourage them to be open to their classmates' views to the contrary. Their emerging political identities, as well as their own national origins and loyalties, may influence their views, so it is helpful to remind them of Point 4 in the Discussion Guidelines (p. 18 and Appendix J): "Reflect on how your own experiences and biases affect your views."

Participation in this summit may require students to do a bit more outside research than for others, depending on their level of knowledge of geography and world events. The summit includes an interesting mix of "hawks" and "doves"—anti-imperialists and proponents of American global supremacy—which should make for lively discussion. As students are likely to be proficient with the summit by now, teachers may wish to add an additional level of difficulty, such as including a quotation from the person they are representing, or adding background information about the country outside the United States to which they will be referring.

CHAPTER 6

Civil Liberties and Public Safety

UNIT QUESTION: Under What Conditions, If Any, Should Citizens' Freedoms Be Restricted?

Current Issue Question: Can reforming gun laws make Americans safer? If so, how? If not, why not?

Unit Introduction: In this unit, students will consider the balance between freedom and security. Starting with the Declaration of Independence and the Bill of Rights, they will learn which liberties were promised to Americans. Presidents who have restricted these freedoms, from John Adams to George Bush, will try to explain why, and citizens who have protested these restrictions (Paul Robeson) or sought greater limitations on freedom (Carrie Nation) will challenge their reasoning. In what students may find one of the most striking documents in the book, Huey Newton will lay out the Black Panther Party's demands. Congress's investigation of the Federal Bureau of Investigation's Counterintelligence Program, which surveilled the Panthers, provides context.

Our current issue, on government attempts to reduce gun violence through legislation, is likely to be controversial. If students come from gun-owning families or have been personally affected by gun violence, emotions may run high. Teachers might remind students that everyone, including the historical figures in this unit, want both civil liberties and public safety, although we may disagree about how to protect both.

LESSON 6.1
WHAT WAS BARACK OBAMA'S PLAN TO REDUCE GUN VIOLENCE?

Historical Figure: Barack Obama

Event: Aurora movie theater shooting, 2012

Introduction: What right guaranteed by the Constitution is most important to you, and why? You may refer to the Bill of Rights in Lesson 6.3.

UNIT QUESTION: Under What Conditions, If Any, Should Citizens' Freedoms Be Restricted?

Mini-Lecture:

- The 2nd Amendment guarantees the right to bear arms (to have guns).
- In 2012 James Holmes killed 12 people in a mass shooting in a movie theater in Aurora, Colorado.
- He was undergoing treatment for mental illness; he bought guns and ammunition both over the Internet and in gun stores after passing a background check.
- Our document comes from a speech Obama gave in 2016 in which he references the Aurora shooting when explaining what he planned to do to reduce gun violence.

Vocabulary:

constraint: limit
background check: examination by authorities of someone's criminal record before the person is allowed to buy a product or get a job
infringement: violation
proponent: person in favor of something

confiscation: authorities taking property
felon: someone who has committed a felony, a serious crime
ATF: Alcohol, Tobacco, and Firearms Bureau, the federal agency that regulates the sale of these items
relevant: connected to the issue

Document: Remarks by the President on Common-Sense Gun Safety Reform, Barack Obama, 2016

> Every single year, more than 30,000 Americans have their lives cut short by guns—30,000. Suicides. Domestic violence. Gang shootouts. Accidents. . . .
> I believe in the Second Amendment. . . . It guarantees a right to bear arms. . . . But I also believe that we can find ways to reduce gun violence consistent with the Second Amendment.
> I mean, think about it. We all believe in the First Amendment, the guarantee of free speech, but we accept that you can't yell "fire" in a theater. We understand there are some constraints on our freedom in order to protect innocent people. . . .
> Today, background checks are required at gun stores. If a father wants to teach his daughter how to hunt, he can walk into a gun store, get a background check, purchase his weapon safely and responsibly. This is not seen as an infringement on the Second Amendment. Contrary to the claims of what some gun rights proponents have suggested, this hasn't been the first step in some slippery slope to mass confiscation. . . . You pass a background check; you purchase a firearm.
> The problem is some gun sellers have been operating under a different set of rules. A violent felon can buy the exact same weapon over the Internet with no background check, no questions asked. . . .
> So we've created a system in which dangerous people are allowed to play by a different set of rules than a responsible gun owner who buys his or her gun

the right way and subjects themselves to a background check. That doesn't make sense. Everybody should have to abide by the same rules. Most Americans and gun owners agree. . . .

So let me outline what we're going to be doing. Number one, anybody in the business of selling firearms must get a license and conduct background checks, or be subject to criminal prosecutions. . . .

Number two, we're going to do everything we can to ensure the smart and effective enforcement of gun safety laws that are already on the books, which means we're going to add 200 more ATF agents and investigators. . . .

Number three, we're going to do more to help those suffering from mental illness get the help that they need. . . . We're going to ensure that federal mental health records are submitted to the background check system, and remove barriers that prevent states from reporting relevant information. . . .

Number four, we're going to boost gun safety technology. . . . If we can set it up so you can't unlock your phone unless you've got the right fingerprint, why can't we do the same thing for our guns? . . .

. . . Second Amendment rights are important, but there are other rights that we care about as well. And we have to be able to balance them. . . . Our right to peaceful assembly—that right was robbed from moviegoers in Aurora and Lafayette.

Source: The White House, Office of the Press Secretary. (2016, January 5). The President's remarks on common-sense gun safety reform. Retrieved from whitehouse.gov/the-press-office/2016/01/05/remarks-president-common-sense-gun-safety-reform

Comprehension Questions:

1. On what basis does Obama argue that 2nd Amendment rights should be limited?
2. Why is Obama concerned about gun sales on the Internet?

Activities:

1. Of Obama's four plans, which do you think would be most effective at reducing gun violence? Least effective? Why?
2. Divide the class in half and debate this proposition: Obama's plan to include mental health records in the background check system would violate people's 4th Amendment right to privacy.

Reflection: What kind of plan for reducing gun violence would you suggest to the current president?

Resources:

Cable News Network. (2016, June 21). A visual guide: Mass shootings in America. Retrieved from cnn.com/2016/06/13/health/mass-shootings-in-america-in-charts-and-graphs-trnd/
National Rifle Association of America. (2017). Background checks: NICS. Retrieved from nraila.org/issues/background-checks-nics/

Unit Question: Under What Conditions, If Any, Should Citizens' Freedoms Be Restricted?

LESSON 6.2

How Did the United States Explain Its Decision to Declare Independence from Britain?

Historical Figure: Thomas Jefferson

Event: Declaration of Independence, 1776

Introduction: Describe a situation in which you would consider rebelling against the government.

Mini-Lecture:

- In 1775, the Revolutionary War broke out when colonists rebelled against British authorities.
- Thomas Jefferson was a member of the Second Continental Congress, a group of representatives from the 13 colonies who worked together to gain independence from Great Britain.
- Our document is from the Declaration of Independence, of which Jefferson was the main author.
- Jefferson was later president from 1801 to 1809.

Vocabulary:

endowed: provided	*usurpation:* taking power unfairly by force
unalienable: can't be taken away	*object:* goal
institute: to set up	*evince:* to show
ends: goals	*design:* plan
prudence: wisdom	*despotism:* rule by a tyrant
dictate: to give a command	*sufferance:* suffering
transient: temporary	*candid:* honest
hath shewn: has shown	
disposed to: likely to	

Document: Declaration of Independence, Thomas Jefferson, 1776

> We hold these truths to be self-evident, that all men are created equal, that they are endowed by their Creator with certain unalienable Rights, that among these are Life, Liberty and the pursuit of Happiness. — That to secure these rights, Governments are instituted among Men, deriving their just powers from the consent of the governed, — That whenever any Form of Government becomes destructive of these ends, it is the Right of the People to alter or to abolish it, and to institute new Government, laying its foundation on such principles and organizing its powers in such form, as to them shall seem most likely to effect their Safety and Happiness. Prudence, indeed, will dictate that Governments long established should not be changed for light and transient causes; and accordingly all experience hath shewn that mankind are more disposed to suffer, while evils are sufferable than to right themselves by abolishing the forms to which they are accustomed. But when a long train of abuses and

usurpations, pursuing invariably the same Object evinces a design to reduce them under absolute Despotism, it is their right, it is their duty, to throw off such Government, and to provide new Guards for their future security. — Such has been the patient sufferance of these Colonies; and such is now the necessity which constrains them to alter their former Systems of Government. The history of the present King of Great Britain is a history of repeated injuries and usurpations, all having in direct object the establishment of an absolute Tyranny over these States. To prove this, let Facts be submitted to a candid world.

Source: The U.S. National Archives and Records Administration. (n.d.). Declaration of Independence: A transcription. Retrieved from archives.gov/founding-docs/declaration-transcript

Comprehension Questions:

1. Work with a partner to put this document into your own words.

Activities:

1. What would be an example of "transient causes" for replacing a government? What would be an example of causes that are not transient? Create a T-chart.
2. Jefferson wrote that people are endowed with rights "by their Creator." What do you think that phrase meant to him? What does it mean to you? Can people disagree on that point and still support the Declaration of Independence as a whole?

Reflection: What "unalienable rights" do you believe you have (if any)?

Resources:

National Humanities Center. (n.d.). Declaration of Independence: Grievances annotated. Retrieved from americainclass.org/sources/makingrevolution/rebellion/text8/decindep.pdf

LESSON 6.3

WHAT DOES THE BILL OF RIGHTS GUARANTEE?

Historical Figure: James Madison

Event: Bill of Rights, 1791

Introduction: List all the rights you can remember that the Constitution guarantees, then brainstorm with the class to create as complete a list as you can.

Mini-Lecture:

- The Constitution was created in 1787.
- The Bill of Rights, which consists of the first 10 amendments to the Constitution, was ratified in 1791.
- The principal author was James Madison, who was in the House of Representatives for Virginia.

UNIT QUESTION: Under What Conditions, If Any, Should Citizens' Freedoms Be Restricted?

- James Madison was later president from 1809 to 1817.

Vocabulary:

establishment: institution
therof: of it
abridge: to limit
redress: to correct mistakes
grievance: a problem people want authorities to fix
militia: a group of citizens who have weapons
state: country
quarter: to order citizens to give soldiers lodging and food
effects: property
seizure: having property taken by authorities
probable cause: reasons to suspect someone of a crime
capital: a crime for which one could be sentenced to death
presentment: a statement accusing someone of a crime
indictment: a formal accusation in a criminal case

grand jury: a group of 12 to 23 people who can try a case outside of the court system
jeopardy: danger
limb: body part
be a witness against himself: to give testimony in court that could count against yourself
due process of law: fair treatment in the legal system
ascertain: to determine
counsel: a lawyer
common law: laws governing civil (not criminal) cases, in which one person or group is suing another
bail: money people accused of crimes can pay so they don't have to await trial in jail
enumeration: listing
construed: to be taken to mean
disparage: count against

Document: Bill of Rights, James Madison, 1791

   Amendment I: Congress shall make no law respecting an establishment of religion, or prohibiting the free exercise thereof; or abridging the freedom of speech, or of the press; or the right of the people peaceably to assemble, and to petition the government for a redress of grievances.

   Amendment II: A well regulated militia, being necessary to the security of a free state, the right of the people to keep and bear arms, shall not be infringed.

   Amendment III: No soldier shall, in time of peace be quartered in any house, without the consent of the owner, nor in time of war, but in a manner to be prescribed by law.

   Amendment IV: The right of the people to be secure in their persons, houses, papers, and effects, against unreasonable searches and seizures, shall not be violated, and no warrants shall issue, but upon probable cause, supported by oath or affirmation, and particularly describing the place to be searched, and the persons or things to be seized.

   Amendment V: No person shall be held to answer for a capital, or otherwise infamous crime, unless on a presentment or indictment of a grand jury, except in cases arising in the land or naval forces, or in the militia, when in actual service in time of war or public danger; nor shall any person be subject for the same offense to be twice put in jeopardy of life or limb; nor shall be compelled in any criminal case to be a witness against himself, nor be deprived of life, liberty, or property, without due process of law; nor shall private property be taken for public use, without just compensation.

Amendment VI: In all criminal prosecutions, the accused shall enjoy the right to a speedy and public trial, by an impartial jury of the state and district wherein the crime shall have been committed, which district shall have been previously ascertained by law, and to be informed of the nature and cause of the accusation; to be confronted with the witnesses against him; to have compulsory process for obtaining witnesses in his favor, and to have the assistance of counsel for his defense.

Amendment VII: In suits at common law, where the value in controversy shall exceed twenty dollars, the right of trial by jury shall be preserved, and no fact tried by a jury, shall be otherwise reexamined in any court of the United States, than according to the rules of the common law.

Amendment VIII: Excessive bail shall not be required, nor excessive fines imposed, nor cruel and unusual punishments inflicted.

Amendment IX: The enumeration in the Constitution, of certain rights, shall not be construed to deny or disparage others retained by the people.

Amendment X: The powers not delegated to the United States by the Constitution, nor prohibited by it to the states, are reserved to the states respectively, or to the people.

Source: Bill of Rights Institute. (2017). Bill of Rights (full text). Retrieved from billofrightsinstitute.org/founding-documents/bill-of-rights/

Comprehension Questions:

1. Create a title of less than five words for each of the amendments.
2. Which amendment would you cite if the government built a road on your land and didn't pay you?

Activities:

1. Write a short story in which someone has rights from each of the first 10 amendments violated.
2. With a small group, think of a situation in which one person's exercising a right may conflict with another person's exercising another right. Then act it out for the class.

Reflection: What additional rights do you wish Madison had included?

Resources:

Ashbrook Center. (2017). The fate of Madison's proposals for the Bill of Rights. Retrieved from teachingamericanhistory.org/bor/fate-of-madison/

UNIT QUESTION: Under What Conditions, If Any, Should Citizens' Freedoms Be Restricted?

LESSON 6.4
How Did John Adams Restrict Freedom of the Press?

Historical Figure: John Adams

Event: Sedition Act, 1798

Introduction: How do you usually respond when someone criticizes you? Why?

Mini-Lecture:

- John Adams was president from 1797 to 1801.
- During that time, there was a rivalry between Adams's party, the Federalists, and the Democratic-Republicans, led by Thomas Jefferson.
- The French and the British were at war; the Democratic-Republican Party supported the French while the Federalist Party supported the British.
- After the French foreign minister insulted some diplomats whom Adams had sent to negotiate with the minister, many people became angry at and suspicious of French people who were living in the United States.
- Congress passed the Alien and Sedition Acts, four laws that allowed foreigners to be deported, and that allowed anyone who criticized the government to be imprisoned or fined.
- Adams signed the bill into law and his administration used the Sedition Act to imprison Democratic-Republican newspaper editors and politicians who criticized Adams.
- Adams's critics objected that the Sedition Act was a violation of the First Amendment rights to freedom of speech and freedom of the press. The acts were repealed or allowed to expire by 1802.

Vocabulary:

enact: to make law
utter: to speak
procure: to get
scandalous: offensive or alarming to the public
malicious: with bad intentions

defame: to damage someone's reputation
disrepute: dislike
sedition: encouraging rebellion against a government
combinations: actions

Document: Sedition Act, 1798

> SECT. 2. And be it further enacted, That if any person shall write, print, utter, or publish, or shall cause or procure to be written, printed, uttered, or published, or shall knowingly and willingly assist or aid in writing, printing, uttering, or publishing any false, scandalous and malicious writing or writings against the government of the United States, or either House of the Congress of the United States, or the President of the United States, with intent to defame the said

government, or either House of the said Congress, or the said President, or to bring them, or either of them, into contempt or disrepute; or to excite against them, or either or any of them, the hatred of the good people of the United States, or to stir up sedition within the United States; or to excite any unlawful combinations therein, for opposing or resisting any law of the United States, or any act of the President of the United States, done in pursuance of any such law, or of the powers in him vested by the Constitution of the United States; or to resist, oppose, or defeat any such law or act; or to aid, encourage or abet any hostile designs of any foreign nation against the United States, their people or government, then such person, being thereof convicted before any court of the United States having jurisdiction thereof, shall be punished by a fine not exceeding two thousand dollars, and by imprisonment not exceeding two years.

Source: Lillian Goldman Law Library. (2008). An act in addition to the act. Retrieved from avalon.law.yale.edu/18th_century/sedact.asp

Comprehension Questions:

1. Explain in your own words four kinds of speech, writing, printing, and publication that the Sedition Act outlawed.
2. What would happen to people who committed these actions?

Activities:

1. List some things Democratic-Republicans might have wanted to say but could have been prosecuted for saying.
2. Work with a partner to write and act out a dialogue between Adams and James Madison (Lesson 6.3) about whether or not the Sedition Act was constitutional.

Reflection: Do you think there are any situations in which the president should restrict freedom of the press? Describe, or explain why not.

Resources:

CRF-USA. (2017). The Alien and Sedition Acts: Defining American freedom. Retrieved from crf-usa.org/america-responds-to-terrorism/the-alien-and-sedition-acts.html

LESSON 6.5

WHAT WAS ABRAHAM LINCOLN'S ARGUMENT FOR SUSPENDING HABEAS CORPUS RIGHTS DURING THE CIVIL WAR?

Historical Figure: Abraham Lincoln

Event: Civil War, 1861–1865

Introduction: Name three rights that a president would be most likely to suspend in a time of war, and explain why.

UNIT QUESTION: Under What Conditions, If Any, Should Citizens' Freedoms Be Restricted?

Mini-Lecture:

- Abraham Lincoln was president from 1861 to 1865, during the Civil War, in which Southern states seceded from the Union in order to protect the institution of slavery and joined together to form the Confederacy.
- Lincoln first suspended the right of habeas corpus in 1861, when citizens who were against the war attacked Union troops in Baltimore; without habeas corpus, those people could be held without being tried or charged.
- The Supreme Court found Lincoln's actions unconstitutional, but Congress supported him.
- Many people were arrested for deserting the Union Army or spying for or supporting the Confederacy, and the judicial system had difficulty charging and trying all of them quickly.
- Lincoln wrote our document in 1863 suspending habeas corpus again.

Vocabulary:

writ: law
habeas corpus: the right of people accused of a crime not to be imprisoned indefinitely without being charged or tried
insurrection: rebellion
abettor: someone who helps a criminal
muster: to assemble people for military service
article: law
therefrom: from there
draft: mandatory military service

Document: Proclamation 104, Abraham Lincoln, 1863

> Whereas the Constitution of the United States has ordained that the privilege of the writ of habeas corpus shall not be suspended unless when, in cases of rebellion or invasion, the public safety may require it; and
>
> Whereas a rebellion was existing on the 3d day of March, 1863, which rebellion is still existing; and
>
> Whereas by a statute which was approved on that day it was enacted by the Senate and House of Representatives of the United States in Congress assembled that during the present insurrection the President of the United States, whenever in his judgment the public safety may require, is authorized to suspend the privilege of the writ of habeas corpus in any case throughout the United States or any part thereof; and
>
> Whereas, in the judgment of the President, the public safety does require that the privilege of the said writ shall now be suspended throughout the United States in the cases where, by the authority of the President of the United States, military, naval, and civil officers of the United States, or any of them, hold persons under their command or in their custody, either as prisoners of war, spies, or aiders or abettors of the enemy, or officers, soldiers, or seamen enrolled or drafted or mustered or enlisted in or belonging to the land or naval forces of the United States, or as deserters therefrom, or otherwise amenable to military law or the rules and articles of war or the rules or regulations prescribed for the

military or naval services by authority of the President of the United States, or for resisting a draft, or for any other offense against the military or naval service.

> *Source: The New York Times.* (2017). President's proclamation; The habeas corpus suspended throughout the United States in certain specified cases. Retrieved from nytimes.com/1863/09/16/news/president-s-proclamation-habeas-corpus-suspended-throughout-united-states.html

Comprehension Questions:

1. According to Lincoln, why do the current circumstances allow him to suspend habeas corpus?
2. Whose right of habeas corpus is being suspended?

Activities:

1. Work with a partner to create a cartoon with thought and speech bubbles in which Lincoln and John Adams (Lesson 6.4) discuss who had better reasons to suspend constitutional rights.
2. Describe a situation in which the right of habeas corpus would be important to ensure fairness.

Reflection: Do you support Lincoln's decision? Why or why not?

Resources:

Ewers, J. (2009, February 2). Revoking civil liberties: Lincoln's constitutional dilemma. *U.S. News and World Report.* Retrieved from usnews.com/news/history/articles/2009/02/10/revoking-civil-liberties-lincolns-constitutional-dilemma

LESSON 6.6

WAS CARRIE NATION'S TEMPERANCE ACTIVISM PROTECTED BY THE CONSTITUTION?

Historical Figure: Carrie Nation

Event: Prohibition, 1920–1933

Introduction: Do people have a constitutional right to drink alcohol? Why or why not?

Mini-Lecture:

- Carrie Nation (1846–1911) was an activist in the temperance movement, which opposed the sale of alcohol.
- Her first husband was an alcoholic, and her second husband was a minister who supported her activism.
- Nation was a leader in the Women's Christian Temperance Union, which succeeded in banning the sale of alcohol in Kansas, where she lived.
- In 1900, Nation said she was called by God to close down illegal bars in Kansas; she smashed liquor bottles and destroyed property.

UNIT QUESTION: Under What Conditions, If Any, Should Citizens' Freedoms Be Restricted?

- Our document comes from Nation's autobiography, in which she explains this incident.
- In 1920, the United States banned the sale of alcohol with a constitutional amendment, yet illegal trade in alcohol continued.
- "Prohibition" lasted until 1933, when it was ended due to its unpopularity.

Vocabulary:

buggy: horse-drawn carriage
brick-bat: a piece of brick used as a weapon
remonstrance: warning

vice: sin or bad behavior
saloon: place where alcohol is served
dive: place where alcohol is served
jointist: someone who owns an illegal bar

Document: *The Use and Need of Carrie A. Nation*, Carrie A. Nation, 1904

I got a box that would fit under my buggy seat, and every time I thought no one would see me, I went out in the yard and picked up some brick-bats, for rocks are scarce around Medicine Lodge [Kansas], and I wrapped them up in newspapers to pack in the box under my buggy seat. . . . Early next morning I had my horse put to the buggy and drove to the first place, kept by Mr. Dobson. I put the smashers on my right arm and went in. He and another man were standing behind the bar. I said: "Mr. Dobson, I told you last spring . . . to close this place, and you didn't do it. Now I have come with another remonstrance. Get out of the way. I don't want to strike you, but I am going to break up this den of vice." I began to throw at the mirror and the bottles below the mirror. Mr. Dobson and his companion jumped into a corner, seeming very much terrified. From that I went to another saloon, until I had destroyed three, breaking some of the windows in the front of the building. . . .

    The other dive keepers closed up, stood in front of their places and would not let me come in. By this time, the streets were crowded with people; most of them seemed to look puzzled. . . . I stood in the middle of the street and spoke in this way: "I have destroyed three of your places of business, and if I have broken a statute of Kansas, put me in jail; if I am not a law-breaker your mayor and councilmen are. You must arrest one of us, for if I am not a criminal, they are." One of the councilmen, who was a butcher, said: "Don't you think we can attend to our business." "Yes," I said, "You can, but you won't. . . . I know you have manufactured many criminals and this county is burdened down with taxes to prosecute the results of these dives. Two murders have been committed in the last five years in this county, one in a dive I have just destroyed. You are a butcher of hogs and cattle, but they are butchering men, women and children . . . and the mayor and councilmen are more to blame than the jointist, and now if I have done wrong in any particular, arrest me." When I was through with my speech I got in my buggy and said: "I'll go home."

Source: Nation, Carrie A. (1904). *The use and need of Carry A. Nation*. Topeka, KS: F. M. Steves & Sons, pp. 60–62.

Comprehension Questions:

1. According to Nation, what are two negative effects of alcohol on the community?
2. Why does Nation say that the mayor and councilmen were lawbreakers?

Activities:

1. The 1st Amendment protects the right to "petition the government for a redress of grievances." Did Nation's actions fit that description? Why or why not?
2. The 4th Amendment guarantees that people can be "secure in their persons, houses, papers, and effects, against unreasonable searches and seizures." Did Nation violate the bar owners' rights? Why or why not?

Reflection: Was Nation right to take the law into her own hands, if the authorities wouldn't enforce it? Why or why not? Can you think of other circumstances in which citizens can or should enforce laws?

Resources:

State Historical Society of Missouri. (n.d.). Carrie Amelia Nation. Retrieved from shsmo.org/historicmissourians/name/n/nation/

LESSON 6.7

HOW DID HERBERT HOOVER EXPLAIN HIS DECISION TO DISPERSE THE BONUS ARMY?

Historical Figure: Herbert Hoover

Event: Bonus Army protests, 1932

Introduction: Do protesters sometimes go too far in an effort to make their point? Does the government sometimes violate citizens' right to protest? Try to give an example of both situations.

Mini-Lecture:

- Herbert Hoover was president from 1929 to 1933, during the Great Depression, when many people were unemployed.
- Veterans of World War I were especially hard hit by the depression.
- The government had promised veterans a bonus of $1,000, but then told them it would not be delivered until 1945, nearly 20 years after the end of their service in the war.
- About 15,000 veterans, calling themselves the "Bonus Army," came to Washington, DC, and set up makeshift camps; they asked Congress to give them their bonuses right away.
- Congress voted not to do so, but many of the Bonus Army veterans stayed in the capitol.
- Hoover told them to go home, and when they didn't, he ordered the military to set their camps on fire and force them to leave; several veterans were killed.

Unit Question: Under What Conditions, If Any, Should Citizens' Freedoms Be Restricted?

Vocabulary:

encamp: to set up temporary places to live
billeted: when soldiers stay in people's houses
coerce: to force
riot: a violent disturbance by a large group of people
adjourn: to close session
appalling: terrible
overawe: to scare
seat of government: capitol
discharge: to carry out
alleged: supposed
assemblage: gathering

Document: Statement on the Justice Department Investigation of the Bonus Army, Herbert Hoover, 1932

> This experience demonstrates that it is intolerable that organized bodies of men having a grievance or demand upon the Government should be allowed to encamp in the city and attempt to live off the community like soldiers billeted in an enemy country. Attempts by such groups to intimidate or coerce Congress into granting their demands hurt rather than help their cause, and can only end as this one did, in riot and disorder. The available facts demonstrate that the bonus marchers who remained in the city after Congress adjourned represented no fair cross-section of ex-service men. Prior to the adjournment of Congress, law-abiding ex-service men dominated this gathering and preserved order. Afterwards, the proportion of disorderly and criminal elements among these men steadily increased. Such of their leaders as were well-intentioned lost control over them entirely. It is appalling to think of the disorder and bloodshed that would have occurred if darkness had fallen on the city with the police hopelessly overwhelmed at the scene of the disturbance, and the balance of the community without police protection. The prompt use of the military to outnumber and overawe the disturbers prevented a calamity. The principal reason why the Federal Government was given exclusive jurisdiction over the Capital City was to enable it to preserve order at the seat of government and to protect the Congress and other public officials from unlawful interference while in the discharge of their duties. The right peaceably to petition Congress for redress of alleged grievances does not include assemblage of disorderly thousands at the seat of the government for purposes of coercion. . . .
>
> *Source:* Peters, G. H., & Woolley, J. T. (n.d.). Herbert Hoover: "Statement on the Justice Department Investigation of the Bonus Army." American Presidency Project. Retrieved from presidency.ucsb.edu/ws/?pid=23227

Comprehension Questions:

1. Whom is Hoover addressing in this document, and what is his primary purpose in writing it?
2. According to Hoover, why was it necessary to use force to disperse the protesters?

Activities:

1. Do you trust Hoover's description of the protesters as "disorderly" and "criminal"? Why or why not?
2. Work with a partner to write and act out a dialogue between Hoover and Carrie Nation (Lesson 6.6) about balancing the right to protest with public safety.

Reflection: Think of recent protests in your area or around the country. Have the authorities balanced protesters' rights with the rights of other people? Give examples.

Resources:

Eyewitness to History. (2006). The Bonus Army invades Washington, D.C., 1932. Retrieved from eyewitnesstohistory.com/bonusarmy.htm

LESSON 6.8

HOW DID FRANKLIN D. ROOSEVELT JUSTIFY THE INTERNMENT OF JAPANESE AMERICANS?

Historical Figure: Franklin D. Roosevelt

Event: Japanese internment, 1942–1946

Introduction: Could you imagine a situation where the government rounded up a certain group of Americans and kept them in camps? If not, why not? If so, how would it come about and who might be targeted?

Mini-Lecture:

- Franklin D. Roosevelt was president from 1933 to 1945, during World War II.
- After Japanese forces attacked Pearl Harbor, Roosevelt issued an executive order (from which our document is taken) authorizing the creation of internment camps.
- The government forced more than 100,000 people of Japanese descent, many of whom were U.S. citizens, to give up their homes and property and move to these camps.
- Smaller numbers of German Americans and Italian Americans were also interned.

Vocabulary:

prosecution: carrying out
espionage: spying
premises: areas
discretion: judgment

Document: Executive Order 9066, Franklin D. Roosevelt, 1942

> Whereas the successful prosecution of the war requires every possible protection against espionage and against sabotage to national-defense material, national-defense premises, and national-defense utilities as defined in Section 4, Act of April 20, 1918, . . .

Now, therefore, by virtue of the authority vested in me as President of the United States, and Commander in Chief of the Army and Navy, I hereby authorize and direct the Secretary of War, and the Military Commanders whom he may from time to time designate, whenever he or any designated Commander deems such action necessary or desirable, to prescribe military areas in such places and of such extent as he or the appropriate Military Commander may determine, from which any or all persons may be excluded, and with respect to which, the right of any person to enter, remain in, or leave shall be subject to whatever restrictions the Secretary of War or the appropriate Military Commander may impose in his discretion. The Secretary of War is hereby authorized to provide for residents of any such area who are excluded therefrom, such transportation, food, shelter, and other accommodations as may be necessary, in the judgment of the Secretary of War or the said Military Commander, and until other arrangements are made, to accomplish the purpose of this order.

Source: History Matters. (n.d.). Executive order 9066: The president authorizes Japanese relocation. Retrieved from historymatters.gmu.edu/d/5154

Comprehension Questions:

1. Summarize in your own words the concerns about national security that Roosevelt outlines in Paragraph 1.
2. List the powers that Roosevelt gives to the secretary of war.

Activities:

1. Did Roosevelt violate the 4th or 5th Amendments? Why or why not?
2. Work with a partner to write and act out a dialogue between Roosevelt and Thomas Jefferson (Lesson 6.2) about whether Japanese Americans would have been justified in trying to overthrow or turn against the government because Roosevelt had interned them. Look back at Lesson 5.7 for more details on the Pearl Harbor attacks.

Reflection: Do you agree with Roosevelt that national security concerns justified his actions? Why or why not?

Resources:

Houston, J. W. (1983). *Farewell to Manzanar: A true story of Japanese American experience during and after the World War II internment.* New York, NY: Laurel Leaf.

WETA. (2007). Civil rights: Japanese Americans. Retrieved from pbs.org/thewar/at_home_civil_rights_japanese_american.htm

LESSON 6.9

How Did Paul Robeson Defend Himself Against Joseph McCarthy's Accusation That He Was a Communist?

Historical Figure: Paul Robeson

Event: McCarthy era, 1950–1956

Introduction: Are there any beliefs or ideas a U.S. citizen could hold that would justify the government's investigating or punishing him or her? If not, why not? If so, which beliefs?

Mini-Lecture:

- Paul Robeson (1898–1976) was a singer, actor, and athlete who was active in the civil rights movement; he also sympathized with the Soviet Union and communist ideas.
- Robeson believed that communism might offer better living conditions to poor people and workers than capitalism could.
- Joseph McCarthy was a senator from Wisconsin from 1947 to 1957.
- McCarthy believed that communism was "subversive," or threatening to national security, and he used the House Un-American Activities Committee (HUAC) to investigate and punish U.S. citizens suspected of communist sympathies.
- Hundreds of people, especially in the entertainment industry, were investigated. A few were found to be spying for the Soviet Union; many others were "blacklisted" (prevented from working) even if there was little evidence to show they were communists.
- The period from 1950 to 1956 is sometimes called "the McCarthy era," and McCarthy's tactics of accusing people of subversive beliefs without sufficient evidence is called "McCarthyism."
- Our document is from Robeson's testimony before HUAC.

Vocabulary:

apprehend: to believe
invoke: to use to justify one's behavior
laud: to admire

Document: Testimony of Paul Robeson before the House Committee on Un-American Activities, 1956

> Mr. ARENS: Are you now a member of the Communist Party? . . .
> Mr. ROBESON: What do you mean by the Communist Party? As far as I know it is a legal party like the Republican Party and the Democratic Party. Do you mean a party of people who have sacrificed for my people, and for all Americans and workers, that they can live in dignity? Do you mean that party?

Mr. ARENS: Are you now a member of the Communist Party?

Mr. ROBESON: Would you like to come to the ballot box when I vote and take out the ballot and see?

Mr. ARENS: Mr. Chairman, I respectfully suggest that the witness be ordered and directed to answer that question. . . .

Mr. ROBESON: I stand upon the Fifth Amendment of the American Constitution. . . .

Mr. ARENS: Do you honestly apprehend that if you told this Committee truthfully—

Mr. ROBESON: I have no desire to consider anything. I invoke the Fifth Amendment, and it is none of your business what I would like to do, and I invoke the Fifth Amendment. And forget it.

THE CHAIRMAN: You are directed to answer that question.

Mr. ROBESON: I invoke the Fifth Amendment, and so I am answering it, am I not? . . .

THE CHAIRMAN: You are directed to answer that question, Mr. Robeson.

Mr. ROBESON: Gentlemen, in the first place, wherever I have been in the world, Scandinavia, England, and many places, the first to die in the struggle against Fascism were the Communists and I laid many wreaths upon graves of Communists. It is not criminal, and the Fifth Amendment has nothing to do with criminality. . . .

The other reason that I am here today, again from the State Department and from the court record of the court of appeals, is that when I am abroad I speak out against the injustices against the Negro people of this land. . . . I am not being tried for whether I am a Communist, I am being tried for fighting for the rights of my people, who are still second-class citizens in this United States of America. . . .

Mr. ARENS: Now I would invite your attention, if you please, to the Daily Worker of June 29, 1949, with reference to a get-together with you and Ben Davis. Do you know Ben Davis?

Mr. ROBESON: One of my dearest friends, one of the finest Americans you can imagine, born of a fine family, who went to Amherst and was a great man.

THE CHAIRMAN: The answer is yes?

Mr. ROBESON: Nothing could make me prouder than to know him.

THE CHAIRMAN: That answers the question.

Mr. ARENS: Did I understand you to laud his patriotism?

Mr. ROBESON: I say that he is as patriotic an American as there can be, and you gentlemen belong with the Alien and Sedition Acts, and you are the nonpatriots, and you are the un-Americans, and you ought to be ashamed of yourselves.

Source: History Matters. (n.d.). "You are the un-Americans, and you ought to be ashamed of yourselves." Retrieved from historymatters.gmu.edu/d/6440

Comprehension Questions:

1. According to Robeson, why was he called before the HUAC?
2. Look back at the 5th Amendment (Lesson 6.3). Find the phrase in it that Robeson is invoking.

Activities:

1. Robeson compares McCarthyism with the Sedition Act (Lesson 6.4). Work with a partner to create a Venn diagram comparing the similarities and differences.
2. What did Robeson mean when he called members of HUAC "un-American"? Work with a group to list some evidence he might have used. List some evidence HUAC might have provided that Robeson was un-American. Then discuss who had a stronger case.

Reflection: Do you think the House Un-American Activities Committee could be revived in the future? If no, why not? If yes, what groups might it target?

Resources:

American Rhetoric. (2017). Edward R. Murrow: Response to Senator Joe McCarthy on CBS' See It Now. Retrieved from americanrhetoric.com/speeches/edwardrmurrowtomccarthy.htm

LESSON 6.10

How Did COINTELPRO Justify Its Surveillance of U.S. Citizens?

Historical Figure: J. Edgar Hoover

Event: COINTELPRO founded, 1956

Introduction: Which (if any) U.S. citizens should the U.S. government investigate and spy on? Why?

Mini-Lecture:

- J. Edgar Hoover was director of the Federal Bureau of Investigation (FBI) from 1935 to 1972.
- In 1956, Hoover launched a secret program called COINTELPRO (Counterintelligence Program), which investigated and tried to discredit groups or people he thought threatened national security, especially communists.
- In 1971, COINTELPRO ended, after activists revealed its activities by stealing FBI files and giving them to the media.
- In 1976, Senator Frank Church led an investigation of COINTELPRO; his committee released a report, the Church Report, from which our document is taken.

Vocabulary:

domestic: inside the United States
intelligence: information, often secret, that is gathered through investigation and is used by policymakers
neutralize: to remove a danger
trivial: unimportant
degrading: embarrassing
poison pen letter: a letter that contains accusations that a person has done something wrong, sent to that person's acquaintances in order to disrupt that person's life

overtly: openly
dissident: disagreeing with the government
vigilante: a group that tries to seek justice by taking the law into their own hands
propagation: spreading
intolerable: unacceptable
clandestine: secret
militant: using extreme or violent tactics
messiah: someone who is seen as a savior or hero

Document: Church Report on COINTELPRO, 1976

> COINTELPRO is the FBI acronym for a series of covert action programs directed against domestic groups. In these programs, the Bureau went beyond the collection of intelligence to secret action defined to "disrupt" and "neutralize" target groups and individuals. The techniques were adopted wholesale from wartime counterintelligence, and ranged from the trivial (mailing reprints of Reader's Digest articles to college administrators) to the degrading (sending anonymous poison-pen letters intended to break up marriages) and the dangerous (encouraging gang warfare and falsely labeling members of a violent group as police informers).
>
> COINTELPRO began in 1956, in part because of frustration with Supreme Court rulings limiting the Government's power to proceed overtly against dissident groups; it ended in 1971 with the threat of public exposure. In the intervening 15 years, the Bureau conducted a sophisticated vigilante operation aimed squarely at preventing the exercise of First Amendment rights of speech and association, on the theory that preventing the growth of dangerous groups and the propagation of dangerous ideas would protect the national security and deter violence.
>
> Many of the techniques used would be intolerable in a democratic society even if all of the targets had been involved in violent activity, but COINTELPRO went far beyond that. The unexpressed major premise of the programs was that a law enforcement agency has the duty to do whatever is necessary to combat perceived threats to the existing social and political order. . . . "Covert action" is the label applied to clandestine activities intended to influence political choices and social values. . . .
>
> B. Who Were the Targets? 1. The Five Targeted Groups
> The Bureau's covert action programs were aimed at five perceived threats to domestic tranquility: the "Communist Party, USA" program (1956–71); the

"Socialist Workers Party" program (1961–69); the "White Hate Group" [e.g., the Klan] program (1964–71); the "Black Nationalist-Hate Group" program [e.g., the Black Panther Party] (1967–71); and the "New Left" program [e.g., communists/socialists] (1968–71).

. . . On March 4, 1968, the program was expanded. . . . The letter expanding the program lists five long-range goals for the program: (1) to prevent the "coalition of militant black nationalist groups," . . . ; (2) to prevent the rise of a "messiah" who could "unify, and electrify," the movement, naming specifically Martin Luther King, Stokely Carmichael, and Elijah Muhammed; (3) to prevent violence on the part of black nationalist groups, by pinpointing "potential troublemakers" and neutralizing them "before they exercise their potential for violence"; (4) to prevent groups and leaders from gaining "respectability" by discrediting them to the "responsible" Negro community, to the white community (both the responsible community and the "liberals"—the distinction is the Bureau's), and to Negro radicals; and (5) to prevent the long range growth of these organizations, especially among youth, by developing specific tactics to "prevent these groups from recruiting young people." . . .

Source: Wolf, P. (2002). Supplementary detailed staff reports on intelligence activities and the rights of Americans. Retrieved from terrasol.home.igc.org/HooverPlan.htm

Comprehension Questions:

1. Who wrote this report, who are they addressing, and what is their main message?
2. According to this report, why did Hoover and the FBI launch COINTELPRO?

Activities:

1. Work with a partner to write and act out a dialogue between Hoover and Paul Robeson (Lesson 6.9) about balancing civil liberties and public safety.
2. Most people think of Martin Luther King (Lesson 5.10) as a nonviolent activist. Does seeing his name among the targets of COINTELPRO make you suspect that he engaged in activities that endangered public safety, or does it make you suspect that COINTELPRO was mistaken in its targets? Why?

Reflection: Do you think the FBI or other government agencies today have programs or goals similar to COINTELPRO? What evidence would you provide for your answer?

Resources:

Independent Television Service. (2014). *1971*. USA: Independent Lens.

UNIT QUESTION: Under What Conditions, If Any, Should Citizens' Freedoms Be Restricted?

LESSON 6.11
WHAT RIGHTS DID THE BLACK PANTHER PARTY DEMAND, AND WHY?

Historical Figure: Huey P. Newton

Event: Black Panther Party founded, 1966

Introduction: In what way, if any, should the government compensate groups of people whose rights have been denied in the past?

Mini-Lesson:

- The Black Panther Party for Self-Defense was a Black nationalist and socialist organization founded in 1966 by Huey P. Newton and Bobby Seale.
- Huey P. Newton (1942–1989) was a self-described revolutionary who wanted to transform racial and economic power structures.
- Newton was accused of killing a police officer, and imprisoned, but released on appeal.
- Our document comes from the party platform he and fellow activist Bobby Seale wrote when forming the party in 1966; Newton included this document in the dissertation he wrote when earning a PhD in social philosophy from the University of Santa Cruz.
- The document references the "forty acres and two mules" that the government promised but did not provide to freed slaves during Reconstruction (see Lesson 4.5).

Vocabulary:

means of production: resources needed to produce goods, for example, factories

cooperative: property owned by residents and run collectively

decadent: wasteful or corrupt

Document: The Ten-Point Program, Huey P. Newton and Bobby Seale, 1966

1. **We Want Freedom. We Want Power To Determine The Destiny Of Our Black Community.** We believe that Black people will not be free until we are able to determine our destiny.
2. **We Want Full Employment For Our People.** We believe that the federal government is responsible and obligated to give every man employment or a guaranteed income. We believe that if the White American businessmen will not give full employment, then the means of production should be taken from the businessmen and placed in the community so that the people of the community can organize and employ all of its people and give a high standard of living.
3. **We Want An End To The Robbery By The Capitalists Of Our Black Community.** We believe that this racist government has robbed us, and now we are demanding the overdue debt of forty acres and two mules. Forty acres and two mules were promised 100 years ago as restitution for slave labor and

mass murder of Black people. We will accept the payment in currency which will be distributed to our many communities. The Germans are now aiding the Jews in Israel for the genocide of the Jewish people. The Germans murdered six million Jews. The American racist has taken part in the slaughter of over fifty million Black people; therefore, we feel that this is a modest demand that we make.

4. **We Want Decent Housing Fit For The Shelter Of Human Beings**. We believe that if the White Landlords will not give decent housing to our Black community, then the housing and the land should be made into cooperatives so that our community, with government aid, can build and make decent housing for its people.

5. **We Want Education For Our People That Exposes The True Nature Of This Decadent American Society. We Want Education That Teaches Us Our True History And Our Role In The Present-Day Society**. We believe in an educational system that will give to our people a knowledge of self. If a man does not have knowledge of himself and his position in society and the world, then he has little chance to relate to anything else.

6. **We Want All Black Men To Be Exempt From Military Service**. We believe that Black people should not be forced to fight in the military service to defend a racist government that does not protect us. We will not fight and kill other people of color in the world who, like Black people, are being victimized by the White racist government of America. We will protect ourselves from the force and violence of the racist police and the racist military, by whatever means necessary.

7. **We Want An Immediate End To Police Brutality And Murder Of Black People.** We believe we can end police brutality in our Black community by organizing Black self-defense groups that are dedicated to defending our Black community from racist police oppression and brutality. The Second Amendment to the Constitution of the United States gives a right to bear arms. We therefore believe that all Black people should arm themselves for self-defense.

8. **We Want Freedom For All Black Men Held In Federal, State, County And City Prisons And Jails.** We believe that all Black people should be released from the many jails and prisons because they have not received a fair and impartial trial.

9. **We Want All Black People When Brought To Trial To Be Tried In Court By A Jury Of Their Peer Group Or People From Their Black Communities, As Defined By The Constitution Of The United States.** We believe that the courts should follow the United States Constitution so that Black people will receive fair trials. The Fourteenth Amendment of the U.S. Constitution gives a man a right to be tried by his peer group. A peer is a person from a similar economic, social, religious, geographical, environmental, historical and racial background. To do this the court will be forced to select a jury from the Black community from which the Black defendant came. We have been, and

are being, tried by all-White juries that have no understanding of the "average reasoning man" of the Black community.
10. **We Want Land, Bread, Housing, Education, Clothing, Justice And Peace.**

> Source: Hilliard, D (Ed.). (2007). *The Black Panther.* New York, NY: Atria Books. Copyright © 2007 by David Hilliard. Reprinted with permission of Atria Books, a division of Simon & Schuster, Inc. All Rights Reserved.

Comprehension Questions:

1. According to this document, why haven't Black people received fair trials?
2. What argument does this document present for why Black people should be exempt from military service?

Activities:

1. Following the 10th point, the document quotes the preamble to the Declaration of Independence (Lesson 6.2). With a partner, reread it and identify three similarities and three differences in the grievances the colonists had against King George, and those the Black Panthers had against the U.S. government.
2. Look back through this unit and the others we have studied. Which documents would Newton use as evidence to support his points?

Reflection: Do you believe that your education fits the description in Point 5? Why or why not? Is that a positive or negative thing?

Resources:

Olsson, G. (Director). (2011). *Black Power Mix Tape, 1967–1975.* USA: IFC Films.

LESSON 6.12

HOW DID THE U.S. GOVERNMENT DEFEND THE USA PATRIOT ACT?

Historical Figure: George W. Bush

Event: USA PATRIOT Act, 2001

Introduction: How would you feel if you discovered the government was monitoring what books you checked out from the library? Why would you feel that way?

Mini-Lecture:

- George W. Bush was president from 2001 to 2009.
- In 2001, terrorists affiliated with al-Qaida attacked several sites in the United States.
- Congress passed the USA PATRIOT Act, with Bush's support, shortly after the attack, with the goal of investigating suspected terrorists and preventing another attack.
- The American Civil Liberties Union (ACLU) was founded in 1920 to protect the rights of people in the United States; it provides legal assistance and information.

- The ACLU said that the PATRIOT Act went too far in compromising people's civil liberties.
- The Department of Justice denied that the PATRIOT Act allows the government to violate people's rights; our document comes from a webpage on which the Department of Justice defends itself against the ACLU's accusations.

Vocabulary:

domestic: occurring inside a country, in this case, the United States

surveillance: spying on or observing people suspected of crimes

wiretapping: secretly listening to phone conversations or monitoring other private communications

political advocacy: taking action on behalf of a political goal

dissent: public disagreement with government policies or actions

odious: terrible

subpoena: a legal order requiring someone to give documents to the authorities

detonator: a device used to set off a bomb

Document: Dispelling Some of the Major Myths About the USA PATRIOT Act, U.S. Department of Justice, n.d.

> **Myth:** The ACLU claims that the Patriot Act "expands terrorism laws to include 'domestic terrorism' which could subject political organizations to surveillance, wiretapping, harassment, and criminal action for political advocacy." They also claim that it includes a "provision that might allow the actions of peaceful groups that dissent from government policy, such as Greenpeace, to be treated as 'domestic terrorism.'" . . .
>
> **Reality:** The Patriot Act limits domestic terrorism to conduct that breaks criminal laws, endangering human life. "Peaceful groups that dissent from government policy" without breaking laws cannot be targeted. Peaceful political discourse and dissent is one of America's most cherished freedoms, and is not subject to investigation as domestic terrorism. Under the Patriot Act, the definition of "domestic terrorism" is limited to conduct that (1) violates federal or state criminal law and (2) is dangerous to human life. Therefore, peaceful political organizations engaging in political advocacy will obviously not come under this definition. (Patriot Act, Section 802)
>
> **Myth:** The ACLU has claimed that "Many [people] are unaware that their library habits could become the target of government surveillance. In a free society, such monitoring is odious and unnecessary. . . The secrecy that surrounds section 215 leads us to a society where the 'thought police' can target us for what we choose to read or what Websites we visit." (ACLU, July 22, 2003)
>
> **Reality:** The Patriot Act specifically protects Americans' First Amendment rights, and terrorism investigators have no interest in the library habits of ordinary Americans. Historically, terrorists and spies have used libraries to plan and carry out activities that threaten our national security. If terrorists

or spies use libraries, we should not allow them to become safe havens for their terrorist or clandestine activities. The Patriot Act ensures that business records—whether from a library or any other business—can be obtained in national security investigations with the permission of a federal judge.

Examining business records often provides the key that investigators are looking for to solve a wide range of crimes. Investigators might seek select records from hardware stores or chemical plants, for example, to find out who bought materials to make a bomb, or bank records to see who's sending money to terrorists. Law enforcement authorities have always been able to obtain business records in criminal cases through grand jury subpoenas, and continue to do so in national security cases where appropriate. In a recent domestic terrorism case, for example, a grand jury served a subpoena on a bookseller to obtain records showing that a suspect had purchased a book giving instructions on how to build a particularly unusual detonator that had been used in several bombings. This was important evidence identifying the suspect as the bomber.

In national security cases where use of the grand jury process was not appropriate, investigators previously had limited tools at their disposal to obtain certain business records. Under the Patriot Act, the government can now ask a federal court (the Foreign Intelligence Surveillance Court), if needed to aid an investigation, to order production of the same type of records available through grand jury subpoenas. . . .

Source: The US Department of Justice. (n.d.). Dispelling some of the major myths about the USA Patriot Act. Retrieved from justice.gov/archive/ll/subs/u_myths.htm

Comprehension Questions:

1. Who is the Department of Justice addressing in this document, and what is its main purpose in writing it?
2. According to the Department of Justice, how has the PATRIOT Act helped in investigations of domestic terrorism?

Activities:

1. What evidence would the ACLU have to present to support their accusations about the Patriot Act? What evidence would the Department of Justice have to present to support their defense of the Patriot Act?
2. Work with a partner to write and act out a dialogue between Bush and Barack Obama (Lesson 6.1) about the difficulties of balancing civil liberties and public safety.

Reflection: Whom do you believe about the PATRIOT Act: the Department of Justice or the ACLU? Why?

Resources:

ACLU. (2017). Surveillance under the Patriot Act. Retrieved from aclu.org/infographic/surveillance-under-patriot-act

UNIT CONCLUSION:

In this unit, students have seen the difficult questions that ordinary Americans and their leaders have faced when trying to apply the Bill of Rights. Students may be surprised by how liberals and conservatives have found themselves on either side of the freedom-versus-security debate at different points in history. Indeed, this unit complicates some of the divides that students may take for granted. It may cause them to question figures they've seen as heroes (like Lincoln or Franklin Roosevelt) or admire people they wouldn't have expected to (a prohibitionist like Carrie Nation, or a communist like Paul Robeson).

The summit for this unit is likely to be one of the most complex ones yet, filled with impassioned voices arguing that they know what is best for America. Several of the most intellectually and emotionally challenging issues of the course (e.g., Black nationalism and government surveillance of citizens) appear in this unit. By now students should have both the strong sense of classroom community and the familiarity with the ideas involved to manage these challenges. In this summit, teachers may encourage students to refer back to documents or historical figures from previous units to bolster their points. As students move toward the conclusion of the course, they can start to look back on their work as a whole.

CHAPTER 7

American Identity

UNIT QUESTION AND CURRENT ISSUE QUESTION:
What Do We Mean When We Say "We"?

Unit Introduction: This abbreviated, concluding unit is intended to give students a chance to reflect on what they have learned in the course. These excerpts from some of the documents they have studied present different versions of the we's that coexist, overlap, and clash in our country. Depending on teacher preferences and scheduling, this unit could be an extended reflection or a brief review. Either way, it is a wonderful way for students to consolidate their knowledge and consider how their understanding of our country has changed over the course of the year. (Printable PDFs of these shortened versions are available for free download, alongside their longer versions, at www.tcpress.com/Metro.)

It is possible, but not essential, to have a summit for this unit; if teachers choose to have one, students may wish to bring in voices from other documents as well.

Activities: (remain the same for each referenced document throughout this culminating unit)

1. Who is included in the author's "we" or "us"? Who is excluded?
2. How would the author define an American? Work with a small group to create a visual representation, chart, or description.
3. Do you agree or disagree with the author's definition of an American? Why or why not?

Students can refer back to the lessons in which these documents were originally included for more information on the historical figures, the events that surround these documents, and the documents themselves.

LESSON 7.1
Declaration of Independence, Continental Congress, 1776 (Lesson 6.2)

We hold these truths to be self-evident, that all men are created equal, that they are endowed by their Creator with certain unalienable Rights, that among these are Life, Liberty and the pursuit of Happiness.

LESSON 7.2
Our Hearts Are Sickened, John Ross, 1838 (Lesson 2.3)

By the stipulations of this instrument [the treaty], we are despoiled of our private possessions, the indefeasible property of individuals. We are stripped of every attribute of freedom and eligibility for legal self-defence. Our property may be plundered before our eyes; violence may be committed on our persons; even our lives may be taken away, and there is none to regard our complaints. We are denationalized; we are disfranchised [disenfranchised]. We are deprived of membership in the human family! We have neither land nor home, nor resting place that can be called our own.

LESSON 7.3
Declaration of Immediate Causes, South Carolina Legislature, 1860 (Lesson 3.8)

We, therefore, the People of South Carolina, by our delegates in Convention assembled, appealing to the Supreme Judge of the world for the rectitude of our intentions, have solemnly declared that the Union heretofore existing between this State and the other States of North America, is dissolved, and that the State of South Carolina has resumed her position among the nations of the world, as a separate and independent State; with full power to levy war, conclude peace, contract alliances, establish commerce, and to do all other acts and things which independent States may of right do.

LESSON 7.4
On Women's Right to Vote, Susan B. Anthony, 1872 (Lesson 1.9)

The preamble of the Federal Constitution says: "We, the people of the United States, in order to form a more perfect union, establish justice, insure domestic tranquility, provide for the common defense, promote the general welfare, and secure the blessings of liberty to ourselves and our posterity, do ordain and establish this Constitution for the United States of America."

It was we, the people; not we, the white male citizens; nor yet we, the male citizens; but we, the whole people, who formed the Union. And we formed it, not to give the blessings of liberty, but to secure them; not to the half of ourselves and the half of our posterity, but to the whole people—women as well as men. And it is a downright mockery to talk to women of their enjoyment of the blessings of liberty while they are denied the use of the only means of securing them provided by this democratic-republican government—the ballot.

LESSON 7.5
APPEAL FOR NEUTRALITY, WOODROW WILSON, 1914 (LESSON 5.6)

The people of the United States are drawn from many nations, and chiefly from the nations now at war. It is natural and inevitable that there should be the utmost variety of sympathy and desire among them with regard to the issues and circumstances of the conflict. Some will wish one nation, others another, to succeed in the momentous struggle. It will be easy to excite passion and difficult to allay it. . . . Such divisions amongst us would be fatal to our peace of mind and might seriously stand in the way of the proper performance of our duty as the one great nation at peace, the one people holding itself ready to play a part of impartial mediation and speak the counsels of peace and accommodation not as a partisan, but as a friend. . . .

LESSON 7.6
THE KLAN'S FIGHT FOR AMERICANISM, HIRAM W. EVANS, 1926 (LESSON 2.10)

We [the Klan] are demanding, and we expect, to win, a return of power into the hands of the everyday, not highly cultured, not overly intellectualized, but entirely unspoiled and not de-Americanized, average citizen of the old stock.

LESSON 7.7
DAY OF INFAMY, FRANKLIN D. ROOSEVELT, 1941 (LESSON 5.7)

I believe that I interpret the will of the Congress and of the people when I assert that we will not only defend ourselves to the uttermost, but will make it very certain that this form of treachery shall never again endanger us. Hostilities exist. There is no blinking at the fact that our people, our territory, and our interests are in grave danger. With confidence in our armed forces, with the unbounding determination of our people, we will gain the inevitable triumph—so help us God. I ask that the Congress declare that since the unprovoked and dastardly attack by Japan on Sunday, December 7th, 1941, a state of war has existed between the United States and the Japanese empire.

LESSON 7.8

BY ANY MEANS NECESSARY, MALCOLM X, 1964 (LESSON 2.12)

So we have formed an organization known as the Organization of Afro American Unity which has the same aim and objective—to fight whoever gets in our way, to bring about the complete independence of people of African descent here in the Western Hemisphere, and first here in the United States, and bring about the freedom of these people by any means necessary. That's our motto.

LESSON 7.9

WHY I AM OPPOSED TO THE WAR IN VIETNAM, MARTIN LUTHER KING JR., 1967 (LESSON 5.10)

We were taking the black young men who had been crippled by society and sending them eight thousand miles away to guarantee liberties in Southeast Asia which they had not found in Southwest Georgia and East Harlem. So we have been repeatedly faced with a cruel irony of watching Negro and white boys on TV screens as they kill and die together for a nation that has been unable to seat them together in the same school room. So we watch them in brutal solidarity, burning the huts of a poor village. But we realize that they would hardly live on the same block in Chicago or Atlanta.

LESSON 7.10

A CITY ON A HILL, RONALD REAGAN, 1974 (LESSON 1.11)

One-half of all the economic activity in the entire history of man has taken place in this republic. We have distributed our wealth more widely among our people than any society known to man. Americans work less hours for a higher standard of living than any other people. Ninety-five percent of all our families have an adequate daily intake of nutrients—and a part of the five percent that don't are trying to lose weight! . . .

We cannot escape our destiny, nor should we try to do so. The leadership of the free world was thrust upon us two centuries ago in that little hall of Philadelphia. . . . We are indeed, and we are today, the last best hope of man on earth.

LESSON 7.11

THE WAR ON TERROR, GEORGE W. BUSH, 2001 (LESSON 5.13)

We will starve terrorists of funding, turn them one against another, drive them from place to place, until there is no refuge or no rest. And we will pursue nations that provide aid or safe haven to terrorism. Every nation, in every region, now has a decision to make. Either you are with us, or you are with the terrorists. From this day forward, any nation that continues to harbor or support terrorism will be regarded by the United States as a hostile regime.

LESSON 7.12
A More Perfect Union, Barack Obama, 2008 (Lesson 1.12)

For we have a choice in this country. We can accept a politics that breeds division, and conflict, and cynicism. . . . Or, at this moment, in this election, we can come together and say, "Not this time." This time we want to talk about the crumbling schools that are stealing the future of black children and white children and Asian children and Hispanic children and Native American children. . . . This union may never be perfect, but generation after generation has shown that it can always be perfected.

UNIT CONCLUSION

Having finished the final unit, students can complete the Course Exit Survey, (Appendix C) and compare their answers with the Course Entry Survey (Appendix B) they did at the beginning of the year. This exercise can provide a springboard for a final discussion of course themes. Students can also reflect on how they have developed as a classroom community: are the Discussion Guidelines easier to follow than they were at first? Have they come to understand other students' experiences in unexpected ways?

If a summit is held, teachers may want to acknowledge how far students have come in terms of representing the views of historical figures by showing video of or rereading speeches from the first summit. This acknowledgment of how the students have increased their skills in historical thinking, argument-building, and public speaking is a fine way to end the year.

Appendixes

> **APPENDIX A KEY:**
> 🕐 Event
> 👤 Historical Figure
> 📄 Document

APPENDIX A: QUICK REFERENCE GUIDE

Chapter 1: American Democracy

Unit Question: What is American democracy, and what should it be?

Current Issue Question: What does democracy mean to you today?

1.1 How do ordinary Americans define democracy in the 21st century?
- 🕐 2015: 240th anniversary of the start of the Revolutionary War
- 👤 Ordinary Americans
- 📄 Twitter posts

1.2 How did Native American traditions influence American democracy?
- 🕐 c. 1500: Haudenosaunee confederacy established
- 👤 Dekanawidah
- 📄 The Great Law of Peace, Dekanawidah, c. 1500)

1.3 How did Thomas Paine argue for independence from Britain?
- 🕐 1776: Declaration of Independence
- 👤 Thomas Paine
- *Common Sense*, Thomas Paine, 1776

1.4 What was James Madison's argument for representative democracy?
- 🕐 1787: Constitution created
- 👤 James Madison
- 📄 Federalist Paper No. 10, James Madison, 1787

1.5 What did Thomas Jefferson believe were the main responsibilities of government?
- 🕐 1800: Thomas Jefferson elected
- 👤 Thomas Jefferson
- 📄 Inaugural address, Thomas Jefferson, 1801

1.6 How did Andrew Jackson represent the "common man"?
- 🕐 1828: Andrew Jackson elected
- 👤 Andrew Jackson
- 📄 Political cartoons: Figures 1.1–Figure 1.4

1.7 How did Frederick Douglass criticize American democracy?
- 🕐 1838: Frederick Douglass escapes from slavery
- 👤 Frederick Douglass
- 📄 What to the slave is the Fourth of July?, Fredrick Douglass, 1852

Appendixes

1.8 How did Abraham Lincoln define democracy?
- 1863: Battle of Gettysburg
- Abraham Lincoln
- Gettysburg Address, Abraham Lincoln, 1863

1.9 How did Susan B. Anthony interpret the Constitution?
- 1872: Susan B. Anthony arrested for voting
- Susan B. Anthony
- On women's right to vote, Susan B. Anthony, 1872

1.10 What did John F. Kennedy believe the United States should do for the world?
- 1946–1991: Cold War
- John F. Kennedy
- Inaugural address, John F. Kennedy, 1961

1.11 Why did Ronald Reagan believe America was great?
- 1980: Ronald Reagan elected
- Ronald Reagan
- Shining City on a Hill, Ronald Reagan, 1974

1.12 Why did Barack Obama think the United States was not yet a perfect union?
- 2008: Barack Obama elected
- Barack Obama
- A More Perfect Union, Barack Obama, 2008

Chapter 2: Diversity and Discrimination

Unit Question: What does equality mean?

Current Issue Question: What are your views on same-sex marriage?

2.1 What was the Supreme Court's argument for allowing same-sex marriage?
- 2015: Supreme Court allows same-sex marriage
- John G. Roberts
- *Obergefell v. Hodges*, Supreme Court, 2015

2.2 What did the Constitution say about slavery?
- 1787: Constitutional Convention
- Roger Sherman
- The Constitution, 1787

2.3 How did Native Americans argue for equal rights?
- 1838: Trail of Tears
- John Ross
- Our Hearts Are Sickened, John Ross, 1838

2.4 How did Sojourner Truth define equality?
- 1851: Ohio Women's Rights Convention
- Sojourner Truth
- Ain't I a Woman? Sojourner Truth, 1851

2.5 What was the Supreme Court's rationale for denying Black people citizenship?
- 1856: *Scott v. Sandford*
- Roger Taney
- *Scott v. Sandford*, Supreme Court, 1856

2.6 Why did John Brown think violence was justified to end slavery?
- 1859: John Brown attacks Harper's Ferry, VA
- John Brown
- Address to the Virginia Court, John Brown, 1859

2.7 What was the Supreme Court's reasoning for "separate but equal" facilities?
- 1896: *Plessy v. Ferguson*
- Henry Billings Brown
- *Plessy v. Ferguson*, Supreme Court, 1896

2.8 Why did Elizabeth Cady Stanton believe women deserved the same rights as men?
- 1920: Women's suffrage
- Elizabeth Cady Stanton
- Solitude of the Soul, Elizabeth Cady Stanton, 1892

2.9 What was the Supreme Court's argument for excluding Chinese people from U.S. citizenship?
- 1882: Chinese Exclusion Act
- Lee Joe
- *Fong Yue Ting v. U.S.*, Supreme Court, 1893

2.10 What was the Ku Klux Klan's argument for White supremacy?
- 1920–1929: Roaring Twenties
- Hiram W. Evans
- *The Klan's Fight for Americanism*, Hiram W. Evans, 1926

2.11 How did the Supreme Court explain its decision to overturn the "separate but equal" doctrine?
- 1954: *Brown v. Board of Education*
- Thurgood Marshall
- *Brown v. Board of Education*, Supreme Court, 1954

2.12 How did Malcolm X think racial equality could be achieved?
- 1964: Organization of Afro-American Unity founded
- Malcolm X
- By Any Means Necessary, Malcolm X, 1964)

Chapter 3: States' Rights and Federal Power

Unit Question: How should power be distributed among federal, state, and local governments?

Current Issue Question: Should states be allowed to set their own laws on who can vote?

3.1 On what basis did the NAACP argue that North Carolina law violated the Voting Rights Act?
- 2014: The NAACP sues North Carolina's governor
- William J. Barber II
- *North Carolina State Conference of the NAACP v. Patrick Lloyd McCrory*, North Carolina NAACP, 2014

3.2 What was the balance of power between the states and Congress in the Articles of Confederation?
- 1777: Articles of Confederation
- Patrick Henry
- Articles of Confederation, Articles I, II, III, VIII, and IX, 1777

3.3 How did the Constitution compare with the Articles of Confederation?
- 1787: Constitution
- James Madison
- Constitution, Article I, Article IV, 10th Amendment, 1787

3.4 How did George Washington explain his decision to suppress the Whiskey Rebellion?
- 1791: Whiskey Rebellion
- George Washington
- Minutes of the Meeting at Pittsburgh, unknown author, 1791
- A Proclamation, George Washington, 1792

3.5 How did states' rights and federalist interpretations of the Constitution differ?
- 1819: *McCulloch vs. Maryland*
- John Marshall
- *McCulloch v. Maryland*, Supreme Court, 1819

3.6 Who is responsible for protecting Native American Nations: state or federal governments?
- 1831: *Cherokee Nation v. Georgia*
- John Ross
- *Cherokee Nation v. Georgia*, Supreme Court, 1831

3.7 How did Daniel Webster argue that states couldn't nullify federal laws?
- 1832: Nullification Crisis
- Daniel Webster
- Reply to Robert Hayne, Daniel Webster, 1832

3.8 How did the Southern states explain their decision to secede from the Union?
- 1860: Secession of South Carolina
- Jefferson Davis
- Declaration of Immediate Causes, South Carolina legislature, 1861

3.9 Why did Dwight Eisenhower enforce desegregation?
- 1957: Little Rock Nine
- Dwight Eisenhower
- Desegregation address, Dwight Eisenhower, 1957

3.10 How did Orval Faubus argue for segregation as a "state's right"?
- 1958: Orval Faubus closes Little Rock public schools
- Orval Faubus
- Speech on School Integration, Orval Faubus, 1958)

3.11 Does the state or federal government protect individuals from environmental harm?
- 1992: *New York v. United States*
- Sandra Day O'Connor
- *New York v. United States*, Supreme Court, 1992)

Chapter 4: Government, Business, and Workers

Unit Question: What role should government and businesses play in promoting citizens' well-being?

Current Issue Question: How should the government promote a strong economy?

4.1 How did Donald Trump think the government should promote a strong economy?
- 2016, Donald Trump elected
- Donald Trump
- Bringing Back Jobs and Growth, Donald Trump administration, 2017

4.2 What were Christopher Columbus's economic and social goals?
- 1492, Columbus lands in the Americas
- Christopher Columbus
- Log, Christopher Columbus, 1492

4.3 Why did John Calhoun define slavery as a "positive good"?
- 1807: Britain outlaws slave trade
- John C. Calhoun
- Slavery as a Positive Good, John Calhoun, 1837

4.4 Why did the Lowell mill women go on strike?
- 1834: Lowell mill women strike
- Sarah Bagley
- Investigation of Labor Conditions, Massachusetts House Document no. 50, 1845

4.5 How did W. E. B. Du Bois think that the government succeeded and failed in helping former slaves?
- 1865–1877: Reconstruction
- W. E. B. Du Bois
- *The Souls of Black Folk*, W. E. B. Du Bois, 1903

4.6 What was Andrew Carnegie's argument for social Darwinism?
- 1890: Sherman Anti-Trust Act
- Andrew Carnegie
- The Gospel of Wealth, Andrew Carnegie, 1889

4.7 How did the "other half" live in Jacob Riis's photos?
- 1890–1920: Progressive Era
- Jacob Riis
- Photographs from *How the Other Half Lives*, Jacob Riis, 1890 (Figures 4.1–4.4)

4.8 How did Upton Sinclair want to change the meatpacking industry?
- 1906: Pure Food and Drugs Act
- Upton Sinclair
- *The Jungle*, Upton Sinclair, 1906

4.9 What was Henry Ford's plan for ending poverty?
- 1913: Assembly line invented
- Henry Ford
- *My Life and Work*, Henry Ford, 1922

4.10 What were the aims of the New Deal?
- 1929–1939: Great Depression

Appendixes

- Franklin D. Roosevelt
- The New Deal, Franklin D. Roosevelt, 1932

4.11 Why did Lyndon Johnson launch a War on Poverty?
- 1964: War on Poverty begins
- Lyndon B. Johnson
- State of the Union address, Lyndon B. Johnson, 1964

4.12 Why did Cesar Chavez believe farmworkers should unionize?
- 1965–1979: Delano grape strike
- Cesar Chavez
- Address to the Commonwealth Club of California, Cesar Chavez, 1984)

4.13 What was Reaganomics?
- 1981: Reaganomics launched
- Ronald Reagan
- Address to the Nation on the Economy, Ronald Reagan, 1981

Chapter 5: Foreign Policy

Unit Question: Under what circumstances should the United States intervene in world events?

Current Issue Question: How should the United States react to the civil war in Syria?

5.1 How did Donald Trump explain his decision to bomb Syria?
- 2017: United States bombs Syria
- Donald Trump
- Statement on Syria: Donald Trump administration, 2017)

5.2 Why did George Washington believe the United States should stay neutral?
- 1793: Proclamation of Neutrality
- George Washington
- Proclamation of Neutrality, George Washington, 1793

5.3 How did the Monroe Doctrine change U.S. foreign policy?
- 1823: Monroe Doctrine
- James Monroe
- Monroe Doctrine, James Monroe, 1823

5.4 How was the idea of Manifest Destiny used to justify taking over foreign lands?
- 1846–1848: Mexican-American War
- James K. Polk
- *American Progress*, John Gast, 1872 (Figure 5.1)

5.5 Why did Mark Twain oppose U.S. colonization of the Philippines?
- 1898: U.S. colonization of the Philippines
- Mark Twain
- On American Imperialism, Mark Twain, 1898

5.6 How did Woodrow Wilson try to convince Americans to stay neutral in World War I?
- 1917–1919: United States in World War I
- Woodrow Wilson
- Appeal for Neutrality, Woodrow Wilson, 1914

5.7 How did Franklin D. Roosevelt explain his decision to involve the United States in World War II?
- 1941–1945: United States in World War II
- Franklin D. Roosevelt
- Day of Infamy, Franklin D. Roosevelt, 1941

5.8 How did Eleanor Roosevelt explain the purpose of the United Nations?
- 1945: Creation of the UN
- Eleanor Roosevelt
- The Struggle for Human Rights, Eleanor Roosevelt, 1948

5.9 How did the Truman Doctrine change U.S. foreign policy?
- 1947: Truman Doctrine
- Harry Truman
- Truman Doctrine, Harry Truman, 1947

5.10 Why did Martin Luther King Jr. oppose the Vietnam War?
- 1954–1968: civil rights movement
- Martin Luther King Jr.
- Why I Am Opposed to the War in Vietnam, Martin Luther King Jr., 1967

5.11 On what basis did Henry Kissinger advise Richard Nixon to oppose Chilean president Salvador Allende?
- 1973: Military coup in Chile
- Henry Kissinger
- Memorandum for the President, NSC Meeting, November 6, Chile; Henry Kissinger, 1970

5.12 How did Bill Clinton explain his decision to intervene in the genocide of Bosnian Muslims?
- 1995: Dayton Peace Accords
- Bill Clinton
- On Bosnia, Bill Clinton, 1995

5.13 What was George W. Bush's strategy in the War on Terror?
- 2001: War on Terror begins
- George W. Bush
- The War on Terror, George W. Bush, 2001

Chapter 6: Civil Liberties and Public Safety

Unit Question: Under what conditions, if any, should citizens' freedoms be restricted?

Current Issue Question: Can reforming gun laws make Americans safer? If so, how? If not, why not?

6.1 What was Barack Obama's plan to reduce gun violence?
- 2012: Aurora movie theater shooting
- Barack Obama
- Remarks on Common-Sense Gun Safety Reform, Barack Obama, 2016

6.2 How did the United States explain its decision to declare independence from Britain?

Appendixes

- 1776: Declaration of Independence
- Thomas Jefferson
- Declaration of Independence, Continental Congress, 1776

6.3 What does the Bill of Rights guarantee?
- 1791: Bill of Rights
- James Madison
- Bill of Rights, 1791

6.4 How did John Adams restrict freedom of the press?
- 1798: Alien and Sedition Acts
- John Adams
- Sedition Act, Continental Congress, 1798

6.5 What was Abraham Lincoln's argument for suspending habeas corpus rights during the Civil War?
- 1861–1865: Civil War
- Abraham Lincoln
- Proclamation 104, Abraham Lincoln, 1863

6.6 Was Carrie Nation's temperance activism protected by the Constitution?
- 1920–1933: Prohibition
- Carrie Nation
- *The Use and Need of Carrie Nation*, Carrie Nation, 1904

6.7 How did Herbert Hoover explain his decision to disperse the Bonus Army?
- 1932: Bonus Army protests
- Herbert Hoover
- Statement of the Justice Department Investigation of the Bonus Army, Herbert Hoover, 1932)

6.8 How did Franklin D. Roosevelt justify the internment of Japanese Americans?
- 1942–1946: Internment of Japanese Americans
- Franklin D. Roosevelt
- Executive Order 9066, Franklin D. Roosevelt, 1942

6.9 How did Paul Robeson defend himself against Joseph McCarthy's accusation that he was a communist?
- 1950–1956: McCarthy Era
- Paul Robeson
- Testimony of Paul Robeson Before the House Committee on Un-American Activities, 1956

6.10 How did COINTELPRO justify its surveillance of U.S. citizens?
- 1956: COINTELPRO founded
- J. Edgar Hoover
- Church Report on COINTELPRO, 1976

6.11 What rights did the Black Panther Party demand, and why?
- 1966: Black Panther Party's Ten Point Program
- Huey P. Newton
- The Ten-Point Program, Huey P. Newton and Bobby Seale, 1966

6.12 How did the U.S. government defend the USA PATRIOT Act?
- 2001: USA PATRIOT Act
- George W. Bush
- Dispelling Some of the Major Myths About the USA PATRIOT Act, U.S. Department of Justice, n.d.

Chapter 7: Identity

Unit Question/Current Issue Question: What do we mean when we say "we"?

7.1 Declaration of Independence, Thomas Jefferson, 1776
7.2 Our Hearts Are Sickened, John Ross, 1838
7.3 Declaration of Immediate Causes, South Carolina legislature, 1860
7.4 On Women's Right to Vote, Susan B. Anthony, 1872
7.5 Appeal for Neutrality, Woodrow Wilson, 1914
7.6 *The Klan's Fight for Americanism*, Hiram W. Evans, 1926
7.7 Day of Infamy, Franklin D. Roosevelt, 1941
7.8 By Any Means Necessary, Malcolm X, 1964
7.9 Why I Am Opposed to the Vietnam War, Martin Luther King Jr., 1967
7.10 A Shining City on a Hill, Ronald Reagan, 1974
7.11 The War on Terror, George W. Bush, 2001
7.12 A More Perfect Union, Barack Obama, 2008

APPENDIX B: COURSE ENTRY SURVEY

1. List the top three most important events in U.S. history.
2. Why did you choose each one?
3. List the top three most important historical figures.
4. Why did you choose each one?
5. How would you define an American?
6. Do you consider yourself an American? Why or why not?

APPENDIX C: COURSE EXIT SURVEY

1. List the top three most important events in U.S. history.
2. Why did you choose each one?
3. List the top three most important historical figures.
4. Why did you choose each one?
5. How would you define an American?
6. Do you consider yourself an American? Why or why not?

7. How were your views of the United States changed or reinforced during this course?
8. Which historical figure did you find you agreed most with, and why?

APPENDIX D: UNIT ENTRY SURVEY

1. What do you know about the theme of this unit?
2. What would you like to learn about the theme of this unit?
3. How would you answer the Unit Question?
4. Why would you answer that way?
5. How would you answer the Current Issue Question?
6. Why would you answer that way?

APPENDIX E: BIOGRAPHICAL RESEARCH PAPER INSTRUCTIONS

You will write a research paper about the historical figure you will represent in the summit. Your paper should contain six paragraphs:

1. Explain why this person was important in U.S. history.
2. Provide a brief biography.
3. Describe the person's character traits, supported by examples from his or her life.
4. Present the person's answer to the Unit Question and give an example of something the person did or said that proves they would answer that way. Include a quotation from the document we studied in class to support your answer.
5. Predict how the person would answer the Current Issue Question if he or she were alive today. Explain why the person would have been likely to hold that view.
6. Explain what you learned about U.S. history by studying this person's life.

Add a References section at the end of your paper, including the document we read in class and at least one other source.

APPENDIX F: SUMMIT RESEARCH WORKSHEET

1. I will portray this historical figure in the summit:
2. What I already know about my historical figure:
3. What I want or need to know about my historical figure:
4. Document we will read in class related to my historical figure:
5. Outside sources of information about my historical figure:
6. My historical figure was important in U.S. history because:

7. Three facts about my historical figure's life that are relevant to how they would answer the Unit Question or Current Issue Question:
8. Two characteristics or qualities my historical figure has:
9. How my historical figure would speak or act in the summit:
10. Evidence from the document we read that shows how my historical figure would answer the Unit Question:
11. Evidence from my own research that shows how my historical figure would answer the Unit Question:
12. I think my historical figure would answer the Unit Question by saying:
13. Evidence from the document we read that shows how my historical figure would answer the Current Issue Question:
14. Evidence from my own research that shows how my historical figure would answer the Current Issue Unit Question:
15. I think my historical figure would answer the Current Issue Question by saying:
16. Which other historical figures we studied in this unit would my historical figure be most likely to agree with? Why?
17. Which other historical figures we studied in this unit would my historical figure be most likely to disagree with? Why?
18. One question I think my historical figure will be asked:
19. How my historical figure would answer:
20. Another question I think my historical figure will be asked:
21. How my historical figure would answer:
22. One question my historical figure would have for _____:
23. My historical figure would ask _____ this question because:
24. One question my historical figure would have for _____:
25. My historical figure would ask _____ this question because.

APPENDIX G: UNIT EXIT SURVEY

Look back on your answers to the Unit Entry Survey from the beginning of the unit, and review the lessons we have done.

1. Which event, historical figure, or document that we studied changed or reinforced your opinion on the Unit Question? Why?
2. Which event, historical figure, or document that we studied changed or reinforced your opinion on the Current Issue Question? Why?
3. Which historical figure that we studied did you agree with most? Why?
4. What did you learn about the theme of this unit?
5. Provide one new question you have about the material we studied in this unit.

APPENDIX H: CURRENT ISSUE LETTER INSTRUCTIONS

1. Consider your views on the Current Issue Question for this unit.
2. Decide upon a leader or authority figure who has decision-making power over this issue, and think of an action you would like the leader to take on the issue.
3. Write a respectful letter explaining your views to this leader. Reference at least one historical event you have studied in this unit that provides a comparison or evidence to support your view.
4. Send your letter and share any response you receive with the class!

APPENDIX I: DESIGNING YOUR OWN THEMATIC UNITS

1. Identify an essential question that is relevant in multiple eras of U.S. history.
2. Generate a list of about a dozen people who have offered answers to this question, and/or a list of about a dozen events in which this question came to the fore.
3. Locate a document that illustrates the perspective of each historical figure or relates to the event.
4. Isolate an excerpt of each document that is most relevant to the essential question.
5. Identify vocabulary in each document that may be unfamiliar to students.
6. For each document, generate several comprehension questions that can help you assess whether students have understood what they've read.
7. For each document, generate several questions students can use to do an activity in which they apply higher-order thinking skills.
8. Create appropriate introduction and reflection questions or activities for each document.

APPENDIX J: DISCUSSION GUIDELINES

1. Assume positive intentions and give classmates the benefit of the doubt—disagree with ideas, don't attack people.

    NO: If you don't believe in background checks on gun sales, you don't care about public safety!

    NO: If you believe in background checks on gun sales, you don't care about civil liberties!

    YES: I know we both care about public safety and civil liberties; I think we disagree on the effect of background checks on gun sales.

2. Speak to your classmates as you would to a role model you respect.

    NO: You idiot!

    YES: I strongly disagree with you.

3. Don't blame your classmates for what members of a group they belong to have done, and don't ask classmates to speak for all members of a group they belong to.

   NO: Why do you Black people think violence is necessary?

   NO: Why do you White people always take Native Americans' land?

   YES: I have questions about Malcolm X's idea of armed self-defense.

   YES: As a Native American, I feel upset when I learn that White people took my ancestors' land.

4. Reflect on how your own experiences and biases affect your views—avoid blame and shame.

   NO: I don't see why we need to study women in history; men did most of the important stuff.

   NO: Men should feel guilty about how they have treated women.

   YES: As a male, I realize that I've been seeing history through the eyes of men.

5. If you feel upset, angry, or confused during a discussion, take a break. Take care of yourself and take care of each other.

APPENDIX K: ONLINE CONTENT

www.tcpress.com/Metro

1. Links to most of the full documents that are excerpted in the book (arranged chronologically by historical event)
2. Downloadable, printable copies of most of the documents excerpted in this book, for classroom use (arranged chronologically by historical event)
3. Downloadable, printable copies of Appendixes B–J

www.rosaliemetro.com/bigquestionsmanyanswers

1. Blog about my academic work related to this approach to teaching history, and about my professional development work with teachers
2. Ideas for other thematic units related to U.S. history
3. Reviews and testimonials

References

Casale-Giannola, D. P., & Green, L. S. (2013). *41 active learning strategies for the inclusive classroom, Grades 6–12*. Thousand Oaks, CA: Corwin.

Cohen, E. G., & Lotan, R. A. (2014). *Designing groupwork: Strategies for the heterogeneous classroom* (3rd ed.). New York, NY: Teachers College Press.

Common Core State Standards Initiative. (2016). Frequently asked questions. Retrieved from corestandards.org/about-the-standards/frequently-asked-questions/

Gibbons, P. (2015). *Scaffolding language, scaffolding learning: Teaching second language learners in the mainstream classroom* (2nd ed.). Portsmouth, NH: Heinemann.

Hess, D. E., & McAvoy, P. (2015). *The political classroom: Evidence and ethics in democratic education*. New York, NY: Routledge.

Iowa State University of Science and Technology. (2016). Revised Bloom's Taxonomy. Retrieved from celt.iastate.edu/teaching/effective-teaching-practices/revised-blooms-taxonomy

King, L. (2016). Epilogue: Black history is more than skin color. *Social Studies Journal, 36*, 72–79.

Levstik, L. S. (2000). Articulating the silences: Teachers' and adolescents' conceptions of historical significance. In P. N. Stearns, P. Seixas, & S. Wineburg (Eds.), *Knowing, teaching, and learning history: National and international perspectives* (pp. 284–305). New York, NY: New York University Press.

Levstik, L. S., & Barton, K. C. (2005). *Doing history: Investigating with children in elementary and middle schools*. New York, NY: Routledge.

Loewen, J. (2008). *Lies my teacher told me: Everything your American history textbook got wrong* (2nd ed.). New York, NY: The New Press.

McTighe, J., & Wiggins, G. (2013). *Essential questions: Opening doors to student understanding*. Alexandria, VA: Association for Supervision and Curriculum Development.

Milner, H. R. (2010). *Start where you are, but don't stay there: Understanding diversity, opportunity gaps, and teaching in today's classrooms*. Cambridge, MA: Harvard Education Press.

Rockmore, E. B. (2015, October 21). How Texas teaches history. *The New York Times*. Retrieved from nytimes.com/2015/10/22/opinion/how-texas-teaches-history.html

Stanford History Education Group (SHEG). (n.d.). Reading like a historian curriculum. Retrieved from sheg.stanford.edu/rlh

Takaki, R., & Steffof, R. (2012). *A different mirror for young people: A history of multicultural America*. New York, NY: Seven Stories Press.

Visual Thinking Strategies (VTS). (2016). What is VTS? Retrieved from vtshome.org/

Wineburg, S. (2001). *Historical thinking and other unnatural acts*. Philadelphia, PA: Temple University Press.

Zinn, H. (2003). *A people's history of the United States*. New York, NY: HarperCollins.

Index

About.com, 147–148
Adams, John, "Sedition Act" (1798), 171–172
"Address to the Commonwealth Club of California" (Chavez, 1984), 129–130
"Address to the Nation on the Economy" (Reagan, 1981), 132–133
"Address to the Virginia Court" (J. Brown, 1859), 61–62
AFL-CIO, 113
African Americans. *See also* Slavery
  Black Panther Party, 185–187
  civil rights movement (1954-1968), 153–155, 194
  Little Rock Nine (1957), 97–100
  North Carolina voting rights, 77–80
  Organization of Afro-American Unity (1964), 74–76, 194
  school desegregation, 72–74, 97–100
  Supreme Court on "separate but equal," 63–65
  Supreme Court overturns "separate but equal," 72–74, 97–98
AIM, 4n
"Ain't I a Woman?" (Truth, 1851), 57–58
Alexander, C., 133
Al Jazeera, 137
Allende, Salvador, 156–158
American Civil Liberties Union (ACLU), 187–189
American Progress (Gast), 142
American Rhetoric, 152–153, 182
Anthony, Susan B., 39–41
  "On Womens' Right to Vote" (1872), 40–41, 192
"Appeal for Neutrality" (Wilson, 1914), 145–146, 193
Arkansas, Little Rock Nine (1957), 97–100

Articles of Confederation (1777)
  "Articles of Confederation, Articles I, II, III, VIII, and IX" (1777), 81–82
  balance of power between states and Congress, 80–82
  U.S. Constitution versus, 82–84
Ashbrook Center, 109–110, 170
Assad, Bashar al-, 136
Assembly line invention (1913), 122–124
Assessment, 14–15
Aug, P. H., 57–58
Avalon Project, 81–82, 83–84, 86

Bagley, Sarah, 111–113
  "Investigation of Labor Conditions" (1845), 111–112
Baldwin, James, 4n
Barber, William J., II, 77–80
  North Carolina State Conference of the NAACP v. Patrick Lloyd McCrory, 79–80
Barnes, P., 67
Barton, K. C., 15
Battle of Gettysburg (1863), 37–39
Beals, M. P., 98
"Big Questions Many Answers" (blog), 19
"Bill of Rights" (1791), 169–170
  Civil War habeas corpus rights, 172–174
  Sedition Act (1798), 171–172
  10th Amendment, 84
Bill of Rights Institute, 169–170
Black Panther Party, 185–187
BlackPast.org, 74–75
Black Power Mix Tape (film), 187
Bonus Army protests (1932), 176–178
Brave Boy of the Waxhaws (Currier & Ives), 33
"Bringing Back Jobs and Growth" (Trump, 2017), 105–106

Brown, Henry Billings, 63–65
  Plessy v. Ferguson (Supreme Court, 1896), 63–64
Brown, John, "Address to the Virginia Court" (1859), 61–62
Brown, Oliver, 72–74
Brown v. Board of Education (Supreme Court, 1954), 72–74, 97–98
Burns, K., 67
Bush, George W., 161–163
  USA PATRIOT ACT (2001), 187–189
  "The War on Terror" (2001), 161–162, 194
"By Any Means Necessary" (Malcolm X, 1962), 74–75, 194
Byrd, R. C., 93–94

Calhoun, John C., "Slavery as a Positive Good" (1837), 109–110
California, Delano grape strike (1965-1970), 129–131
Carnegie, Andrew, 115–117
  "The Gospel of Wealth" (1889), 116–117
Carnegie Corporation, 116–117
Carroll, L., 163
Cartoons, political, 33–35
Casale-Giannola, D. P., 14
Central Intelligence Agency (CIA), 46
Cesar Chavez Foundation, 129–130
Chafe, W. H., 65
Chavez, Cesar, 129–131
  "Address to the Commonwealth Club of California" (1984), 129–130
Cherokee Nation v. Georgia (1831), 89–92
Chile, military coup (1973), 156–158
Chinese Exclusion Act (1882), 67–69
Chronological approach, 1–2

Church, Frank, "Church Report on COINTELPRO" (1976), 183–184
"City on a Hill, A" (Reagan, 1974), 45–46, 194
Civil rights movement (1954-1968), 153–155, 194
Civil War (1861-1865)
    Battle of Gettysburg (1863), 37–39
    Harper's Ferry attack (1859), 61–62
    Reconstruction (1865-1877), 113–115
    secession of South Carolina (1860), 94–96, 192
    suspension of habeas corpus rights, 172–174
Classroom climate, 16–18
Clinton, Bill, 158–160
    "On Bosnia" (1995), 159–160
CNN, 137, 159–160, 161–162, 166
Cohen, E. G., 14
COINTELPRO surveillance, 182–184
Cold War (1946-1991), 41–43
Colonial Williamsburg Foundation, 82
Colorado, Aurora movie theater shooting (2012), 164–166
Columbus, Christopher, "Log" (1492), 107–108
Common Core State Standards Initiative, 1, 4–6
Common Sense (Paine, 1776), 26–27
Commons, J., 111–112
Communism
    COINTELPRO surveillance, 182–184
    McCarthy era (1950-1956), 180–182
Constitution. *See* U.S. Constitution
CRF-USA, 172
Crucible of Empire, The (film), 144
Currier & Ives, 33

Davis, Angela, 4n
Davis, Jefferson, 94–96
    "Declaration of Immediate Causes, South Carolina legislature" (1860), 95–96, 192
"Day of Infamy" (F. Roosevelt, 1941), 147–148, 193
Dayton Peace Accords (1995), 158–160
"Declaration of Immediate Causes, South Carolina legislature" (1860), 95–96, 192

Declaration of Independence (1776), 26–28, 167–168, 191
Dekanawidah, 23–26
    "Great Law of Peace" (c. 1500), 24–25
"Desegregation address" (Eisenhower, 1957), 97–98
Designing thematic units, 19
Differentiating instruction, 15–16
Discussion Guidelines, 18
"Dispelling Some of the Major Myths About the USA Patriot Act," 188–189
Douglass, Frederick, "What to the Slave is the Fourth of July?" (1852), 36–37
Du Bois, W. E. B., 113–115
    The Souls of Black Folk, 113–114

Economic policy
    Christopher Columbus economic and social goals (1492), 107–108
    Lyndon B. Johnson War on Poverty (1964), 127–128
    Ronald Reagan economic policy (1981), 131–133
    Franklin D. Roosevelt/New Deal (1932), 124–126
    Donald Trump economic policy (2016), 105–106
Eisenhower, Dwight D., "Desegregation address" (1957), 97–98
El Buri, R., 48
Environmental rights, 100–102
"Essential questions," in U.S. history, 6–7
Evans, Hiram W., 69–72
    "The Klan's Fight for Americanism" (1926), 70–71, 193
Everyday Democracy, 22–23
Ewers, J., 174
"Executive Order 9066" (F. Roosevelt, 1942), 178–179
Eyes on the Prize (film), 100
Eyewitness to History, 178

Facing History, 160
Faubus, Orval
    Little Rock Nine (1957), 97–100
    "Speech on School Integration" (1958), 99–100
Federal Bureau of Investigation (FBI), COINTELPRO surveillance, 182–184
"Federalist Paper No. 10" (Madison, 1787), 29–30
Federal Judicial Center, 41
"First Inaugural Address" (Jefferson, 1801), 31–32
Foner, P. S., 36–37
Fong Yue Ting, Wong Quan, and Lee Joe v. U.S. (Supreme Court, 1893), 68–69
Ford, Henry, 122–124
    My Life and Work (1922), 123–124
Ford Motor Company, 122–124

Gasdik, N. J., 84
Gast, John, 142
George III, King of England, 28
George Washington University, 120, 150–151
Georgia
    Cherokee Nation v. Georgia (1831), 89–92
    Worcester v. Georgia (1832), 90
"Gettysburg Address" (Lincoln, 1863), 38
Gibbons, P., 16
Gilded Age (1877-1900), 115–117
Gilder Lehman Institute of American History, The, 61–62, 87
"Gospel of Wealth, The" (Carnegie, 1889), 116–117
Grade level, accounting for, 15–16
Gray, Horace, 67–69
    Fong Yue Ting, Wong Quan, and Lee Joe v. U.S. (Supreme Court, 1893), 68–69
Great Britain
    Declaration of Independence (1776), 26–28, 167–168, 191
    Proclamation of Neutrality (1793), 138–139
    Revolutionary War anniversary (2015), 22–23
    slave trade outlawed (1807), 109–110
Great Depression (1929-1939)
    Bonus Army protests (1932), 176–178
    New Deal (1932), 124–126
Great Father Andrew (artist unknown), 35
"Great Law of Peace" (Dekanawidah, c. 1500), 24–25
Green, L. S., 14
Gun safety reform (2012), 164–166

Halsall, P., 24–25
Hampton, H., 100
Harper's Ferry attack (1859), 61–62
Harrington, Michael, 127, 128
Harry S. Truman Library and Museum, 153
Haudenosaunee Confederacy, 23–26
Hayne, Robert, 92–94
   "Reply to Robert Hayne, Daniel Webster (1832), 93–94
Henry, Patrick, 80–82
Hess, D. E., 16
Hilliard, D., 185–187
Hispanic Americans, Delano (California) grape strike (1965-1970), 129–131
Historical thinking skills, 14
History.com, 72
History Matters, 178–179, 180–181
History Place, The, 40–41, 126
Hoover, Herbert, 176–178
   "Statement on the Justice Department Investigation of the Bonus Army" (1932), 177
Hoover, J. Edgar, 182–184
Houston, Jean Wakatsuki, 4n, 179
How the Other Half Lives (Riis, 1890), 117–120
Huerta, Dolores, 129
Huffington Post, 47–48

Ibis Communications, Inc., 39
Imbert, Anthony, 34
"Inaugural Address" (Kennedy, 1961), 42–43
Independent Television Service, 184
"Investigation of Labor Conditions" (1845), 111–112
Iowa State University of Science and Technology, 13
Islam/Muslims
   Dayton Peace Accords (1995), 158–160
   ISIS/ISIL (Islamic State of Iraq and Syria/Islamic State of Iraq and the Levant), 135–137
   USA PATRIOT ACT (2001), 187–189
   War on Terror (2001-), 161–163, 194

Jackson, Andrew, 32–35, 55
   Cherokee Nation v. Georgia (1831), 89–92
   Nullification Crisis (1832-1837), 92–94

political cartoons about, 33–35
Trail of Tears (1838), 55–57, 192
Japanese internment (1942-1946), 178–179
Jarecki, E., 158
Jefferson, Thomas, 30–32
   "Declaration of Independence" (1776), 167–168, 191
   "First Inaugural Address" (1801), 31–32
John F. Kennedy Presidential Library and Museum, 43
Johnson, Lyndon B., "State of the Union Address" (1964), 127–128
Johnson, P. N., 84
Jungle, The (Sinclair, 1906), 121–122
Justia, 59–60, 88–89, 101–102

Kennedy, Anthony, 51–53
   Obergefell v. Hodges (Supreme Court, 2015), 52
Kennedy, John F., 41–43
   "Inaugural Address" (1961), 42–43
Kennedy, K., 96
King Andrew (anonymous), 34
King Center, The, 155
King, LaGarrett, 17
King, Martin Luther, Jr., 153–155
   "Why I Am Opposed to the War in Vietnam" (1967), 154–155, 194
Kissinger, Henry, 156–158
   "Memorandum for the President" (1970), 157–158
Ku Klux Klan, 69–72
   "The Klan's Fight for Americanism" (Evans, 1926), 70–71, 193

Lawson, S. F., 97–98
Legal Information Institute, 52, 53, 63–64, 73
Lesson structure, 10–14
   activities, 13–14
   comprehension questions, 13
   documents, 13
   historical figure and event, 12
   introduction, 12
   lesson question, 11–12
   mini-lecture, 12
   reflection, 14
   resources, 14
   setting up the lesson, 11
   vocabulary, 12–13
Levstik, L. S., 7, 15
Liberty Fund, 139

Library of Congress, 144
Lillian Goldman Law Library, 29–30, 31–32, 38, 138–139, 140–141, 171–172
Lincoln (film), 96
Lincoln, Abraham, 37–39, 172–174
   "Gettysburg Address" (1963), 38
   "Proclamation 104" (1863), 173–174
   secession of South Carolina (1860), 94–96, 192
Little Rock Nine (1957)
   "Desegregation address" (Eisenhower, 1957), 97–98
   "Speech on School Integration" (Faubus, 1958), 99–100
Loewen, J., 2, 3
"Log" (Columbus, 1492), 107–108
Lotan, R. A., 14
Lowry, A., 128

Madison, James, 28–30, 82–84, 168–170
   "Bill of Rights" (1791), 169–170
   "Federalist Paper No. 10" (1787), 29–30
   U.S. Constitution, 10th Amendment (1791), 84
   U.S. Constitution, Article 1, Article 4 (1787), 83–84
Malcolm X, 74–76
   "By Any Means Necessary" (1964), 74–75, 194
Mandel, K., 144
Manifest Destiny, 141–143
Marshall, John, 87–89
   McCulloch v. Maryland (Supreme Court, 1819), 88–89
Marshall, Thurgood, 72–74
   Brown v. Board of Education (Supreme Court, 1954), 73
Massachusetts, "Investigation of Labor Conditions" (1845), 111–112
"Master narrative" (Takaki), 3–4
McAvoy, P., 16
McBride, A., 89
McCarthy era (1950-1956), 180–182
McCarthy, Joseph, 180–182
McCrory, Patrick Lloyd, 78, 79–80
McCulloch v. Maryland (Supreme Court, 1819), 87–89
McTighe, J., 6
Meatpacking industry reform (1906), 120–122
Medley, K., 65

Index

"Memorandum for the President" (Kissinger, 1970), 157–158
Mexican-American War (1846-1848), 141–143
Miller, D. A., 144
Milner, H. R., 16
"Minutes of the Meeting at Pittsburgh" (1791), 86
Monroe, James, 139–141
  "Monroe Doctrine" (1823), 140–141
More Perfect Union, A (film), 84
"More Perfect Union, A" (Obama, 2008), 47–48, 195
Museum of Chinese in America, 69
My Life and Work (Ford, 1922), 123–124

NAACP Legal Defense and Educational Fund, 74
National American Woman Suffrage Association (NAWSA), 65
National Association for the Advancement of Colored People (NAACP), 72, 74, 77–80
  North Carolina State Conference of the NAACP v. Patrick Lloyd McCrory (2015), 79–80
National Endowment for the Humanities, 141, 149
National Humanities Center, 168
National LGBTQ Task Force, 53
National Museum of the American Indian, 26
National Park Service, 39, 61
National Rifle Association of America, 166
National Security Administration Archive, 157–158
National Women's History Museum, 58
National World War I Museum and Memorial, 147
Nation, Carrie A., 174–176
  The Use and Need of Carrie A. Nation (1904), 175
Native Americans/Indigenous Peoples
  AIM, 4n
  Cherokee Nation v. Georgia (1831), 89–92
  Christopher Columbus economic and social goals (1492), 107–108
  Haudenosaunee Confederacy (c. 1500), 23–26
  Trail of Tears (1838), 55–57, 192

New Deal, 124–126
  "The New Deal" (F. Roosevelt, 1932), 125–126
Newton, Huey P., "The Ten-Point Program" (1966), 185–187
New York
  How the Other Half Lives (Riis, 1890), 117–120
  New York v. United States (Supreme Court, 1992), 100–102
New York Public Library, 110
New York Times, 132–133, 173–174
Nixon, Richard M., "Memorandum for the President" (Kissinger, 1970), 157–158
North Atlantic Treaty Organization (NATO), 159
North Carolina State Conference of the NAACP v. Patrick Lloyd McCrory (North Carolina, 2015), 79–80
Nullification Crisis (1832-1837), 92–94

Obama, Barack, 46–48, 164–166
  "A More Perfect Union" (2008), 47–48, 195
  "Remarks by the President on Common-Sense Gun Safety Reform" (2016), 165–166
Obama White House Archive, 106
Obergefell v. Hodges (Supreme Court, 2015), 52
O'Connor, Sandra Day, 100–102
  New York v. United States (Supreme Court, 1992), 101–102
Office of Arts and Archives, The Pure Food and Drug Act, 122
Office of the Historian, 160
Ohio Women's Rights Convention (1851), 57–58
Olsson, G., 187
"On American Imperialism" (Twain, 1898), 144
"On Bosnia" (B. Clinton, 1995), 159–160
"On Women's Right to Vote" (Anthony, 1872), 40–41, 192
Organization of Afro-American Unity, 74–76, 194
Other America, The (Harrington), 127, 128
"Our Hearts Are Sickened" (Ross, 1838), 192

Paine, Thomas, 26–28
  Common Sense (1776), 26–27
Pawel, M., 131

Payne, C., 97–98
PBS, 56, 57, 62, 65–66, 115, 117, 124, 126, 147
Pennsylvania
  "Gettysburg Address" (Lincoln, 1863), 38
  "Minutes of the Meeting at Pittsburgh" (1791), 86
Pennsylvania Archives, 86
Pepperdine University, 125–126
Peters, G. H., 177
Pew Research Center, 23, 46
Philippines, Spanish-American War (1898), 143–144
Plessy, Homer, 63–65
Plessy v. Ferguson (Supreme Court, 1896), 63–64
Political cartoons, 33–35
Political spectrum, 21, 44–45
Polk, James K., 141–143
Presidential elections
  Andrew Jackson (1828), 32–35
  Thomas Jefferson (1800), 30–32
  John F. Kennedy (1961), 42–43
  Barack Obama (2008), 46–48, 195
  Ronald Reagan (1980), 44–46, 194
  Donald Trump (2016), 105–106
Primary sources, 4n
"Proclamation 104" (Lincoln, 1863), 173–174
"Proclamation, A" (Washington, 1792), 86
"Proclamation of Neutrality" (Washington, 1793), 138–139
Progressive Era (1890-1920), 117–120
Prohibition (1920-1933), 174–176
Project Gutenberg, 113–114, 123–124
Pure Food and Drug Act (1906), 120–122

Reading like a Historian program (SHEG), 11–12, 14
Reagan, Ronald, 44–46, 131–133
  "Address to the Nation on the Economy" (1981), 132–133
  "A City on a Hill" (1974), 45–46, 194
Reconstruction (1865-1877), 113–115
"Remarks by the President on Common-Sense Gun Safety Reform" (Obama, 2016), 165–166

"Reply to Robert Hayne, Daniel Webster" (1832), 93–94
Revised Bloom's Taxonomy (Iowa State University of Science and Technology), 13
Revolutionary War anniversary (2015), 22–23
Riis, Jacob, *How the Other Half Lives* (1890), 117–120
Robeson, Paul, "Testimony of Paul Robeson before the House Committee on Un-American Activities" (1956), 180–181
Rockmore, E. B., 4
Romagnolo, D. J., 153
Roosevelt, Eleanor, 149–151
  "The Struggle for Human Rights" (1948), 150–151
Roosevelt, Franklin D., 124–126, 147–149
  "Day of Infamy" (1941), 147–148, 193
  "Executive Order 9066" (1942), 178–179
  "The New Deal" (1932), 125–126
Ross, John, 55–57, 89–92
  Cherokee Nation v. Georgia (1831), 90–91
  "Our Hearts Are Sickened" (1838), 192
  "To the Senate and House of Representatives" (1838), 56, 192
Ross, R., 48
Roy Rosenzweig Center, 35

Same-sex marriage, 51–53
Sanders, S., 163
Sandford, John, 59–61
Schulten, K., 163
Scott, Dred, 59–61
Scott v. Sandford (Supreme Court, 1856), 58–61
Seale, Bobby, "The Ten-Point Program" (1966), 185–187
"Sedition Act" (1798), 171–172
Set To Between Old Hickory and Bully Nick (Imbert), 34
Sherman, Roger, 53–55
Sinclair, Upton, 120–122
  The Jungle (1906), 121–122
Slavery. *See also* African Americans; Civil War (1861-1865)
  Constitutional Convention (1787), 53–55
  Frederick Douglass escapes (1838), 36–37

Harper's Ferry attack (1859), 61–62
  as a "positive good" (Calhoun, 1837), 109–110
  Reconstruction (1865-1877), 113–115
"Slavery as a Positive Good" (Calhoun, 1837), 109–110
Smith, L. M., 115
Social Darwinism, 115–117
Socioeconomic status. *See also* Workers and workers' rights
  Great Depression (1929-1939), 124–126, 176–178
  How the Other Half Lives (Riis), 117–120
  New Deal, 124–126
  Reconstruction (1865-1877), 113–115
  Social Darwinism, 115–117
  War on Poverty (1964), 127–128
"Solitude of the Self, The" (Stanton, 1892), 65–66
Souls of Black Folk, The (Du Bois), 113–114
South Carolina
  "Declaration of Immediate Causes, South Carolina legislature" (1860), 95–96, 192
  Nullification Crisis (1832-1837), 92–94
Southern Poverty Law Center, 72
Spanish-American War (1898), 143–144
"Speech on School Integration" (Faubus, 1958), 99–100
Spielberg, S., 96
Stanford University, 69
  Stanford History Education Group (SHEG), 3, 11–12, 14
Stanton, Elizabeth Cady, 65–67
  "The Solitude of the Self" (1892), 65–66
State Historical Society of Missouri, 176
"Statement on Syria" (Trump, 2017), 136–137
"Statement on the Justice Department Investigation of the Bonus Army" (Hoover, 1932), 177
"State of the Union Address" (Johnson, 1964), 127–128
Steffof, R., 3, 55
"Struggle for Human Rights, The" (E. Roosevelt, 1948), 150–151

Suffrage, women's, 39–41, 65–67, 192
Supreme Court. *See* U.S. Supreme Court

Takaki, Ronald, 3, 55
Taney, Roger, 58–61
  Scott v. Sandford (Supreme Court, 1856), 59–60
Teaching U.S. History, 95–96
"The Ten-Point Program" (Newton & Seale, 1966), 185–187
Terrorist attacks of September 11, 2001
  ISIS/ISIL (Islamic State of Iraq and Syria/Islamic State of Iraq and the Levant), 135–137
  USA PATRIOT Act (2001), 187–189
  War on Terror (2001-), 161–163, 194
"Testimony of Paul Robeson before the House Committee on Un-American Activities" (1956), 180–181
Textbook-based approach, 3–4
The Henry Ford, 124
Thematic, document-based approach, 1–19
  assessment, 14–15
  chronological approach versus, 1–2
  classroom climate, 16–18
  Course Entry Survey, 7
  Course Exit Survey, 7
  designing thematic units, 19
  differentiating instruction, 15–16
  discussion guidelines, 18
  "document-based," reasons for, 3–4
  "essential questions" in U.S. history, 6–7
  grade-level instruction, 15–16
  lesson structure, 10–14
  meeting standards, 4–6
  textbook-based approach versus, 3–4
  "thematic," reasons for, 1–2
  unit structure, 8–10
  "we," meaning of, 6–7
"To the Senate and House of Representatives" (Ross, 1838), 56, 192
Trail of Tears (1838), 55–57, 192
Trials of Henry Kissinger, The (film), 158

TributetoRonaldReagan.com, 45–46
Truman, Harry, 151–153
    "Truman Doctrine" (1947), 152–153
Trump, Donald, 135–137
    "Bringing Back Jobs and Growth" (2017), 105–106
    "Statement on Syria" (2017), 136–137
Truth, Sojourner, "Ain't I a Woman?" (1851), 57–58
Twain, Mark, 143–144
    "On American Imperialism" (1898), 144

Union of Concerned Scientists, 102
United Farm Workers (UFW), 129–131
United Nations, created in 1945, 149–151
U.S. Constitution, 54
    Susan B. Anthony interpretation of, 39–41, 192
    Articles of Confederation versus, 82–84
    Bill of Rights (1791), 84, 168–174
    Constitutional Convention (1787), 53–55
    creation in 1787, 28–30
    "Proclamation 104" (Lincoln, 1863), 173–174
    slavery and, 53–55
    states' rights and Federalist interpretations, 87–89
U.S. Department of Justice
    "Dispelling Some of the Major Myths About the USA Patriot Act," 188–189
    "Statement on the Justice Department Investigation of the Bonus Army" (Hoover, 1932), 177
U.S. National Archives and Records Administration, 167–168
United States Senate, 94
U.S. Supreme Court
    Brown v. Board of Education (1954), 72–74, 97–98
    Fong Yue Ting, Wong Quan, and Lee Joe v. U.S. (1893), 68–69
    McCulloch v. Maryland (1819), 88–89
    New York v. United States (1992), 100–102
    Obergefell v. Hodges (2015), 52

Plessy v. Ferguson (1896), 63–64
Scott v. Sandford (Supreme Court, 1856), 58–61
Unit structure, 8–10
    Biographical Papers, 8, 10, 15
    Current Issue Letter Instructions, 10, 15
    Current Issue Question, 8–9, 10, 49
    designing thematic units, 19
    Summit Instructions, 9
    Summit Research Worksheet, 8, 49
    summits, 8–10
    Unit Entry Survey, 8
    Unit Exit Survey, 10, 15
    Unit Question, 8–9, 10, 15, 49
University of Arkansas, 99–100
University of California, Library, 154–155
University of Groningen, 30, 127–128
University of Virginia, Rector and Visitors Center, 145–146
USA PATRIOT Act (2001), 187–189
Use and Need of Carrie A. Nation, The (Nation, 1904), 175
UShistory.org, 133

Vietnam War (1955-1975), 153–155, 194
Virginia, "Address to the Virginia Court" (John Brown, 1859), 61–62
Visual Thinking Strategies (VTS), 13
Voices of Democracy, 42–43
Voting rights, 39–41
    Susan B. Anthony arrested for voting (1872), 39–41, 192
    North Carolina voting rights, 77–80
    Voting Rights Act (1965), 77–80
    women's suffrage, 39–41, 65–67, 192

War on Poverty (1964-), 127–128
"War on Terror, The" (G. W. Bush, 2001), 161–162, 194
Washington, George
    "A Proclamation" (1792), 86
    "Proclamation of Neutrality" (1793), 138–139
    Whiskey Rebellion (1791), 85–87
Webster, Daniel, 92–94
    "Reply to Robert Hayne, Daniel Webster" (1832), 93–94
Wells-Barnett, I. B., 72
WETA, 179
WGBH Educational Foundation, 163
"What Does Democracy Mean to You?" (2015), 22–23
"What to the Slave is the Fourth of July?" (Douglass, 1852), 36–37
Whiskey Rebellion (1791), 85–87
White House, 105–106, 136–137, 165–166
Whitehouse.gov, 32
"Why I Am Opposed to the War in Vietnam" (King, 1967), 154–155, 194
Wiggins, G., 6
Wilson, Woodrow, 145–147
    "Appeal for Neutrality" (1914), 145–146, 193
Wineburg, S., 3
Wisconsin Historical Society, 107–108
Wolf, P., 183–184
Women's rights
    Lowell mill women strike (1834), 111–113
    Ohio Women's Rights Convention (1851), 57–58
    women's suffrage, 39–41, 65–67, 192
Woolley, J. T., 177
Worcester v. Georgia (1832), 90
Workers and workers' rights
    Delano (California) grape strike (1965-1970), 129–131
    Ford assembly line invented (1913), 122–124
    Lowell mill women strike (1834), 111–113
    meatpacking industry reform (1906), 120–122
World War I (1917-1919), 145–147, 193
World War II (1941-1945)
    Japanese internment (1942-1946), 178–179
    U.S. decision to enter war, 147–149, 193

Younge, G., 122
Young Lords, 4n

Zinn, H., 3, 108, 143
Zucchino, D., 80

About the Author

Rosalie Metro is an assistant teaching professor in the College of Education at the University of Missouri-Columbia. She holds a Ph.D. in Learning, Teaching, and Social Policy from Cornell University. She has taught U.S. and world history at the middle and high school levels. Her research has been published in journals, including *Comparative Education Review* and *Anthropology and Education Quarterly*, and in a number of edited volumes.